PRINCE CHARMING
A Memoir
CHRISTOPHER LOGUE

faber and faber

First published in 1999
by Faber and Faber Limited
3 Queen Square WCIN 3AU

Photoset by RefineCatch Limited, Bungay, Suffolk
Printed in England by Clays Ltd, St Ives plc

A CIP record for this book
is available from the British Library

ISBN 0–571–19768–X

2 4 6 8 10 9 7 5 3 1

Contents

ILLUSTRATIONS

ACKNOWLEDGEMENTS

PRINCIPALLY to my wife, Rosemary Hill, and to James Campbell, for their critical attention to the first version of this book. Then to my editor, Christopher Reid, for the improvements that his many detailed notes made to the second version, and to my publisher, Matthew Evans, for spotting evasions in the text less worldly souls might have missed.

Thereafter: to Peter Clarke for lending and allowing me to quote from his diaries for the years 1948 to 1956, to Paul Wallace, my friend since 1949, for his interviews, his cautions, and to Nell Dunn who titled the book after reading and amending parts of it.

Then to those dear friends who were kind enough to give me their memories of myself: the late Patrick Brangwyn, the late Kenny Carter, Alice Carter, his widow, Hugo Claus, J. P. Donleavy, Bamber and Christina Gascoigne, Sir Paul and Lady Getty, Caroline Hobhouse, Candida Lycett Green, Shusha Guppy, Jane Lougee, Elizabeth Luard, the late John Phillips Marquand, Melissa North, George Ames Plimpton, Roger Smith, Bernard Stone, Michael Taylor, Michael and Sarah White, Austryn Wainhouse and Louis de Wet.

And to those who in various respects helped me with various aspects of this book: Fleur Adcock, Gillian Bate, Richard Bates of Discript, Nicholas Bethell, Miss C. Bland of the War Pensions Agency, Dr Alan Borg, CBE, FSA, John Boty, the late Patrick Bowles, Charles Boyle, Mark Boyle, Oliver Bradbury, Philip Brady, Michael Bridges, Mary Briault, Sir Julian Bullard, GCMG, John Calder, Jill Chisholm, William Cookson, Caroline Coon, Artemis Cooper, Ron Costley, the late Robert Dartnell, Derek Drescher of the BBC, Nessie Dunsmuir, Pedruth Emanuel of Teacher, Stern and Selby, Toby Faber, Eleanor Fazan, Jane Feaver, Arnold Feinstein, Hilary Field of the BBC (Bristol), David Gale of the Home Office, David Godwin, my agent, Audrey Gray, Jonathon Green, for referring me to the citation from Roy Jenkins, Martin Green, Jan Hallwood, Dr P. M. Hallwood of Flynn Pharma Ltd, Joyce Harper, Patricia Harris, Michael

ACKNOWLEDGEMENTS

Hastings, John Hawkes, Stephen Heggie, Anthony Hill, Edward
Hill, Joan Hills, Richard Hollis, Edward Horne, BEM, Michael
Horovitz, Tristram Hull, Richard Ingrams, Sir Peter Jay, Paul
Johnson, John de St Jorre, Richard and Vivian King, Tony Kinsey,
Bert Kitchen, Bobby Korner, Jay Landesman, Peter Levi, Inez
T. P. A. Lynn of the London Library, Joanna Mackle, Mildred
Marney of Rowan Script, for her patience, professionalism
and reliability, Sir George Martin, Susan Martin, Margaret
Matheson, Douglas Matthews, Jean Michie, Adrian Mitchell,
Colin Moffat, Elizabeth Moore, Mary Moore, Iris Owens,
Richard Parkes, Brian Patten, Stephen Peet, Alan Powers, Julian
Putkowski, Kathleen Raine, George Ramsden, Margaret
Richardson of the Sir John Soane Museum, M. D. Richardson
of the Fleet Air Arm Museum, Jeremy Robson, Ernest Rodker,
Tony and Anne Marie Rushton, Bill le Sage, John Sankey,
Michael Schmidt, Richard Seaver, Christian Smith, Mary Smith,
Mark Steyn, David Storey, Gay Talese, Brigit Vaughn, Sally
Vincent, Simon Vinkenoog, David Vital, Nicholas Walter,
Arnold Wesker, Richard West, Peter Whitehead and George
Whitman.

FOREWORD

Some of the personal names in what follows are false – those given to my fellow soldiers, for example, as I have forgotten their actual names. Others are falsified to avoid embarrassment or hurt; these names are not indexed.

Though the book's conversations are contrived, and when citing Peter Clarke's diaries, my own diary scraps, or from letters that I received and wrote, I have cut and conflated, nothing in these contexts is made up. From forgetfulness, or for literary reasons, my chronology is somewhat jumbled.

Preferring to live in a castle rather than under a tree, I identified when young with the Sheriff of Nottingham (as played in *The Adventures of Robin Hood* by the incomparable Basil Rathbone, MC) rather than with the rebel outlaw. In middle age, Chu Teh, the opium-smoking ex-warlord who ran the military side of the Long March, was my dream role. Nowadays I see myself as Rowlf, the Muppets' pit-band pianist.

1926–1951

ON MY WAY TO PARIS

ONCE when I was helping my mother to wind her wool she said: 'Your father met me through the Mussons. We were both members of the Finchley Choral Society. Bernard Musson introduced us. I was going to marry Frank Musson, Bernard's brother, a watchmaker from Ipswich whose father painted seascapes.'

'Where are they now?'

'Oh, gone . . . long gone. Frank was silent. I can't abide silent men. Bernard helped me to write the letter breaking it off. "Don't worry, Molly," May – Bernard's wife – said. "He'll find you a good husband. Not one of those ships' captains." Bernard had left the sea by then. He brought your father to our house just before my own father died and your grandmother and I moved to Southsea.

'Your father took his holiday in Southsea. At the Sandringham. A very good hotel. After he and Bernard went home Dad said: "Our Molly will marry that man." Though my mind was by no means made up.

'Mark you, there was no better man in this world than your father, but I was not sure about marrying. I had had my suitors. Chiefly – besides Frank Musson – Mr Langstone, an Islington builder and decorator who worked for Dad. George Langstone was far too mean with his money for my taste.

'Paddy Mannion was mean.' The Mannions' garden backed on to ours. Joan, their daughter, was my first love. 'Mind you, as the manager of a gentlemen's outfitters Paddy had no money to speak of. You saw the state of their house after – thanks to Mr Hitler – we moved to Bournemouth and ran into the Mannions again.

'Things were very different with your father. He had no money of his own, as you know. He had his position. A very good position for those days. With his pension to come. There was nothing unsuitable about Jack Logue.

'He was tall, well turned out, chamois spats, shoes well polished' – looking askance at my own – 'even in the worst weathers. Truth to tell, many people thought him handsome.

3

'Still, I hesitated. Your grandmother and I got along so happily. Especially after my father's death. There was always so much going on. Theatricals. Tennis. Fancy-dress parties. Cissie' – my mother's elder sister – 'had been married to Percy Bridges for some time and there was plenty of room at home.

'But my mother liked Jack. They would sing duets. Then I would sing. Then we would sing together. Something from *The Student Prince*, perhaps – with Percy on the piano. Such a lovely pianist. Why that man never took his gift seriously I shall never understand. Suddenly it was 1924 and I, as I have had to remind you so often, was born on March 25th, 1888.'

'The same year as T. S. Eliot,' I said.

'There you go, writers all the time – the kind of people who are forever at home. Gubbins at a desk. It would do you good to understand that very few people give tuppence for your Mr Eliot, plus all the writers in Christendom. Dancing. Parties. Sport. That is what the world likes.

'Long before I met your father I made a dress called The Web – fancy dress was all the rage. Cissie cut out the pattern. Mr Hughes, the dentist, made the bluebottles to go on it, and Mr Woodstock, a commercial artist keen on Cissie – not that she gave him a second thought – marked the spots where the blue-bottles should go. My brother George made the headdress – a web of silver wire. Of course I took first prize. Though I didn't actually *take* the prize as the fancy was at home. I won other prizes with it – which I did take. Then a girl from down the road asked if she could borrow it. Of course I said yes. And she won a prize with it. So I said, keep the dress. I didn't want to get known by it.'

'What about Dad?'

'Your father proposed to me on South Parade Pier in 1924. Such a lovely pier. We would stand on the upper deck and enjoy a glass of French champagne while we listened to music and watched the moonlight on the sea – until your friend Mr Ken Russell burned it down while making some tin-pot sex film.'

'He didn't burn it down. Its wiring caught fire while the film – not a sex film – was being made.'

We did not remind each other of the day when I persuaded her to remove and hand me her wedding ring. Whereon, aged six or seven, I slipped it through the pier's decking into the sea.

'Anyway, when your grandmother took me to Portsmouth Harbour station she said: "Never mind about me. Marry Jack Logue. He loves you." And on the train I decided that if your father met me at Waterloo with a carnation in his buttonhole and a copy of the *News Chronicle* under his arm, then, yes, I would accept him. And there he was. So well dressed. With his umbrella, his paper, gloves, and flowers for me. Above everything, he looked so kind. He had such a kind face. His dear, kind face. And we were married on April 27th 1924. Me thirty-six, him fifty-three.

'Cissie made my dress. Your uncle Percy played the organ. Bernard gave me away. We lived in the house on the Suburb' – the Hampstead Garden Suburb – 'your father bought over the years. You were born in Southsea two years later on a lovely November day.

'I wanted to be with my mother for the birth. I prayed and prayed for a girl, but you turned out to be a boy, and we must accept what God sends us.

'Oh, your father was so proud of his son. "This is my son, John Christopher," he would say – even to the milkman. He was such a hard-working man, my Jack Logue. So kind. So honest. As honest as the day is long.'

AGED forty, on the top deck of a number 12 bus, Betjeman's line 'Old men who never cheated, never doubted' comes to me. I can hardly see Regent Street for my tears. 'You all right, dear?' says the conductress. 'Yes, thank you. I'm fine. It will go away in a minute.'

LAST Sunday I was reading John Mortimer's memoir *Clinging to the Wreckage*. Over three hundred pages. Then the papers arrived. One has an interview with Mortimer. He rises at 5 a.m., works until 1 p.m., then – after cooking himself a tasty lunch of pheasant or trout – does the shopping.

I cannot cook. I dislike shopping. I have never written three hundred pages of anything.

I light the fire with the Business Section. Mortimer – I know and admire him – considers all is well if he completes ten handwritten pages a day. Ten pages a day!

Allowing for a week to get into it, plus ten days for cooking and shopping, if John starts a book on 1 January his editor will have the finished manuscript by May, whereas – after eight months, five lunches, plus weekly pep talks – my unlucky editor gets five heavily corrected pages on a Friday afternoon and has his weekend ruined by my telephone calls asking him, e.g. to remove a comma at the end of line 3 and to insert a semicolon on page 2a after the words 'with the greatest difficulty'.

Better to have become a painter.

Over lunch, Vivian King – I am staying with the Kings – reminds me that I did once manage more than two hundred pages '. . . in the dirty book you wrote for Girodias. And if you write anything as good as *Voyage Round My Father* we shall have plenty to be thankful for.'

DAME Henrietta Barnett could not have found a couple as well suited for a house on the less expensive slopes of her housing estate, the Hampstead Garden Suburb ('founded to bridge the gap between wealth and want'), as Jack and Molly Logue. Steady people, conscious of good taste, with a love of music, disinclined to take these interests too far.

Besides employing the finest architects of her day – Lutyens, Unwin, Dawson – Dame Henrietta had the Suburb laid out on egalitarian principles. My father's modest house had an ample porch, tiled fireplaces, hardwood block floors, painted wood panelling, gardens back and front. The Suburb affirmed the ideals of Ruskin and of Morris.

Not that my parents were radical.

Knowing, as their wages clerk, how little his fellow Post Office workers were paid – 'Though it was regular' – my father, a devout Irish-English Catholic, was troubled by politics; hearing one thing from the pulpit, another from his conscience; comfortable when reading G. K. Chesterton, realising that Shaw spoke a lot of the truth. Happiest with a ball in his hand, or singing, or in his garden. Once only, putting me – in 1949 or 1950, full of wild political talk – in my place, getting up from his armchair, holding his *News Chronicle*, and saying: 'That is enough from you, my lad. As a boy I learnt that many people were underfed, underpaid, uneducated, with almost no medical help and no life beyond their noses aside for five days a year by the sea – if lucky. Work, marriage, babies. Football, gossip, drink. Bad teeth, early death. Men and women worth less than a new pump. Now look around you. Please be quiet or go to your room.'

I went to my room.

'WHEN you were very young no one would have known you were a boy,' Molly said. 'Not a sound out of you. Out in the garden in all weathers. Snow on the hood of your pram. You have certainly made up for it. Within a year of your being born I lost all my teeth. How did the devil get into you? A lot of people feel sorry for me having you as a son.'

Sometimes when she took me shopping I crawled behind the counter and refused to come out. 'You are so selfish. Not companionable. Then or now. I'm glad I don't have to travel with you, young man.'

FLORRIE James, my mother's helper-cum-cleaner while we lived on the Suburb, was my friend. Married to a railway signalman, living on and in company property, she wheeled me between the rolling stock to the door of their cottage, two down, two up, the floors connected by a staircase entered through a cupboard door. 'You could perform a brain operation on Florrie's kitchen table,' my mother said.

I was allowed to sit upstairs watching the trains go by twenty yards off. Or better, Florrie's husband, Bob, took me to his box, popped me on a shelf beyond the bank of levers, safe and sound in the world of the railways; his fellow signalmen rolling their tobacco, discussing their dogs, while the warning bells rang and trains thundered past.

If Florrie had me for the day we set off from the Suburb, her pushing, sometimes letting go – 'Wheeeee!' – of John Christopher in his pram, 'the world's best mode of transport,' over Child's Hill to Cricklewood Yard; 'and' – so my Irish aunt, my father's sister, Margaret, who taught me to read and write, said – 'if it was a fine day you would stand up in your pram and sing the songs you learnt from your father as he sang you to sleep.'

I hear his voice now, a light Irish tenor: 'From the same range as John McCormack's,' Aunt Margaret said. 'Not to be mentioned in the one sentence with that man's heavenly voice, a gift from God, if ever He gave one. Yet a tunable voice, fit for singing. You had no cares in the world.'

Hilda, my half-sister, collected me.

Until late in life Hilda Logue had no luck. Fifteen in 1920 when her mother died, for four years she was the woman in my father's house, feeding him, seeing him off to work, doing his washing, ironing – though quite unsuited to housework – until he married my mother, a woman not slow to take over both father and house. A poor hand: for Hilda, by temperament nervous, eager to oblige, without good looks or a quick head, a rotten hand. Worsened by my arrival – the apple of everyone's eye.

I flinched at Hilda's wish for closeness. I did not want to hear how she longed to resign from the job my father made her take in the Post Office, and become a chiropodist: ' . . . a freelance, like you.'

She was interested in books, painting, music. I refused to discuss them. Like many half-educated people I suffer from intellectual snobbery. No money was spent on Hilda's education, an advantage that would have saved her untold anxiety. I do not think my father sang Hilda to sleep, or told others how proud of Hilda he was.

'Your mother was not prepared to go to Cricklewood Yard,' Hilda said. 'While Florrie and I had a cup of tea your game was to hide in the staircase. When it was clear we were going home you gripped the stair rail until Florrie prised your fingers off it, then carried you, screaming, to the pram where I strapped you in. A talkative thing when it suited you, I was treated to three miles of silence as I pushed you back to your mother.'

Forty-five years later, taking part in the Cambridge Poetry Festival, I was asked by the owners of Heffers bookshop to read from my work at their new premises, then to lunch upstairs with the shop's manager and his guests. The meal had begun – there must have been ten at the table – when through the door of the dining room, more nervous than the assistant who accompanied her, came Hilda, announcing to one and all that she was my sister, and that she, too, had won a gold medal for reciting poetry

8

when she was young, and that she had come to Cambridge from Felixstowe especially to hear her brother read – an event she had learnt of through the local newspaper.

Instead of welcoming and of offering her my place – as I saw from the manager's look I might – I stood, eyes lowered, a graceless little fellow embarrassed by his awkward, desperate sister's presence, praying for her to vanish. Which of course she did, escorted out of his shop by that courteous manager, while I sat, silent, looking at my plate, remembering one of Hilda's favourite sayings: 'God gives you your relatives, but you choose your friends for yourself.'

In the late 1950s I fell in love with Nell Dunn, whose mother, Lady Mary Campbell, was admired by the property magnate Sir Charles Clore – then owner of what had been our end of the Suburb.

Lady Mary, living in the Ritz, asked to see me. Nell was very much against such establishments. I, on the other hand, though familiar with the name – thanks to Fred Astaire – had never entered the Ritz.

Nell was wearing jeans, a PEACE FOR ME top under an Afghan waistcoat, her fine blonde hair tied up with luminous beads. I was carrying her Moroccan-carpet shoulderbag stocked with leaflets advertising a poetry-and-jazz event, a fundraiser for CND.

Lady Mary occupied a suite overlooking Green Park. She received us in bed. No sooner were we through the door than she looked from me to her daughter and said: 'Darling, how awful for you.'

A month later, thanks to Lady Mary, Sir Charles's firm offered my mother a flat a stone's throw from the house where she and my father had lived until, in 1932, after forty-five years' service, John Dominic ('Jack') Logue retired as Superintendent of the London Postal Service, to Southsea.

'On your father's side', Aunt Margaret said, 'you come from a line of schoolteachers and soldiers.' Opening the lid of my grandfather's field desk, she read from her notebook: '*George Logue* – the name is from Loiguire, son of Niall the high king of Dalriada, a pagan with sense enough to welcome St Patrick to his court in 440 – *born Coleraine, 1835; father, James Patrick Logue, a schoolmaster; enlisted, Royal Artillery, 1856; married Rose McCloskey, father, James Michael McCloskey, a schoolmaster, also of Coleraine, at Coleraine, November 15th 1864; served, Crimea and India* – where he helped to hold down the natives, wrong for an Irishman, albeit they were heathens – *Discharged, Farrier Sergeant 14th Brigade RA, 1878*. This' – taking it out – 'is his long-service and good-conduct medal. Yours to be. But with your atheist/socialist notions you'll have no use for it, so I'll leave it to Father McFee.'

'Isn't McCloskey a Protestant name?'

'No impudence from you, my lad. Rose McCloskey never missed her prayers in her life. A pity his eldest, not George himself, was your father. He would have tanned the devil out of you. Straight as a sword. A glass of water before he went to bed at 9.30 p.m., first standing to attention to sing the national anthem, then saluting the old Queen's picture, then kissing each of us goodnight, to be up at 4.30 a.m.

'He died in his sleep. When the Brigade came for him, Child's Way – where we lived while the Suburb was built around us – was too narrow for the gun carriage. So the burial party knocked out the walls at its mouth and off he went under the Union flag.'

'And where is he now?'

'In Heaven – a place you'll never see if you continue as you are. Atheism? There's no such thing. A silly boast God finds no trouble in forgiving. Hilda tells me you're a poet – or you like to be called one. Very well. Mark what Jonathan Swift says – though he's a lost soul: "Poets are like singers – either very good or no good."

'Take the medal. I am not long for this world and no tears over that. You're not so bad as you like to be thought. I say it only for your father's sake. My brother Jack.'

'Jack is very Irish,' my mother said to her Southsea friend Elsie Curran. 'Give him his way, everything would be done in the kitchen.

'When John Christopher was learning to go to the lavatory he liked to be alone near by. Jack sat him on his pot under the kitchen table with yesterday's *News Chronicle* draped down around the edges. We had no trouble with him in that direction.'

Although I saw little of him until he retired, my father's easiness with the world, his belief that God had made the world and so, despite everything, it was a good place, influenced me. He saw himself as one of a decent lot that I was to join as soon as may be, encouraged from the age of seven to go out on my own, and not just to school or the shops.

'He has been to the lavatory,' my mother heard from Dad, 'has a tongue in his head and money in his pocket' (not more than sixpence). 'He knows how far he is allowed to go and the time he has to be home.' And to me: 'Do not be afraid. Look whoever speaks to you straight in the face. Use your head.'

Earlier, me three or four, us out together during his holiday, him having seen enough of the bowling, the sea, when it was time to go home to my grandmother's he'd clap his hands and call: 'Old John!' Tuned to his voice, taking my face out of this old paint pot, or dragging a treasure – some lump of seaweedy driftwood, say – I would come trotting up, confident his presence protected me from my mother's: 'How is it you get your shoes into such a state?'

On his discharge, Grandfather Logue became chief veterinarian to the 600 horses belonging to a livery stables at Dudden Hill Farm, Willesden. It was there that he and Rose raised their eight children. My dad loved Jim, his nearest brother, Rose McCloskey's second child.

'Jim knew no fear,' Dad said. 'Though your grandfather forbade it, Jim and I went to the boxing booths at Willesden Fair. Jim would raise his hand, give me his shirt, then go under the rope into the ring, sixteen, eleven stone, brave as the brave. He always took his fists to them, never a pause.

'The boxers wanted him for one of their own. Not Jim. He was already a Communist. God knows where he learnt such wickedness. When your grandfather heard of it he never mentioned Jim's name again. The Farm loved him, so your grandfather heard of the fights. "John Dominic, James Patrick, follow me," he'd say, leading us to the harness room where he took down a leather strap and beat us. Neither of us uttered a word or shed a tear. He never asked Jim for his purse – three or four shillings – entitled to it though he was. Jim saved or gave away his money. Your aunt Margaret, ten, bandaged his knuckles and bathed his face. She worshipped Jim. When she heard he'd turned Communist, she wept for two days. Two whole days. He should have been a missionary.'

The brother John Dominic did not mention was Constant. 'Your father and I have no common ground with Constant and his wife Jean,' my mother said. 'Constant has left the Church. If you must hear more, ask your aunt Margaret.'

'Your uncle Constant is employed by Willesden Borough Council,' was all I learnt from her.

It was from my mother's brother, George Chapman, my favourite uncle, I heard the truth. 'Your uncle Constant', George said, 'is in charge of the gentlemen's convenience at Willesden Green Station.'

A half-fare from Temple Fortune to Willesden Green was tuppence, or if you were lucky – ' You mean dishonest,' Aunt Margaret said – gazing straight ahead when the conductor came round, free.

Willesden was further than allowed. More, though he had shown me how to use them, Dad forbade me to enter public lavatories. 'If you are taken short, go behind a bush. You were not born silly.'

Getting off at Willesden Green station I felt anxious. There was the Gentlemen's. A small crowd at its entrance. I thought of Jim going under the rope and went down the stairs. At the bottom there was a queue crossing the lavatory to a wooden cubicle with a stable door behind which I was thankful to see someone who looked like a chubby version of Dad putting the money he took from the man at the head of the queue into a Gladstone bag.

Edging in I said: 'Uncle Constant? I'm John Christopher, your brother Jack's son.' 'God Almighty,' said Constant Logue, letting me in, lowering the bag to my feet, 'if your mother finds out you're here she'll kill me. Put the money I pass you into the bag. Yes, Mr Myers, he's my nephew, a fine boy. That's three shillings to win on Runnymede in the two-thirty at Newmarket. A wise choice.'

When Uncle Constant closed his book we went upstairs to his car. A car! The first I had entered.

'This is your auntie Jean,' Uncle Constant said. Auntie Jean was a looker. Blonde. Plump. Red lipstick. Smoking. 'Connie, ring his mother and tell her he's here,' she said.

'We're not on the telephone,' I said, wishing we were.

'Then you'll drive him home the moment he's had something to eat, or the police will have been told and we'll be in the papers.'

Uncle Constant tipped the money on to the kitchen table. Jean ('No Auntie for me, please') counted it while Constant had a gin and tonic. A gin and tonic! And it wasn't Christmas. And the wireless was on. And not the Home Service. Radio Luxembourg! Dance music! Interviews with film stars! And they had a dog, Biscuit. And Biscuit's basket was *in the kitchen*. And then their daughter, Eric – 'We wanted a boy so we called her Eric' – wearing a very tight top, came in from work and gave me a kiss and a cuddle.

This is the life for me, I thought. This is definitely the life for me. Never to think so again until I learnt how to survive in Paris.

On the way home I asked about Jim. I knew Jim had visited us at least once, because a pair of big brown well-polished boots – 'Jim's boots, they're here when he wants them,' Dad said – were kept in our hall.

'Ah . . . Jim,' Constant said. 'Jim was the best of us after your dad. He went to Russia. Met Lenin, so they say. Spoke on the wireless and said the revolution was coming here. Your father had a postcard from him. He lives in South Africa now. A founder member of their Communist Party, I'm told.' I was proud of this until I learnt that in its first days one of the South African Communist Party's slogans ran: Workers of the World Unite for a White South Africa.

My mother was polite to Constant. I was sent upstairs to wash my hands. He called out goodbye.

I lay on my bed thinking that Eric might, just might, take all her clothes off for me if I could find a really good way to put it to her. The only woman I knew well enough to ask for advice was my mother. That was out. We were not friends, Molly and me. I never asked for her advice. Never confided in her. We were two headstrong people, neither that good at making the best of things. Me, troubled, unable to find my way. She, happy in a happy marriage, which was clouded by a worrisome son.

When the most difficult times of his life were over – he hoped –
by the late fifties, say, he saw her each Saturday to avoid feeling
guilt. Visits she accepted as her due, and, on occasions,
enjoyed.

That we had scarcely three or four ten-second fellow-to-fellow
conversations in our entire lives was my fault more than hers.

At eleven, keen on Leslie Charteris's gentleman hero, I marked
the Saint's height on the edge of the door of my room. Seeing my
mother seeing me measuring my four-foot-seven-inches against
Simon Templar's six-foot-two, love broke my never-say-what-
you-are-up-to rule, and in a rush I described the Saint to her, then
asked if she thought I would grow to be as tall as him. 'Let us
wait and see. Your eyes are as blue,' she said. Next day we
resumed our long quarrel.

When, shortly before I joined the army, she said: 'We are selling our bed. Your father sleeps so badly. After all these years we
shall have to have single beds now,' I said nothing.

'YOUR father should have risen far, far higher,' Molly said.
'But how could a farrier sergeant's son sit the Civil Service
examination?'

John Dominic left school at fourteen. Had the Civil Service
examination been open to him it is likely he would have entered a
different branch of 'the Service' – as he called it – from the Post
Office. This would not have made him happier. He was proud of
the Post Office. The staggered nature of the work allowed him to
organize a team of harriers, to raise and tour his own cricket
eleven. In retirement, he administered Portsmouth's four-county,
open bowls tournament. 'Of course, he was secure when many
were losing their work,' Molly said. They could chart their
future.

I see my mother at Bournemouth at the end of the 1940s, her
knitting set aside, rubbing mentholated embrocation into my
elderly father's chest as he sat in his chair before their fire, while
saying: 'When this is done, and you've had your nap, we'll go for
a walk along the cliffs to the links.' Then he would spread the
News Chronicle over his face, settle in his chair, and nap for forty
minutes.

John Dominic was expert at paperwork. Cushioning the lead

of a pencil against the ball of his thumb he sharpened, then pointed it with the small blade of the penknife bought when he and my mother sailed up the Rhine in 1932, their only trip abroad.

'Between Cologne and Koblenz we fell into conversation with a German couple,' Dad said. 'After a while the man opened his coat and took a silver pin topped by a swastika from his lapel and gave it to your mother, saying: "You may not have heard of us up to now, but you will before long."'

'It was a beautiful pin,' my mother said, 'yet I never cared for it. It lay in one of the drawers of your father's desk for donkey's years and came to light when he was making blackout screens for our windows during the war. The dustmen had it.'

When – we were still in London – he had pointed the lead, Dad set his cylindrical ebony rule across a blank writing pad, lining its top sheet by rolling the ebony downwards with the fingertips of his left hand while drawing the pencil across its width with his right. His lines were evenly spaced, unblistered, soon done.

Sitting beside him at his desk I practised writing. 'Hold the pen lightly, dip it evenly, not too far in, keep the words flowing forward, a touch above the lines. Let your hand float along the page. That's good, that's the trick, patience does it.'

Each year my parents went to Southsea for Dad's annual holiday, and, on Dad's retirement, they went to live there.

Hidden from the rest of England by Portsdown Hill, guarded by its marine forts, Horse Sand and Spitbank, with its three-mile-long seafront, two piers, the Fleet on the Solent, the Canoe Lake Park, its Royal Naval Dockyard and its shingle beaches, the municipality of Portsmouth & Southsea was an agreeable place for a boy. As a three-year-old visitor, Sunday mornings were my favourite. Then, sitting on my father's shoulders, we followed the band of the Royal Marines as they marched along the Front to church parade, on our left the Solent, on our right their silver instruments, us – at my insistence – always level with the big drum's bandsman in his leopard-skin apron twirling leather-headed sticks, and then, after a silence paced by rim shots from the drummer boy: one, two, three –

'A life on the ocean wave
A home on the rolling deep . . .'

Epes Sargent's exhilarating march broke forth, whose words
John C. learnt from John D. so they sang them as the one strode
and other was carried along.

IT was at Southsea, aged around eight, I began to lie and to
steal. My father was surprised to hear from another member
of his local church, St Swithin's, congregation of his son's trip
to New York with his uncle Constant, 'the professional card
player'. This romancing preceded less innocent misrepresenta-
tions, backed up, when challenged, by denials.

My thefts began at home: money from my father's pockets, my
mother's purse. Then sweets and toys from shops. I knew that it
was wrong to steal. I had what a child could want. I was not led
astray. Indeed, I led others, my friends Peter and Raymond
Kerswell, astray. My parents knew I stole and lied.

As people who believed that lying and stealing were sinful, and
that theft was a serious crime, they must have been dismayed.
Being falsely accused of theft by a fellow wages clerk was the
worst experience of my father's life. He must have lived in
expectation of my being, as, eight years later, I was – and you
will hear – caught, charged, brought before a juvenile court, and
punished.

Because they had bought their house with their savings my
parents' only income was my father's pension, much of which
went on my school fees, though my first Southsea school, that of
St Swithin's, was free.

The first thing I learnt there was the difference between work
and play. I had no words to explain my instinctive rejection of
what, in our time, to those of my class, was a given: work on the
one hand, play on the other.

Levelled at me today, the command 'Get a proper job' still
hurts. In those early years, and for long after, such thoughts were
like a hidden chorus declaring that I was workshy, parasitical.
Now and again the chorus might add that I was stuck-up, a
show-off, thinking myself 'too good for the ordinary things of
life'. Worse, it described the activities I liked – larking about,

playing games, parties, fancy dress, recitations, etc. – as 'not matters to be taken seriously', 'silly things that would not survive childhood,' things that had no place 'in the real world'.

Echoes of that chorus persist. A young woman at a party saying – when I confessed I felt low: 'Well, you do just what you like, so put up with it.' Elsie Curran had little time for me: 'The boy who swallowed the dictionary.'

It is difficult for a child to show that preoccupations with no direct connection to what is known as work are not a waste of time. Matters are worsened by sarcasms: 'Well, what is it his lordship *wants* to do, then?' Having no answer, and flustered by the thought that there might be no answer (as for eighteen years I had no answer), you raise the drawbridge and post your faithful retainers along the battlements before answering: 'Nothing.'

'Then go to your room.'

Blest I could be so told.

My army days excepted, I have always had that precious godsend, a room of my own. If, as an eccentric child, I lacked someone to teach me how to distance myself from reality, at least I had my room, and in my room, my things.

Mostly I have forgotten what I learnt at school. Drawing, carpentry and English were agreeable, offset by that cold, dirty punishment called 'sport', where, on pain of death from a ball on the head or suffocation by mud, you were obliged to pay attention.

I was of some use to St Swithin's. There is a photograph of me bewigged, frock-coated, silk breeches tied just below the knee with ribbons, patent-leather pumps, left hand on hip, all got up for my part as Prince Charming in the school's 1934 production of *Cinderella*.

I hear my mother telling Elsie Curran: 'You'll not believe it, I have to drag him away from school. He knows all the parts.'

'And his own?'

'It does seem to get bigger as the days go by . . .'

'Then now we know what to do with you, young man, don't we?'

My odd (deep, rather loud) voice persuaded my mother to enrol me with Miss Crowe, an elocution mistress, for extra lessons. Miss Crowe combined literary taste with physical attractiveness. Anxious to be in her favour, I memorized the poems she set me: 'The Lady of Shalott', a shortened version of 'The Pied Piper', 'The Walrus and the Carpenter', 'Gunga Din'. And thanks to her I learnt that in the hands of a master the musical quality of words (their movement, their contrasts) combined with their meaning, made poetic thought: 'Which', she said – as we sat on the floor of her studio room, me doing my best to look up her skirt – 'is its own kind of thought, related to musical thought.'

As well, I discovered that a way of memorizing a text was to copy it out. This led me to find my handwriting insufficiently dignified for 'The Lady of Shalott'. So my father, having filled and wiped the nib of his Swann fountain pen, and standing me by his desk to repeat the poem line by line, made a fair copy of it in his elegant hand, asking, as we moved along, for the significance Miss Crowe gave to this or that punctuation mark, thus adding notational to logical power. The next time he and I went out together, always to me a slightly worrying turn for he sang aloud in the street and spat into the gutter, we visited an art suppliers – instantly my preferred kind of shop – where we bought a card of mixed nibs, pen holder attached, scripts illustrated verso, plus a sheet of cartridge paper and a bottle of Indian ink.

At a stroke I had received poetic, syntactical, performance and design standards.

Secretly I put my name, not Kipling's, at the end of my fair copy of 'Gunga Din'. I took care that Miss Crowe did not learn of this. An act as wilful led to our parting.

I LOVED the sea. Molly knitted me a blue swimming costume with a gold anchor on its side.

After lunch, Dad returned to the bowling tournament's office while my mother and I went via the Canoe Lake to the beach with sandwiches and a thermos of tea in a basket covered by a check cloth. Uncle George had promised me half a crown when I had learnt to swim. I was keen to get my hands on the money because Uncle Percy had given me a gramophone record of Bing Crosby and Johnny Mercer singing 'Mr Gallagher and Mr Shean' which I could take around to my friends the Kerswells' house and play on their radiogram. The snag was: no privacy to learn how 'Bing', as he was in our conversations, did his 'Ohhhhh, Mr Mercer – Mr Mercer – Mr Mercer' flourish. I had spotted a second-hand wind-up portable gramophone in the Hidyhole in Highlands Road for the give-away price of ten shillings and sixpence, which – if I could throw in that half-crown – my savings would cover.

Knowing her son, my mother was not taken in by my one-foot-on-the-bottom claims to the money. Suddenly, though, I could swim. Not a bather herself, Molly asked another middle-aged lady (swim-suited, rubber-capped, greased) who was about to enter the Solent, if she would be kind enough to check my claim. Nothing loath, the dame plunged in, swam underneath me and surfaced to call, 'Afloat and on the move,' before overarming towards the Isle of Wight.

AUNT Cissie and Uncle Percy were to have me while my parents sailed up the Rhine. I did not look forward to this alteration. Not that I disliked Cissie's house. Full of rare clocks, it had a fruiting orange tree and a water tank visited by newts in its greenhouse. When I put it to him, Dad said I could take my Fairy cycle with me.

Comparing notes, my parents found I had asked to take my soldiers, my fort, my box of shells, two large pieces of driftwood, my cast iron six-gun, a set of Rupert Bear annuals, my stamp collection, my gramophone, my records, my ex-WD water bottle ('Who knows when an explorer may have to cross the Sahara by night?') and even my bed with me. Told I must limit myself to what could be carried in a pillow case, I lost my temper, shouted with rage, wept, and was sent to bed.

Aunt Cissie was a dressmaker. She made me nervous. There was no question of playing her up, or, if crossed, talking her round.

'It was a pleasure to watch that girl sew,' my mother said. 'Stuff over one hand, in-out-in-out went her needle, no matter how small, even a No. 1, drawing the thread after it with her little finger, next length ready between her lips. Such stitches – you'd think a machine had made them.'

Before she married Percy Bridges, Cissie travelled the world as lady's maid to the Duchess of Manchester. 'I lent money to the Duke,' she said. 'I pitied the man. Nice but weak. The Duchess had the money – that's why the family took her. Stingy. She would hire me out for a fee. I cut and sewed six shirts for Queen Isabel of Spain, yet got not a penny extra. The Duke said he wanted the money for spare parts – cars were his hobby – but I knew he wanted it for drink.'

Tiring of employment, she decided on Percy, an industrial chemist earning 'a good screw in mines' – that is to say, from working on explosives in the Portsmouth Naval Dockyard.

Percy was the first man I knew whose circumstances broke him. He might have earned a living as a jobbing pianist-composer. He wrote marches, novelty and patter songs. He could 'do' Winston Churchill and Anthony Eden. Finding me in a rage about some trifle or other he 'did' me to my face – criticism I have never forgotten.

'When he played, Percy's hands just flew over the keys,' Molly said. 'We would stand around the piano and sing and sing until we could sing no more. His job disgusted him. Cissie would not hear of his leaving. He told your father so. Not another soul. He said he stopped playing because he wasn't as good as a famous performer like Hutch. The truth was that his work stained his fingers. He couldn't look at them.'

Percy had a car. 'We are going for a spin in the car,' Molly said, getting me ready. But at the end of the road Percy stopped, got out, and then walked back to the house to make sure that the gas or the water was off, or to be certain he had given the key of the greenhouse door two full turns.

After war was declared my parents and I sat together while the German air force flattened half our road. I had never felt so huge a fear, nor, coincidentally, so close to my parents. Nor after-wards, so dejected.

The bombing drove Percy mad. During daylight air raids he sat on a chair in the middle of the road. Cissie could not get him indoors. When Cissie died of cancer, 'six years plus a complete house redecoration after being given a month to live' – her grandson, my cousin Michael told me – 'Percy moved in with my parents. My mother' – I had to call her 'Auntie Gladys' – 'couldn't handle him, so he became an in-patient at Napsbury

Hospital. He would walk the twenty miles back to us. My father' – Uncle Lionel to me – 'telephoned for the nurses. He stopped coming in the end. But not the walking out. He was missing for two days, then found dying in a field.'

MY arrival for the three weeks at Cissie's went smoothly. I was shown the spare room. My six-gun went under the pillow. I was permitted to hang my water bottle on one of the bedposts. To my own surprise, when the moment came for my parents to leave, I threw myself into my father's arms and begged to be taken with him.

Trouble came at breakfast the next day.

The sisters liked everything cleared up. As one who often left his plate half full, I had learnt how to manage my mother's: 'You will remain at this table until you clear your plate. Millions of Chinese children would thank God for what I put before you.' Thereafter we would sit in silence, my mother staring at me, me staring at my knees, until Dad, fed up with it, ordered me down.

Having tasted the piece of toast Cissie buttered for me, my appetite vanished. Asked why, I said I wasn't hungry and we didn't have toast for breakfast at home. 'Well,' Cissie said in her waxed-twine voice, 'you are not at home and I am not your mother. I expect you to make a good breakfast and you will sit at the table until you do.'

As (a usually reliable) opening move in the battle to come, I spun my knife on the tablecloth. No good. Cissie stood over me, cut the toast into fingers, and included the knife in her clearing away. During one of her trips to the kitchen I pumped my breath back down into my stomach to see what chance there was of vomiting if (say) I ate one of the fingers. No hint of a heave, never mind the deep retching I was after. By now Cissie had cleared the tablecloth, leaving me alone before a plateful of cold toast fingers on the polished mahogany. Through the door to the kitchen she said: 'As I am making pastry when the washing-up's done, I see we shall be enjoying each other's company until lunch time.'

I had lost. While Aunt Cissie was out at the dustbin, I put the fingers into my pockets and took my plate to the kitchen. Safe upstairs I popped the fingers into the back of the floral china clock on the dressing table. So it continued, with different clocks for the daily toast.

On the day my parents came to collect me I was ready, and standing by the front door for an hour by the grandfather clock in the hall (three portions of toast), before they were due.

'We have had our words, but on balance he has been no trouble,' Cissie said, as, gun in belt, water bottle over shoulder, dying to open my presents, I hurried into the taxi.

'Say goodbye to your auntie Cissie,' my mother said.

'Goodbye, Auntie Cissie.'

Two days later my mother confronted me with a paper bagful of warped toast fingers.

'Have you seen these before?'

Silence.

'How could you do such a thing?'

Silence.

'As nobody else would, your aunt Cissie was kind enough to take you off our hands during the only proper holiday of our lives – and this is what we come back to.'

Silence.

'You are just too much for us. What fools we are to spend what little money we have on your education. Where do you get it from? That's what I ask myself. Not from your father. And certainly not from me, your poor mother.'

Silence.

'And don't tell me you're sorry. I can see how sorry you are by the look on your face. Sorry for yourself. Never for anybody else. That's you, my son. Though you're no son of mine. One of these fine days you'll have something to be sorry for, make no mistake. Go to your room this minute and pray to God for His forgiveness.'

Shortly after this incident I came down with measles and mumps, my first illness. I could not sleep. My mother sat by my bed all night, every night, for a week.

'I wish I could bear the pain for you,' she said. 'Be a soldier. Ask God for His help. God never denies His help to those who ask.'

Walking by the sea twenty-five years later with Isobel, whom I loved, I saw she looked doubtful when I said, not that I had stopped believing in God, but that I had never believed in Him.

'Not as a child?'

'Not really.'

'You never saw Him as a little old man with a long ginger beard?'

'Certainly not.'

'Surely children believe everything they are told?'

At home, or at St Swithin's, it was assumed (by me as well) that I believed in God. To have announced that one did not believe in God would have appeared a vain, truthless boast, as well as an insult to the entire community to which one's parents belonged. Even in a rage I could not have said: 'I do not believe in your God or in any other god,' to my mother or to my father.

I am sure my parents realized I ceased to attend Mass or to go to confession as soon as I had left boarding school. Supposedly off to church on Sunday mornings, I would sit in a beach shelter, reading, or walk by the sea. And this was several years after I had understood that, by nature, I disbelieved.

Born without religious faith, I prefer the company of those whom, though they seldom mention it, I know to be religious. I am not impressed by my atheism. Cosmology has something to do with it. I find the idea of a beginning as impossible to credit as that of an end. The phrase, 'the edge of the Universe', tempts me to ask, what is the Universe 'in'? If asked: 'Are you an atheist?' I am tempted to reply: 'Yes. Are you a godist?' or, if irritable, '-ite?'

Did the ancient Greeks believe in their gods as I believe in the existence of the ancient Greeks? I am not sure how people form their religious beliefs. To hold such beliefs but lack a sense of humour can be dangerous. There are those who search for God in creation. Were I religious, this would be my position. And there are people who are holy. They are rare. But they exist.

GOD was everywhere at my second school, the de la Salle Brothers' St John's College, Southsea. You sat, you stood, you were taught and were punished in God's name.

BROTHER JOHN: 'Who made you?'
    THE CLASS: 'God made me.'
BROTHER JOHN: 'Why did God make you?'
    THE CLASS: 'God made me to know and to love Him.'

Only when you walked out through the College gates were you free of the Brothers, their ubiquity, their indoctrination.

I had beliefs. I believed in the Lady of the Lake; in ghosts; that my thefts were wrong; that girls were special. Fifty years old before I read George Saville's remark to his daughter, Elizabeth, 'that he believed as much as he could, and imagined that God would forgive him if, unlike the ostrich, he could not eat iron', I did my best as a schoolchild to believe in God. Of the power of the Brothers themselves there was no doubt.

This power echoed that of the hidden chorus declaring work and play to be opposites. You could confront the chorus, saying to yourself: 'Wait until my face is on a cigarette card, or I am one of those people who stop the roar of London's traffic to be interviewed on *In Town Tonight*.' Dealing with the Brothers was more difficult. What they believed, you must believe. My conclusion was, apart from my parents, I would steer clear of people who believed in God.

I had my code. Stealing was wrong. Breaking your word was wrong. Hitting people was wrong. Hitting animals, one of my father's few inflexible rules, was worse.

'All animals?'

'All.'

'Even sharks?'

'Even sharks.'

'Even if you have to walk the plank?'

'You don't have to walk the plank.'

'You do if you're a pirate.'

Dad fanned himself with his hat.

'I agree that piracy is an outdoor job and that outdoor jobs are best,' he said. 'So you could start with something like the Ordnance Survey and work your way up.'

This raised the worrying subject of jobs, and the irreconcilability of work and play. We walked on in silence. Me nine, him sixty-four.

The Brothers helped me to solve the work/play split during what was called a 'free period'. In such, a Brother talked to us on a non-curricular subject close to his heart.

Brother John spoke of architecture, explaining that all the great English cathedrals had been built by, then stolen from, us Catholics by the Tudor king, Henry VIII. Brother John said: 'Every part of a cathedral, including its roof, is holy. Few besides God will ever see the rooftop carvings, while the common people, whose labour paid for the building, knew in their hearts that the carvings were up there, safe in the sight of God until Judgement Day.'

These words struck home. From now on, whatever I did, I would do in that spirit. For its own sake. For no other reason. As the medieval carvers had carved for God. No justification was needed. None would be offered. That I did not know what I wanted to do was unimportant.

A YEAR ahead of me at St John's, Vernon Pine was a corpulent boy, slow speaking, his head always slightly tipped back, and a voice that seemed to come through his nose. His father, a bank manager, made, and on Sunday mornings raced, his self-steering model J-class yacht on the Canoe Lake.

To house these lovely things Portsmouth and Southsea Council provided a locker shed, where their lacquered or varnished hulls sat on padded stands, their masts racked above, their sails taken home to be washed and ironed for next weekend's competition.

It was behind the locker shed that Vernon proposed we should 'kiss dicks'. In other words, rub our penises together. Somewhat prudish then, as I am still, I did not fancy his offer. Besides, I was very much under the spell of that popular form of child abuse: the association of wickedness with whatever goes on at the top of one's legs.

Had Vernon been a girl making a comparable offer, I might have acted, and avoided much grief later in life. What he was, was my first fan. When I proposed this or that as the game of the day, Vernon always agreed. He played hard, and never uttered real-world spoiler-talk of the 'it's only a game' variety. I liked, and needed, him.

There was a further consideration. Between the Kerswells, Vernon and myself, the price of one cheap-afternoon cinema ticket (fourpence) could usually be raised. As the most present-able of us, Vernon was the one to persuade whoever was in charge of the Odeon's, the Apollo's or the Gaiety's box office of his being 'just turned fourteen': meaning, allowed to see 'A' films unaccompanied.

Once inside the cinema Vernon made his way to the rear doors and pushed up the exit bar. In we came, waiting until the gunfire or the music swelled before tiptoe-crouching through the dark-ness to the seats.

We saw *The Crusades*. Richard the Lionheart (Henry Wilcoxon), sword in hand, a winged helmet on his head, storming the walls of Acre Castle on the shore of Palestine. We sat through it twice.

Vernon's penis was half hard; mine was flabby. All I had to do to get mine going was to think about Miss Crowe's stocking tops or the teenaged girl where I bought Dad's daily packet of twenty Players Old Navy Cut, a rounded beauty, pleased – despite my mother's dictum that girls disliked being looked at – to flaunt herself for me as long as there was no one else in the shop.

We rubbed our penises together while I, determined to stay soft, pictured us caught by a park keeper. Then I put my penis away, expecting Vernon to be fed up.

He was not. Sitting by the Lake I tried out my 'I do it for nothing, it is an end in itself', death-blow to the work-versus-play, jobs-for-life brigade.

When he finished his mouthful of the Mars bar we were sharing, Vernon said:

'It's good. But just do it – whatever "it" is – and keep quiet is better.'

'Why?'

'I've noticed it.'

'Then they'll think they've won,' I said.

'They've only won if you give in.'

'I'll never give in,' I said, starting to feel sorry for myself. 'I'd rather die.'

'Then they really have won,' Vernon said, folding the Mars

bar's wrapper into a triangle. 'The point is, if you don't have a job, what are you going to do for money?'

'I'll steal it,' I said.

'That is wrong,' Vernon said. 'Think of the person whose money you'll be stealing. In any case, my father says only the stupid steal.'

'Then I'll starve,' I said, resisting the temptation to add: 'And when I'm dead you'll all be sorry.'

'Don't worry about money,' Vernon said. 'I'll find the money for you. Finding money is easy.'

His words amazed me. I had never heard anyone speak of money in so familiar a way.

Money, in our house, was a powerful thing you could not do without, over which you had no – or very little – control. We had enough for our needs. My parents did not think of having more. You earned your 'screw' and your pension. That was that. There was something indecent about money. If you inherited it – well and good. The thought that you could just come by it, easy as that, was exciting.

'Vernon,' I said, trying to keep the wonder out of my voice, 'how are you going to get it?'

'I'm not sure how,' Vernon said, in a serious tone. 'Perhaps I'll advertise. Put up a sign: The Vernon Pine Trust Company. Dad says the first thing people do if they get a lot of money they didn't expect to get is panic. The next thing they do is to bring it to him.'

'Don't you have to ask permission to put up a sign like that?'

'Baron Rothschild didn't ask permission.'

Vernon spoke of Baron Rothschild with the same tone of reverence as boys like me spoke of the Red Baron, von Richthofen, the First World War air ace.

'Vernon,' I said as we walked along the side of the Lake, 'I'm sorry about that business with our dicks. Not joining in, I mean.'

'You won't say anything about it, will you?'

'Never,' I said.

And I never have until now.

PETER and Raymond Kerswell were my best friends; daily in the holidays I walked round to their house. Mrs Kerswell, the wife of a soldier, was a small Irishwoman with bright brown eyes and dark brown hair kept in a bun hidden by a round brown straw hat when she went shopping.

If the boys were busy with her messages, or tending the altar at St Swithin's – she trained them for housework, homework and church work – Mrs Kerswell either sent me home or sat me in her front room until they were free.

Here – Sergeant Kerswell had served several years in Gibraltar – I waited among her souvenir tambourines, castanets, and embroidered views of the Rock, overseen by a large coloured lithograph of Jesus Christ holding his robe open to reveal his chest, which in turn was open to show, where his heart should have been, a heart-shaped lamp radiating golden beams.

Among the Kerswells' books was a quarto, *Covenants With Death*, reproducing photographs taken on the Western Front during the First World War. Close-ups of dead, rotting soldiers, from both armies. Some wearing gas masks, still holding their weapons. Some in each other's arms under miles of barbed wire, itself under miles of low cloud that stretched into the book's gutter.

Here was a terrible thing, neither work nor play, that made me do what otherwise I would not have dared to do: go uninvited with the book in my hands from the front room to the kitchen.

George, Mrs Kerswell's eldest, six-foot-three, already a soldier, was having a strip wash at the sink. Seeing my face he dried himself, put the book up on a high ledge, and led me back to the front room where we played his orchestral recording of the *Blue Danube* on the radiogram, while he taught me the waltz.

DURING summer at Southsea, the Front was the place where thousands of visitors strolled, watching the Fleet, the regattas, booking excursions on Royal Blue charabancs to Rowlands Castle or Chichester, listening to the music from the bandstands and dipping from the shingle, while stalwarts armed with balloons knocked each other off the Greasy Pole and bathing beauty contests were judged by King Neptune. Laughter mixed with the sound of the waves when, as one of the great ocean-going liners steamed up the Solent towards Southampton, those who had not read the Sailing Tables posted along the Front were swooshed by its wash into the water, still sitting in the deck chairs they had placed too close to the sea's edge.

By the end of June, Peter, Raymond and I had so toughened the soles of our feet we ran uncaring on hot asphalt, our sport to beg from smokers: 'Please can I have your cigarette card, Mister?' Kensitas smokers were top, for Kensitas issued the 'Flags of All Nations' set, printed on silk, and meant, when complete, to be sewn on to the surface of a cushion. Tired of begging, we stacked empty ice-cream tubs into a column as high as Raymond (the youngest) or me, then asked the beach photographers to take us. Who laughed and looked elsewhere.

Raymond had to be home by four. Peter and I went to my house for tea.

'My mum says you may be sent to boarding school,' he said.

'Did she?'

'Raymond heard your mum talking to ours about it.'

'I don't want to go.'

'Stop stealing then.'

'I haven't stolen anything for ages.'

'What about those darts?'

'Oh, those. I threw them away.'

Not far from Hidyhole was a baker's shop where on Saturday mornings one might buy for a penny a bagful of broken biscuits, then go to the beach and, if it was raining, gorge on them inside a shelter assembled from deck chairs. Or, if it was sunny, in the damp semi-darkness among the iron stanchions supporting the pier. There, even if the wind was up and there were white horses on the sea, the air was salty and still.

THE only place at St John's where the spirit of the Brothers did not prevail was the gym. Though none of us knew it, the word for the aura of this hall where we were taught by a man, not a Brother, was sensual.

Rope-climbing was my speciality. Twisting the rope into a tread with one's instep, then push/pull up to the crossbeams, before a long, loose-gripped slide back down, the last yard jumped – easy as kiss your hand. Except for once, when, somehow, as I slid down, the underside of my half-hard penis fast rubbed against the length of the rope and – SLAM! – for the first time in my waking life, I came. Feeling that my penis was exploding, I let go of the rope and fell six feet on to the mat.

The gym master sent me to shower. My spunk tasted salty.

Here was another great power. And there was an extra. It had a powerful servant: secrecy. Without a word being said I understood that, just as I had no one to talk to about coming, if I kept quiet about it no more would be said. I kept quiet.

EACH year the pupils of the Southsea schools of dancing and elocution competed on the stage of Portsmouth's Theatre Royal. To represent her studio in 1935, Miss Crowe chose Yvonne Hunter and me.

Listing our repertoires as we walked home via the Lake, Yvonne – on whom I was fairly keen – said she wished to recite 'Wynken, Blynken and Nod' by Eugene Field as her first poem, then Bunyan's 'My Little Bird' if she went forward for a prize. My first was to be 'Gunga Din' with 'The Walrus and the Carpenter' to follow.

'You must give the poet's name: "'Gunga Din' by Rudyard Kipling",' said Yvonne.

'What about the gestures?' I said.

Miss Crowe was keen on gestures. 'When Gunga lifts his water bag to the lips of the soldier, raise an imaginary water bag.' As if the words came from Heaven, I knew that gestures were No Good.

Then the blow fell.

Miss Crowe announced that Yvonne was to recite 'Wynken, Blynken and Nod' while I was to start with 'Christopher Robin Is Saying His Prayers' by A. A. Milne, with Joyce Kilmer's equally embarrassing (and very short) 'Trees' to follow. And I had to make gestures.

'When the poem says that Christopher Robin kneels at the foot of his bed, you kneel. When Christopher Robin droops his little gold head on to his hands, you droop yours on to your hands.'

How could Miss Crowe do this to someone who loved her – the pupil who would have taken first prize only to lay it at his teacher's feet?

Thirty-six years later, having given an adequate performance as Cardinal Richelieu in Ken Russell's film *The Devils*, I boasted to Lindsay Anderson of my future as the only English poet/film star.

'You', Lindsay said – with a sigh – 'will never be a star. You might become a featured player specializing at intellectual villains, artistic misfits, etc.'

Came the day of the competition. Miss Crowe was wearing red high heels, a black two-piece suit and a black and red pillbox hat. I recited the Milne without gestures. I did not reach the final. After the competition Miss Crowe came up to my mother and said: 'I am sorry, Mrs Logue, as your son is determined to indulge himself at the expense of my studio he and I must go separate ways.'

'That's typical of you,' Isobel said. 'It would have cost you nothing to make the gestures. Miss Crowe would have kissed you.'

My mother was upset.

'I'm sorry,' I said through my tears. 'I can't do the gestures. Even alone in my room.'

'There is no such word as "can't". Wait until you get out into the world. Then you will know what for. Tomorrow I shall have one of my heads.'

I was sent to bed.

Half an hour later Dad brought me up a cup of hot milk and some biscuits. He saw I was miserable.

'Never mind, old John,' he said. 'It will be forgotten in the morning. You can write a letter to Miss Crowe. She'll have you back.'

She did. It wasn't the same.

Worse followed.

One Sunday morning an angry father knocked on my parents' door demanding to see me. He declared that I had robbed his young daughter at toy-pistol point of the ice cream she had been eating in the street. What he said was true.

My father marched me to the shop to buy, and then to deliver, with proper apologies to the girl, to her mother and to her father, a replacement for the ice cream I had stolen. When Vernon came around he was told I was in disgrace. He was not to come again until hearing otherwise. On Monday, at my father's request, a uniformed policeman called at the house to inform me that, if I did such a thing again, I would go to prison.

Then I was sent away to school.

P RIOR Park, a Palladian villa, was built for Ralph Allen, the friend of Alexander Pope, a self-made millionaire whose wealth came first from organizing an efficient postal service between London and the west of England, thereafter from trade in the honey-coloured Bath stone out of which Prior was built – the envious said – 'seeing all Bath, for all Bath to see', above a funnel-shaped valley to the city's south, whose slopes, Allen – advised by Pope and Capability Brown – planted, whose streams he dammed into three stepped lakes, crowning the bank between the topmost with a Palladian bridge in 1755.

By the 1930s Prior Park College had become a boarding school with fees of £100 a year, 'including extras', run by the Irish Christian Brothers, a teaching order founded to create an educated Catholic middle class for Ireland.

I HAD put being sent away out of my mind. When the day came I travelled to Prior thinking about other things.

The truth struck at bedtime. I could not drink my cocoa. I refused to get into my pyjamas.

New boys slept in the Nurse's dormitory which had a small window high up on one of its walls enabling Nurse to keep an eye on the year's intake. She stood over me while I got undressed. I had never slept in a room with strangers. I dreamt I was fastened to her by an illuminated tube.

To say I was unhappy, though true, would be too knowing. I was lost. My room, my friends, were gone. Worst of all, in this foreign place I was never alone, a luxury I had, without knowing it, cherished.

Throughout my childhood I thought of happiness as a state of affairs found in films. When I was alone in my room, playing with my things, or down by the Lake with my friends, I was happy as people in films were happy. For the moment these blessings had been removed. In the future, if I was lucky, things would improve. If not, I would kill myself.

It took me sixty years to understand that, in my mind, from the day I went to Prior, I no longer had a home. True, in both the early and the late 1940s I lived again under my parents' roof. It was not the same.

If to feel at home is to feel, as well as belonging, you are of use,

I did not feel at home again until I lived among the French in the company of my American and British friends in Paris in the 1950s.

THERE was a rough kindness about the Irish Christian Brothers of Prior Park. Firm in their celibacy, sincere in their beliefs, well-trained, wanting, I feel sure, the affection and loyalty of their pupils, they would teach you, if you wished to learn. Peter Levi, my fellow poet, entered Prior a year after me and is properly educated – in Greek, Latin, French, our country's history, good manners. There was no bullying of pupils by pupils. No realized sexual abuse.

There was, however, no escape from the Brothers. These men in black soutanes with their belief in, and inculcation of, guilt. With their reliance on physical punishment. Their ignorance of sex. Their fear of intellectual freedom. Redemption (for having been born) through prayer, pain, daily attendance at Mass – plus regular confession – had a significance in their heads and hearts far above that of friendship, physical affection, and sympathy with the human lot. Their nasty god was everywhere. We were sent into the confessional – a dark, smelly, wooden crate of a place – to retail our so-called sins to a hairy ear.

Once inside the crate you knelt, then said: 'Father, forgive me, for I have sinned.' If you lied, you were lying to God. If you lied to God, you would go to Hell. Here was a puzzle. From what I had found in illustrated books, Hell had naked women in it (mostly upside down). That was a lot better than being stuck in Heaven for all eternity with the Brothers. How many sins got you a place in Hell? Of course, there was Limbo. Perhaps Limbo was best. It was difficult to find out anything about Limbo.

There is something to be said for confession. The belief that Catholics sin, confess, and are then free to re-sin without increasing their badness-balance, is mistaken. The point of confession is to examine your conscience, decide what you have done, or thought, that is actually wrong, and then, displeased with oneself, try to do better. The Brothers missed the point. Their method – proscription rather than examination, the cultivation of guilt, the awarding of punishment and blame – was cruel, abusive; even – if you countenance the thought – sinful in itself.

33

To the Kerswells and to Vernon I invented one or two Prior Park friends. In fact, I made no friends. Peter Levi might have become one. We were both to some extent *déclassé*. His father was a middle-class Jew who had fought as a ranker in the First World War, mine an Irish/English Catholic raised in the army.

'My dad was expected to succeed in business,' Peter told me fifty-eight years later. 'One morning his uncles gave him £100 and told him to do what he could with it. By midday he had managed to lose £15,000.

'You were not a popular boy with us nine-year-olds,' Peter said. 'There was a film out called *The Frog* – about a man who led a mysterious criminal organization. We formed an anti-Logue secret society. Each member had a frog inked on to his wrist. There was nothing very personal about it. The Frog spoke with a deep, funny-sounding voice. So did you. Only now do I break our society's oath of silence.'

B Y my third year at Prior I had learnt to escape surveillance. For pleasure, there was the Park itself, 160 acres of it, with the grotto Allen built for Pope – its roof fallen in, its pool exhaling marsh gas when stirred. I visited Allen's valley. Wandering between pieces of weathered statuary and twenty-foot-high stands of bamboo, you came to the lakes: black, rank, undredged for two hundred years, still deep. One Christmas a young postman drowned himself in the lower lake for love of a girl. He was from Coombe Down. The pike ate his body before it could be recovered. Quiet, you might catch a glimpse of a pike's head breaking the surface.

Home from Prior, I set out my army, paged through my books, played my records, went round to the Kerswells.

Peter, a year older than me, was soon to leave school.

'What are you going to do?'

'Look for a job.'

'What job?'

'Any old job.'

Vernon had become a fan of Shirley Temple's. 'Just seven and she's earning $200,000 a year. Take her song "The Good Ship Lollipop". She sang it to 40,000 Hawaiians and immediately afterwards they fell down on their knees and prayed for her good health.'

Artie Shaw was my star. He had appeared in a newsreel playing 'Begin the Beguine' on his clarinet, pointing it into the air, while his big band swung behind him.

Seeing *The Adventures of Robin Hood* was the best moment of the holiday. I quite liked Errol Flynn. But Basil Rathbone was my man. I forgot I would soon be back waking to the sound of Brother James's massive handbell and then forced to go to Mass, longing all the while to be married to Olivia de Havilland and resident in Nottingham Castle.

TOWARDS the end of the thirties, my parents had decided to spend their Christmases in family hotels. As my father explained: 'The extra work is too much for your mother.' The work was less of an issue than, in Molly's words, 'your uncle George's atheistic theosophy', and the fact that, 'George and your half-sister Hilda see far too much of each other. He should spend Christmas with his wife. Poor Edie.' Staying in a hotel meant that they avoided inviting, or not inviting them.

What Molly Logue omitted to say was that, with her leading, she and Cissie had encouraged George to marry their friend Edie Langford, a pretty, nervous, delicate young woman, always care-fully made up, dressed as if for an outing, no more cut out to be the wife of an unworldly engineer than he, their brother, was to be a conventional husband.

In 1938 we went to Eastbourne where Astaire and Rogers' *Carefree* was showing. My Christmas money took me there every day from twelve noon until the second show ended. I wished to float for ever with Fred and Ginger over black glass floors.

On Boxing Day the guests entertained each other with their party pieces. The hotel's proprietor served free champagne, lem-onade for the children. I offered to recite. A young couple sang 'Two Sleepy People'. The proprietor told a number of rather daring jokes about Herr Hitler, before announcing: 'And next, Master John Logue will recite Robert Browning's famous poem *The Pied Piper of Hamelin*.'

At the beginning of the third stanza I realized my mistake.

Even in a shortened version, the poem was too long. I began to speed up. I felt the tears rising. Then the gods came to my aid. A thought I never thought before told me: 'Cut it.' Twenty lines later I stopped, and said 'So when the townspeople refused to pay the Piper for getting rid of the rats, he kidnapped all their children and went on his way,' and sat down.

SUMMER 1939: the Kerswells and I had our last outing. Mrs Kerswell wanted a parcel delivered to her friend Mrs O'Malley who lived at Hayling Island. Mr O'Malley had served in the First World War. He gave us tea and sugared bread, coughing as he sliced the loaf.

As we were about to go, Mr O'Malley said: 'I'll show you boys something.' Fetching what looked like an ordinary walking stick, he unscrewed the handle and detached from the rod that was the stick's spine a few round washers of thin paper covered with handwriting.

'I made this stick from the letters Mrs O'Malley and I wrote to each other while she was still Miss Jenkins in munitions and I was in the trenches,' he said. 'When we married I cut the letters into squares, pressed them down this rifle's cleaning rod, rounded off and varnished them.'

IN my last term at Prior, Emmet O'Hagan and I bet another boy, Tubby Walsh, two Crunchie bars he couldn't hold a glass marble in his mouth during the short church service of Benediction. Benediction began, and Fatty Walsh seemed likely to win, when, suddenly, Emmet released a high-pitched fart. This was too much for Tubby. His eyes bulged and, with a look of dismay on his face, he rose and staggered from the pew with his finger down his throat, blurting: 'It's gone down.'

He sneaked. Logue and O'Hagan were sent to the Round Room for punishment.

This the Brothers inflicted by striking the palms of a culprit's hands with a thick fourteen-inch-long (including handgrip) black leather strap.

The Round Room – the place where the strappings were carried out – was a circular lecture hall heated by iron radiators between whose glands, while we listened out for the punisher

Brother's step, we numbed our hands to take the blows without flinching. When Brother Burke came into the Round Room he seized me by the right wrist and brought the strap down on my palm hard six times. Then the same on my left. Then the same for Emmet. Then he sent us back into the refectory for supper. Nobody turned to look at us. We sat with our hands under our armpits. After thirty minutes the pain had dwindled to a burning sensation.

Strapping was frequent. I asked Peter Levi to confirm this.

'Oh yes' he said, 'you and I, quite different children, were strapped all the time. Often for looking in the wrong direction. It was worse if, like me, you had chilblains.'

ONE day during the summer term of 1939 I was sent to see Brother Doyle, the headmaster. Ostensibly, I was summoned for playing 'Heaven and Hell', a game of mine in which St Peter (me) condemned 'the newly dead' (smaller boys) to be sent to Heaven or to Hell by 'angels' (my gang). If the dead were sent to Heaven (seldom) they had to laugh and clap their hands. If to Hell (the bottom of a grassy bank) they were pushed down the bank while they uttered cries of agony.

Coming from behind his desk Brother Doyle bent down and looked me straight in the eyes. Then he said:

'Do you believe in God, John?'

'Yes, Brother Doyle.'

'Are you sure you believe in God, John?'

'Yes, Brother Doyle.'

'Quite sure?'

'Yes, Brother Doyle.'

'Sure in your heart of hearts?'

'Yes, Brother Doyle.'

Dad came to collect me 'for good' a few days later.

One day before leaving I passed the Round Room, where I heard Brother Burke taking the junior-school choir through Jerome Kern and Dorothy Fields' 'The Way You Look Tonight' and was so struck by the beauty of that famous song, and by the loveliness of my schoolfellows' voices, I hear them to this day.

I HAD expected to be at home and to stay there. My parents had found me a place at Portsmouth Grammar School. On 1 September Germany invaded Poland; two days later Britain and France declared war on Germany. As a naval town, Portsmouth would be bombed. The governors decided to evacuate the school. I was fitted for a gas mask by men in brown uniforms. With the mask in its brown cardboard box hanging from my shoulder, I waved goodbye to my parents through the window of a coach and landed up in one of the billets that the school found for its pupils in Southbourne, a suburb of Bournemouth.

A moment from the holidays preceding this departure. I was discussing birthday presents with Lorna Tyndall, the daughter of my mother's church friends, in her mother's kitchen, when her brother Kevin came in and Lorna asked him what he wanted for his: 'A thermometer,' he said.

I felt envy. To know his want so precisely meant that the thermometer was more than a toy. Kevin knew, roughly, what his occupation was going to be. He was already a scientist, say. There was no thermometer in my life.

I have always envied precocious achievers like Pope, who at twelve is supposed to have written the poem beginning:

> Happy the man, whose wish and care
> A few paternal acres bound,
> Content to breathe his native air
> In his own ground.

Or like Mozart, or Gauss. Or like my friend Ken Tynan, who by the time he was ten knew he belonged in the theatre.

The nine years between Kevin's thermometer and my first typewriter were my worst. From 1940 to 1944, between my fourteenth and my eighteenth birthdays, that is, I felt I knew nothing. I understood nothing. Liking solitude, I did not realize that, even so, the lack of mental companionship, and the criticism that is a natural part of it, made me suffer from loneliness. Sometimes, when drawing, I was able to forget myself. Or I copied out chapters of Basil Lubbock's books on clipper ships, learning the names of the sails, of the rigging. I treasured my bicycle. Sometimes I went no further than the river Stour at Tuckton and I watched the sand martins and kingfishers fly in and out of the burrows they had made in the low, sheer banks. On other days I rode as far afield as the western edges of the New Forest, there to wander about its heaths for an hour or two. Anything to get out of the house, to avoid my parents' eyes, to not have to speak. Weeks of silence. Me locked inside my troublesome self. There was a girl whose parents knew mine. Left alone in her family's house I went to her bedroom and kissed the insides of her bras and pants. She liked me. Once when we were alone she dropped an earring down the front of her blouse and dared me to get it. Sullen, I refused.

Cinemas were my refuge. During the advertisements, while I waited for the big picture to start, waves of impatience swept through me. Then the picture was over; or the drawing was finished; and my wearisome self returned.

I had my room, and my postcards. Years later, on my first visit to Florence, when the scale of Botticelli's *Spring* struck me, I loved the memory of my postcard of it. I sat on the terrace of a Florentine café thinking of the little *Primavera* on the shelf beside my bed, and of my oil stove's occasional gulp.

THERE was, as well, this enormous thing: the war. Though we knew that, far away in Russia, in North Africa, tremendous battles, and the terrifying, overwhelming noise that such battles create, filled the world, here in Bournemouth, over and above its natural climate of repose a mood of silent, immovable stillness filled the air. It was unnecessary to tell me to keep my voice down. Although there were rolls of barbed wire in almost every open space, you could go more or less where you wanted to go, and do what you were inclined to do.

Like other stretches of British coastline, Bournemouth's cliff tops were closed to visitors. After dark, sentries with rifles patrolled them. Locals – as we evacuees had become – were allowed down on to the undercliff roads during daylight hours, but only via 'restricted entries', the lifts being dismantled, the zig-zags blocked. Twenty yards out from the low-water line there was a double row of iron stanchions, 'coastal defence works', with sharpened heads.

Few ventured on to the sands. There were no bands or steamer ships, just the noise of the waves on the shingle. Now and again – though this was rare – elderly couples opened their beach huts and sat with travelling rugs over their knees sipping the tea they poured from Thermos flasks into china cups.

To the west of Bournemouth pier lay the chines. Never much visited, darkened by untended conifers and broad-leafed shrubs, in these wartime days they were deserted, their paths crumbling away, the wooden foot bridges over their ravines decayed.

Far to the east of the pier, where the promenade gave way to the bare beach, and the four daily tides ate away at the sandy cliffs so that they tumbled on to, and into, the waves, I found a soft gully leading up to the cliff tops, that, with a little help, could be extended under the rolls of wire lining the nose of the cliff. Then one made one's way home through several lines of anti-tank teeth. There was no traffic to speak of. Cars had been laid up. You might be asked to show your identity card. Only councillors and doctors had petrol.

Authority was transformed. It was everywhere. Unquestioned. And you were part of it. Events such as when our local priest, Father Widowson, first lost his ration book, then had it returned but with its sweet coupons replaced by a copy of the gospel of St John, helped. More so when Aunt Margaret came to Southbourne for a week's holiday, and asked him what penance he would impose should the thief come to him for confession – for by this time my parents had followed me from Portsmouth to Bournemouth.

I disliked and feared Father Widowson. When he cornered me into being alone with him, he insisted on talking about sex. He took me to visit the corpse of one of his parishioners, an old lady, and forced me to put my hand on her cold forehead. I thought: Why are we allowed into her peaceful room?

Once, when he was about to photograph his Sunday-school children on the lawn of the house belonging to Dr and Mrs Watson on whom, prior to the arrival of my parents, I was billeted, having watched him assemble them from the window of my room, I took one of my selection of magazines that included photographs of naked female beauties and began to masturbate over the picture of a friendly looking poser.

Just as I was about to come, Father Widowson, who must have hurried indoors from the garden and crept up the stairs and along the landing to my room, burst in on me, pulled back the counterpane under which I tried to hide myself, and shouting: 'Filth! Filth!', removed my supply of shop-lifted *Men Only* and *The Naturist* from my suitcase with his foot. Then stalked out with them.

Later, I thought: He must have known about my magazines, and guessed what I was doing. Mrs Watson must have told him about the former. And the thought of him thinking about the matter was as bad as his abuse of me. If, too, he suspected I had stolen the magazines – as he might well have done – he never asked me.

PERHAPS the Watsons complained to my parents about it. In any event, they decided to sell up in Southsea and move to Bournemouth, thus avoiding the blitz, and housing me, in one.

Night after night during 1940 when I had returned home to Portsmouth for the first school holidays of the war, we were bombed. My parents and I could not bear to go down into our cellar. We sat at the head of its stairs while every twenty minutes a wave of bombers dropped its load and the ground shook around us. Two houses close by were destroyed. There were craters in the road leading to the Canoe Lake. The smell of household gas hung over them. Against incendiary bombs we kept a stirrup pump and a bucket of sand in the hall. My mother asked what of mine they should bring with them to Bournemouth. I could not decide. Only the books came.

As it was sunny on moving day, Dad asked the removal men to set his easy chair inside the tail gate of their van. There he sat reading his paper, smoking, no doubt giving an occasional wave to a passer-by as the van drove to Southampton, then on through the New Forest to Southbourne.

ONE summer evening in 1939 my parents had taken me to the community singing at Southsea's bandstand. Folding chairs surrounded the stand, where, as twilight fell, we paid a shilling for a chair and another for a copy of the *News Chronicle Song*

Book – 'including Sea Shanties, Negro Spirituals, Hymns, Carols and Children's Songs'. Then our Master of Ceremonies, dressed in a blue blazer over a white roll-top jersey, his accompanist in a long white frock, led us into:

'A song you all know. "There is a Tavern in the Town". Page 43.'

By the time we reached: 'Adieu, kind friends, adieu, adieu, adieu, adieu . . .' our assembly was in full voice. This was followed by 'The Minstrel Boy', then 'High-ho' – a round: 'Those on my left to wait for a beat from my hand before they sing.' Lamps were lit. Drinks and ice creams were served by young ladies. Well after 10 p.m. we closed with: '"Jerusalem" by William Blake to be followed by "God Save The King" for which we will stand.'

'Dear, dear Southsea,' my mother said. All that was gone.

D URING the winter of 1941, the Japanese bombed Pearl Harbor, our form had *Henry V* as its set text, and for the only time in my life I saw my parents weep. A letter from Bernard Musson arrived to say that Jack, their only son, my father's godson, named after my father, a pilot officer in the Fleet Air Arm whose photograph stood on our sideboard, was dead. While flying over Crete his plane had crashed into the ground. My parents sat beside each other at the kitchen table, crying. The Allied advance in Italy was halted. Yachts, dismasted for the duration, stood on the water near Christchurch Priory quay.

Besides the choruses of *Henry V*, all I remember of my Bournemouth schooling is the Grammar's caretaker, Burden, among whose duties was that of leading those to be caned to the office of the man who would deliver the blows, Mr Stork, the headmaster.

Burden was stooped. He had a large, pale face no broader than his neck, heavy lips, hooded eyes. He knocked at the classroom door, entered, then stood silent, until a look bade him forward to whisper the name of the canee into the ear of the teacher taking the class, then: 'Logue' – were it he – 'Mr Stork will see you in his office,' was heard. And Burden led you out of the classroom, up the stairs with: 'This way, lad. He won't be long, lad. He's seeing a parent. Something serious, I believe. Let's hope it's not an expulsion.'

THE war news was bad. The Germans were driving us back in North Africa. In Russia, they had reached Leningrad. Each day we listened to the one o'clock news, Dad with my school atlas open on his knees, noting the German advances. A man who detested communism, he knew our fate depended on Russian soldiers. If the Germans could conquer Russia they could conquer us. To the north-east, on certain clear nights, the sky over Southampton glowed red from the fires started by German bombers.

Then, in 1942, came the victories of El Alamein and Stalingrad. Almost every day someone on the radio sang 'My Lovely Russian Rose'.

> 'I will come and find you,
> Break the chains that bind you,
> Where the river Volga flows;
> You will surely bloom again
> My lovely Russian rose.'

The government forged a sword to be presented by Britain to Stalingrad. The Sword of Stalingrad. A tall, beautiful, silver sword. Its picture appeared in all the newspapers. It was even suggested that the big diamond, the Star of India, be removed from the crown of England and set as the pommel to its hilt.

The sword was exhibited in Westminster Abbey. Many queued to see it. Evelyn Waugh wrote: 'The people were suffused with gratitude to their remote allies and they venerated the sword as the symbol of their own generous and spontaneous emotion.' Stalin was known as Uncle Joe.

AMONG the less attractive features of my character is a tendency to give provocative views for no good reason. Now and then – much to my own surprise, of course – I provoke unintentionally. Once – quite recently, at supper with relative strangers – I did so by saying what I thought, and think, is true: despite Britain's losses – 326,000 dead, 480,000 wounded, to say nothing of our material contributions – the Russian Front was the decisive arena of the war against Nazi Germany. Its battles overshadowed with horrific violence the worst battles fought on the Western Front of the First World War. The defeat of the Nazi forces represented a triumph over adversity of a kind that we, Russia's allies, have merely read about.

When these thoughts drew explosive dissent from two of my fellow guests, I felt astonishment, and shut up, going next day to the library to make sure my views were shared – which, broadly speaking, they were – by serious military historians.

Vernon, though I did not hear of it until much later, was lost in 1943 when his ship was torpedoed on the way to Murmansk.

Bournemouth was not wholly spared. There were daylight air raids. Cinemas flashed warnings of these raids on their screens. Those who wished to leave, did so. Not many did. Twenty Messerschmitt fighter-bombers mounted the worst of these raids. They hit the Metropole Hotel, killing 101 people. The hotel's proprietors left the bloodstains on the walls of the saloon bar. R. L. Stevenson's house was destroyed in the same raid.

I was picked up on Christchurch quay by two twenty-two-year-old women, one middle-, one working-class, both married to soldiers serving abroad. They were having a good war. Freedom. Jobs. Money. They took me to a bar and bought Pimms, with fruit in the mixture. I had never felt so happy. The working-class Jane – a local – confessed to fearing her husband's return. It was going to spoil 'everything'. She reminded me of Eric, Constant's daughter. She wore tight tops. Her breasts stood out. How was I going to get my hands on them? All I had to do was be patient, agreeable and lucky. But I didn't learn this for years and years. The other Jane – plump, jolly – told me her land-girl sister's story. How she had fallen in love with a German POW who had been sent to work on the same Northumbrian farm as herself. She got pregnant. The neighbours found out about it all. She was almost lynched. Pitchforked. The police saved her.

Soon I was drunk, and had to be taken to my front door. In the morning I woke up helplessly in love with both women. Dizzy with yearning, I wrote each of them a long, passionate letter, revised with care. When I cycled to the stable block at Mudeford where they lodged, I found its doors open, them gone, and a man with a shotgun warned me off.

Black American soldiers, extraordinary men of six foot four who shouted their thoughts out while they played dice in the street and drove sixteen-wheel trucks at eighty miles an hour through the New Forest, took me to see Bob Hope in a US army concert at Bournemouth Pavilion.

I scraped through School Certificate. Justly, I was not the kind of boy Mr Stork thought suitable for further education. I knew I must leave school. My father had told me he would no longer pay my fees once I had reached seventeen. Asked what I wanted, blessed with the strength to answer, I would have said: to stay in the stable block with the two Janes, emerging only to board the black-hulled staysail yacht moored on the Tuckton bank of the Stour at Christchurch, never to return.

I masturbated over my magazines twice, sometimes three times a day. In part I stole them out of shame, lacking the courage to pay straight out. I was caught. The police were called. I was charged with theft and summoned to appear before the juvenile court.

On the day appointed, my father, now seventy-two, dressed in his best, came with me on the trolley bus with his retirement certificate – 'desiring to express to you my appreciation of the faithful service you have rendered to the State during a period of more than forty-five years', framed, signed by the Postmaster General and wrapped in brown paper under his arm.

Mr Stork was waiting at the court. When the magistrates heard that I did not deny the charge, he spoke up for me, as did Dad. Flicking through the magazine that lay on their table, one of the magistrates asked nobody in particular if the photographs 'have anything to do with the case?' The answer was no. Again, I kept quiet. I was given six months' probation.

My parents were not people who asked a lot of life. They hoped, as he grew up, to find a friend in their son. Someone with beliefs they shared. A man who saw and respected them for what they were, holding, perhaps, the sort of position his father, if educated, might have gained, married to a decent woman his mother could shop with, sharing tales of his infancy and reliving her motherhood through grandmotherliness.

From time to time I thought of volunteering for the army. As a refuge rather than as a vocation. A place where I could be until the war was over. I would be safe in the army. Fed, housed, clothed. I would not have to find a job. The army was not a job. It was a way of life. If hard, no harder than life at Prior. I might be killed. That would solve everything.

I had read that after basic training you could apply to join the army commandos from where it was a short step to strange units such as Popski's Private Army, among whose heroes I imagined myself, whose doings I followed.

In May 1944 I went to the Services Recruiting Office in Bournemouth, passed my medical and signed up 'for the duration' as the saying went. The warrant officer who recruited me asked which regiment I wished to join. I told him the Commandos.

'That's Combined Ops, lad,' he said. 'You have to have a substantive unit to be detached from before you can join them' – looking my podgy five foot seven up and down – 'if they'll have you, that is. So what's it to be?'

'The Black Watch,' I said, naming the only regimental name I knew.

'The Black Watch,' he said, writing it in. 'Well, lad, you'll hear from Aldershot two weeks from now. Just follow your orders. Good luck to you.'

I went for a coffee. Then I walked home along the cliffs knowing I need never look at the Situations Vacant columns again.

CAMERON Barracks, Inverness, 1944.
Dear Mum and Dad,

I did not write yesterday as is usually my custom, because all over the week-end I have been 'C.B.' (confined to barracks) which means reporting at various times at which a bugle is blown. Whilst you are doing this you are known as a 'defaulter'. All this arises from the fact that I had dusty boots by my bed Friday morning. One of the jobs I was given was Officers' Mess orderly. So I belted over to the 'wallahs' mess and told them who I was. Well, when I had finished scrubbing tables and floors the cook in charge told me to come and get something to eat and by gosh what a meal it was!!, fish and chips, jelly and cream, coffee and cream crackers. I was amazingly pleased with life. Did you,

Dad, know anybody in Portsmouth by the name of Brangwyn, the son went to Oxford and has been called up and sent here. He is a very nice fellow.

A note from Brangwyn:

Bexley Heath, 1997

At Cameron Barracks we were told to put our kit in Hut 12. Sitting on one of the beds with a mop and pail beside him was a short soldier dressed in dirty fatigues which smelt of disinfectant, his sleeves wet, his forage cap dead straight on his head. When I gave him the light he asked for he discharged the smoke from his cigarette so violently that Armstrong, one of our party, asked him if he needed help. He said thank you, no, he was just learning to smoke, then took up his cleaning gear and coughed his way out of the hut.

'He can't be one of us,' Armstrong said.

'No chance,' I said. 'This is a commissioning camp. That fellow is part of the Permanent Duty Company. We'll not see him again.'

This was my first meeting with you, Christopher.

Six weeks earlier I received a railway warrant and a postal order for five shillings enabling me, plus my ration book and identity card, to join the colours at Cameron Barracks.

On the journey, courtesy of a handful of young northern working-class men going to Inverness for the same reason, I entered the larger world, puzzled to find myself so out of register. They were so easy with life, with one another.

'3.40 p.m. was the time we reached Inverness', I wrote home, 'and were marched to the barracks.'

Everybody smoked. You learnt badges and ranks. Everybody drank. Talk centred on sex and violence. You were expected to be good at both. It took the hut seconds to spot I knew nothing of either. I spoke with a la-di-da voice. I walked in a pansified way. I was christened 'Charlotte'.

I modified my walk and said as little as possible.

Training together, keeping yourself, and others, out of harm's way, altered me. Everyone else had left school at fourteen. I was helpless. My webbing was always twisted. On route marches,

when my turn came to carry the platoon's Bren gun – 23 lb –
someone shouldered it for me. I had never been in a fight. I could
not bear to go to the lavatory in public.

It was around about this time I invented an elder brother, an
SAS war hero always acting bravely under adverse circumstances.
'Once I get into the Commandos it will be all right,' I told myself.

In December 1985 Robert Dartnell, once my fellow soldier,
wrote to me, saying:

> I saw you on the TV and was certain that you were Chris
> Logue of 25 Platoon. Your voice left me in no doubt. Do you
> remember Sgt Davis' dog who accompanied us on route
> marches? And Bill Ostler who played the mandolin? Yes,
> Chris, in spite of your somewhat pompous attitude to all and
> sundry in those days of yore, there was another side to your
> character . . .

Patrick Brangwyn and I became friends. He was well built with
a thick bushy head of brown hair and a broad boyish grin. We
both liked poetry. Neither of us cared for the communal latrines.
We bumped into each other when going to use them late one
night. Now we were walking into Inverness together, Patrick
carrying a book.

'W. B. Yeats.'

'Who?'

'I thought you said you went to a public school?'

'A boarding school.'

'And you never heard of Yeats?'

'It was an Irish school.'

'Yeats *was* Irish.'

'Was he a Catholic?'

'God, you are ignorant.'

Patrick was an Oxford undergraduate on an officers' training
course. I had never met anyone who had been to Oxford. Even
so, I had always supported Oxford in the Boat Race. Privately, I
had decided that Oxford was the place for me. I had discussed
the matter with my brother. As soon as the war was over he
would leave the SAS and go to Oxford. Then I would join him.

Brangwyn and me walking past a ruin:

'Do you know whose castle that was?' I said.

'No.'

'Macbeth's.'

'Are you sure?'

'Absolutely. My brother told me. He's in the SAS.'

'I thought we'd have a drink in the Caledonian Hotel,' Patrick said.

I had never had an alcoholic drink in a hotel.

'Only if they have vodka,' I said.

'Of course they'll have vodka,' Pat said. 'You really mustn't say that sort of thing, old man.'

'You mean about vodka?' I said.

'Yes. And admitting you never heard of Yeats.'

'What *was* Yeats, then?'

'What do you mean – what *was* he?'

'What I say: what *was* he?'

'Oh . . . You mean what *religion* was he?'

'Yes.'

'He was a Theosophist.'

'Like my uncle George,' I said. 'Someone who aims at everything and hits nothing' – Aunt Margaret's joke against George.

After our second drink Patrick vanished up the Caledonian's main stairs.

I started on Yeats.

Three minutes later Patrick returned, looked round the bar, then led me up to the first floor and into a large bathroom. 'Lavvy's next door,' he said, taking off his uniform. 'I'm having a bath.' I took Yeats with me for my first decent shit since I joined up. Yeats was good. Even his sloppy stuff. If your sloppy stuffs good you're probably in the first division. Then it was my turn for a bath. We dried ourselves on the bath mats and parted at the guard room.

JUNE 6th – D-Day – the Allies landed on the beaches of northern France.

YMCA 'With His Majesty's Forces' Inverness

Dear Mum and Dad,

Today at lunch time I had your parcel given to me, I was delighted. Everything I asked for was in it, thank you very much indeed. Nearly everyone had a piece of cake and there was very little left but everybody shares alike. Soon I will pack up the tin and send it back to you but at the moment there seems to be a terrible shortage of string in our hut.

I cannot remember if I told you before, but Sergeant 'Nobby' Clark, one of our Education instructors wrote me an exceptionally nice letter and enclosed in it his first lesson in the art of being a journalist. He, in peacetime, was a reporter in Poole.

This letter I am writing in the Catholics' canteen attached to St Mary's, Inverness. It's very friendly and easy to feel at home. Upstairs is a wizard reading room with piles of novels, etc., so I go to the YMCA and collect some of their writing paper and then come back here. It is amazing how much us chaps come to rely on these places and the people who run them are absolute Gods in our esteem.

Now, Mum, here is a list of my wants. Don't be surprised if you find it a little long but I assure you all the things are really necessary.

(1) Some Rags for cleaning.
(2) A small artist's sketch book.
(3) Nail scissors (essential).
(4) Anadin tablets.
(5) Some tin boxes (v. important to keep my many many odds and ends in).
(6) A small prayer book.
(7) Some Air Mail Letters to write to Jimmy.
(8) Some spare buttons.
(9) A long thin bed-sheet which I will return with the next tin.

And don't forget to write at *least* twice a week.

Lots of love,
John C.

Jimmy (Logue) was my cousin. In the Middle East with the RAF.

CORPORAL Broxbourne, newly married, joined the camp's permanent strength. 'Study him, Chris' – 'Charlotte' had been dropped – said Larry Titchfield. 'You see a shagged-out man. On the nest at breakfast, lunch time, tea time. Whip it in, whip it out, wipe it, whip it in again. He's on his way to a discharge for premature exhaustion. That poor woman doesn't have a chance to wear her knickers. The thought of him having it makes mine stiff enough to hang a Bren gun on. How about you?'

'Definitely.'

'Then have a wank. Get the dirty water off your chest. Fuck going blind. I've wanked from nine and I'm one of the best shots in Northern Command. It's hard to find a place for a decent wank in Cameron Barracks. I use the Padre's rest room. Very few people go there.'

To my fellow soldiers, my understanding – that girls were doing a favour if they as much as let you kiss them – was true ignorance. They assumed that girls were as keen on fucking as boys. Getting pregnant was the only danger. Fifteen was a reasonable starting age. Perhaps a touch younger.

'Chris, when you're coming, you wish your pipe was a mile long,' said the blond lad who got into Airborne and died in France.

Then there was violence. 'The Argylls' (the Argyll and Sutherland Highlanders), Larry said, 'are around so there's sure to be a fight in the NAAFI. Probably tonight. When you see me stand up, so do you. Feel this' – slapping his forehead – 'an inch thick. Grab a jacket, pull the head to you, bang his nose with your head hard as you can. It's a terrible terrible pain you give when you hit that little part here,' touching the underside of his nose.

Our platoon shared Huts 5 and 6. Sergeant Davis – on detachment from the Queen's Own Regiment – expected his hut (5) to be the best.

'You will look smart at all times. In town, and in the cinema where you think nobody is looking, you will keep your collars done up because I, Sergeant John Michael Davis of the Queen's Own, will be looking.

'You do not have to like each other. You have to support each other. And me. Privates Titchfield and Regget, fighting over dominoes? If it happens again it's down to the gym, gloves on, and under the ropes for both, with you lot looking on.'

In one of his letters Bob Dartnell recalled part of our 'battle inoculation' – as Company Orders had it. We were trucked to a ruined village for sham house-to-house fighting. The climax of the exercise was a bayonet charge across a field while giving hideous roars, plus a final, dreadful shriek as we thrust our points into straw bags topped with threatening cardboard faces.

Having got us into line Sergeant Davis said:

'Don't plunge your point in too deep. Three inches of cold steel is sufficient for anybody. Jab it in. Stir it about for a couple of seconds, use the butt to stun the chap next to him, boot the third gentleman in the balls. Got it? Jab. Slam. Boot. And remember, noise is a weapon. I want plenty of horrible noise. Colonel Marker, Captain Tweedie and Staff-Sergeant Berg will be observing – and so will I. Right.'

Pause.

'Platoon, fix bayonets!'

Pause. Then:

'Charge!'

Off we went, with Sergeant Davis running in parallel with us.

Halfway to the straw bags, when we were about to start our screaming, the safety-pin I had replaced my missing waistband button with came undone and my trousers fell down.

As I stooped to pull up my trousers Sergeant Davis shouted, 'Don't put your rifle down, Logue. Finish the charge bum bare!'

A week later, on a similar exercise, Staff-Sergeant Berg stood us at ease and announced: 'Today we are going to combine movement and leadership. Twenty-four Platoon will be taken to a spur they will defend against an attack by Twenty-five Platoon. They will be told who will lead their defence on reaching the spur. Twenty-five Platoon's attack will be led by Private Logue. Out here, Logue.'

My hut looked at me, smiling. Some members of the platoon sat down.

This saved me. I felt cross. Staff-Sergeant Berg had said nothing about sitting down. And there they were on their arses, puffing away, chatting. As if in a dream, I heard my pansy-posh strangulated voice saying: 'On your feet, Twenty-five Platoon, and stop smoking.' Nobody moved.

'Right,' Staff Sergeant Berg said, ' Twenty-five Platoon is on a charge. Disobeying orders. Maybe mutiny. Seventy-two days' detention at the very least . . . ' By which time they were on their feet, cigarettes out, looking straight ahead.

Having ordered them into their transport, I doubled over to Sergeant Davis, came to attention, almost saluted, and said: 'Sergeant, what shall I do?'

'Split the Platoon. Keep the ten you know best. Put Roberts in charge of the others. Tell him to take them round the spur. No noise. Take yours up through the trees on to the slope behind it. When you're ready, charge the spur making as much noise as possible. Twenty-four will turn in their slit trenches and waste their blanks on you. That's Roberts's signal to advance slowly, letting Twenty-four have it with all he's got while you drop flat and crawl. Bayonets fixed.

'Don't let your ten fire their blanks. If they were live you'd be shooting Roberts's lot.'

Everything went well, except that, as we charged, the branch of a sapling caught on the pack of the soldier running to my left, and sprang back, hitting my left eye.

Dear Mum and Dad,

I fear this will not be a very cheerful letter as I have been detained in the camp infirmary for ten days the reason being I have injured my left eye. I may have to wear glasses, but I would have to wear them only while shooting.

I had two visitors: a sergeant of the Army Education Corps who asked me if I would like to go on a course with the chance of joining that unit at the end of it; and Brangwyn, soon leaving Inverness for his regiment.

I asked him how I would get into Oxford University.

'You have to matriculate and make a good impression on the chap who interviews you, old man.'

'Have you got to have money?'

'It doesn't do any harm.'

'My dad hasn't got any money.'

'Don't worry about it. We're friends. I'll be back there when the war's over. I'll show you what to do.'

'Will you really, Pat?'

'Of course I will, old man.'

53

That was the last time I saw Patrick until he, Charles Fox and I started a literary magazine together in the early fifties.

Between the Bayonet Charge and the Battle of the Spur I applied to join the Commandos and was interviewed by a major from Combined Operations who accepted me although my eye was not what it had been. As I packed my kit Sergeant Davis came into the hut.

'I hear you're joining the Commandos.'

'Yes, Sergeant.'

'What about the education course? The war is good as over. There won't be any Commandos soon. You're educated. Build on it. You're the type. You think I'd be here if I was educated?'

'You'd be an officer, a colonel, Sergeant.'

'You're thicker than you sound, lad.'

I went on leave. I rode my bike to Christchurch. The black-hulled yacht had gone. I bought a badge I was not entitled to wear, a pair of blue wings centred on an open parachute, the insignia of the Parachute Regiment. I asked my mother to sew it on to the shoulder of my battledress jacket.

My father was concerned over the flying bombs.

'They are hard to destroy. They could make the war last years more.'

He looked so worried. Rare in him. Although I did not sense it, perhaps what he was thinking was: even at this late stage we might be destroyed.

I have a note in his handwriting that says: 'Telegram from John C. His new address is: Holding Operational Commando, Hermitage Camp, Wrexham, North Wales.'

I had picked the badge off my jacket.

One day at Wrexham we were having arms instruction in a field bordered by a lane. As we listened, three teenaged girls came down the lane laughing, talking together. When they were abreast of us – with our instructor's back towards them – they stopped, and then, without a word, lifted their skirts and flashed their knickerless tufts at us, just like that, then ran off down the lane, giggling.

AT the end of April 1945 Hitler committed suicide. My diary says:

I saw Captain Farr, a member of Popski's Army. He said that as soon as I am old enough I can join Popski but it would be better if I joined the SAS first. But though I have written I have had no news from the SAS.

I had a friend called Harry who was going into Airborne. One night in Wrexham we were lucky enough to pick up two girls. By the time it came for them to go home my girl and I were in a dark corner of the bus station enjoying long kisses and paying no heed to her friend's warning that their last bus had arrived. Then, all at once, we found our teeth being knocked together as I was beaten over the head from behind with an umbrella wielded by an eighty-year-old woman, 'an aged crone', as Harry put it later. Chivvied by the aged – and recognized – crone, my girl slipped out of my arms, on to the bus. We waved to each other as it pulled away.

I learnt a term of the (for me) once-heard-seldom-fogotten kind: 'escape outfit.'

'He got fourteen days for stealing Sergeant Arrowsmith's escape outfit'.

'His what?'

'That's the pack the SAS sergeants get when they're being dropped behind enemy lines. It's got a compass, a silk map that folds down to the size of a stamp, gold coins for bribes and a cyanide pill with which to escape the tortures of the Gestapo.'

'Really?'

'Ask at the Quartermaster's if you don't believe me.'

As no one at the Quartermaster's knew of the item, I decided to make my own: a watertight tobacco tin, watch-chain compass, miniature French dictionary, and well-folded £5 note. The tin went everywhere with me.

DIARY SCRAP

The Japanese are taking a long time to surrender. I hope we drop another atomic bomb soon.

At the time, Britain had 4,500,000 men and 500,000 women under arms.

Hermitage Camp filled up with soldiers from the European, Middle and Far Eastern Combined Operation units due for disbandment. Some wore Military Medal or Distinguished Service Medal ribbons. As you made your way to the bar of the NAAFI you noticed thirty-five to fifty-year-olds bidding one another goodbye before they returned to their wives, their children and jobs.

In July of 1945 ballot boxes sealed for three weeks to admit the postal votes of servicemen and women overseas were opened, and a Labour government was returned to power with a majority of 183. Even I, with hardly a political thought in my head, realized that something important had occurred. Harry and I went into Chester for a drink. It is no overstatement to say that there was a tingle in the air. Fifty-two years were to pass before, in May 1997, when New Labour was elected, I felt that common, political tingle – an unusual variety of happiness – once again. In 1945 it presaged a steady reduction of inequality among us, a gradual improvement in our health, and, overall, an enlargement of hope.

Harry and I were surprised at the lack of enthusiasm for this victory among our fellow soldiers. Some were vexed by the rejection of Churchill. Mostly, comments on the change produced a shrug. Our lot wandered unwanted about the camp. Airborne were no longer recruiting. I was made one of the clerks at the camp's headquarters office. When a unit was disbanded, its clerks would deliver their surplus blank travel warrants, maps, notebooks, typewriters, etc. to us for disposal. From these stores I took, among other things, six blank paybooks – AB64s to give them their official name – a wallet-like document establishing the identity and pay of soldiers below the rank of Warrant Officer. One went into my escape outfit.

After five weeks I was posted from Hermitage Camp to my substantive unit, the 4th Battalion of the Black Watch, at Swansea. Then the 4th was posted to the Middle East, destination Palestine, sailing from Liverpool during December 1945, 'in misty weather' as the battalion's war diary states.

During my embarkation leave, Dad suggested we go to the cinema – an invitation never offered before. The film, released by the government, comprised footage by Allied cameramen of the concentration camp at Belsen. We walked home in silence.

IT cannot be said that the 4th battalion of the Black Watch had had a distinguished war record.

Until 1943 it was assigned to cutting tunnels through the Rock of Gibraltar – its doings noticed by the world only when one of its sentries arrested and, with the knowledge of his superiors, imprisoned an American in plain clothes who turned out to be General Eisenhower, the Allied Supreme Commander.

The situation when the 4th reached Palestine was as follows. For the British, governing by mandate, the power was a curse. By 1939 the government had decided that for the next six years no more than 75,000 Jewish immigrants would be admitted to Palestine. Five years later, the discovery of the death camps in southern Poland helped to make this policy as good as indefensible.

Seven weeks before we reached our camp at Binyamina, 30,000 Tel Avivians, including a number of thugs and thieves, demonstrated, and then rioted, against the imposition of this policy. After two days of stoning, the 6th Airborne Division opened fire, killing six, and injuring sixty, of the crowd.

The 4th saw none of this. Unlike Jerusalem or Tel Aviv, Binyamina was not a dangerous place.

Binyamina

Dear Mum and Dad,

Only now do I realize what an utter fool I was at school in not learning more than I did. I now realize that I could quite easily have learned anything that I thought difficult. I have an intense desire to go to Oxford and take a degree in Philosophy and Economics. I wonder if I shall ever be able to manage it.

THE weather was warm, with occasional downpours of rain. I became the lance-corporal in charge of the Unit Library – for which, see later. We gorged on musk melons scrumped from the farm beside our camp. A corporal in the Motor Transport Unit gave me driving lessons. Donkeys roamed between our tents. If you tickled a donkey's balls with a long bamboo which still had a few leaves sticking out at the top, its impressive pink and black penis would appear, and then it would look at us with reproachful eyes before retracting and wandering off. Rumours said the 4th was to be disbanded, returned to Swansea, sent to Burma.

Binyamina

Dear Mum and Dad,

I have started to write poetry in quite a big way, on the whole it is mainly about ships and the sea, and I have been using as a model, Masefield and Conrad. Thank you very much for my *Reader's Digest* and *Yachting World*.

Fifty of us went on leave to Beirut. A day there, and I understood the phrase 'a high standard of living'. On the city's west, the Mediterranean. On its east, the snow-topped mountains of Lebanon. Swimming in the morning. Skiing in the afternoon. Delicious street food. Cafés, shops with things unseen in Britain. And – particularly enticing to me – bookstores and shops that sold paintings, ancient marble heads, icons.

Sergeant Steven Heggie, one of my six tent mates, liked me. It must have been a shock to him when, on the morning of Sunday 4 April 1946, Private Slee of the Intelligence Section, also of our tent, hurried into it to whisper: 'Chris Logue has gone into Haifa to sell paybooks to the Jews. Lieutenant Ross' – the battalion's Intelligence Officer – 'says you are to come at once. We must find him. Arrest him.'

In 1980 George Steiner invited me to read excerpts from the *Iliad* to illustrate a talk on English versions of Homer's poem which he was to give at that year's Edinburgh Festival. During the lunch that followed George's lecture, I was handed this note:

Enjoyed the learned Steiner's talk and your readings. Shall we meet for a drink? Yours Steve Heggie (ex-4th BW)

We met that evening.

'Slee was a pompous chap,' Steven said. 'Large, waxy, not so bright. You used to argue with him and beat him at it, very unfairly. He would walk out of the tent in a huff. You liked doing it. You were a bully. We all argued all the time, of course. You went a lot further than the others.

'Slee and Ross were very agitated on the way to Haifa. They scanned the windows of the buses we passed. Slee repeated what he had told Ross. That you had taken some blank AB64s out of your kitbag and made them up into a small parcel addressed to your mother while telling Slee that you were, in fact, going into Haifa "to sell them to the Jews for not less than £4 and ten shillings each". When Slee said this might have serious consequences, you replied: "If I had twenty rifles I would sell them too."

'We found you sitting in the NAAFI bar, or rather, I found you. Slee and Ross had gone into another room.

'The place was busy. As soon as you saw me, you threw the parcel away behind a pot palm.

'Then Slee and Ross came in and stood over you, Ross saying, in a breathless sort of voice, that you had better come outside with them. I retrieved the parcel and gave it to Ross before we got into the jeep. Otherwise we would have gone back and searched the place. It was best for you Ross had them. Then we drove to Haifa's railway-station yard. Ross took you to one side, tore the parcel open and asked if the paybooks had come from you. You said yes. He said something like: "How could you do such a thing? How could you?" Then he hit you once on the face, not very hard. He was upset.

'On Monday morning you appeared on Commanding Officer's Orders and were remanded on open arrest while he looked into the matter and decided what to do with you. Most of us thought Colonel Maitland would give you seventy-two days' detention.'

IT was at this point that my luck ran out. I learnt I was to be court-martialled. Until then I would be held in close arrest – that is to say, locked up.

In Palestine matters were going from bad to worse. The Lehi ('Fighters For the Freedom of Israel') shot seven members of the 6th Airborne Division in Tel Aviv. Next day the Division rioted, demanding revenge.

At the end of the month the 4th was sent to Egypt for disbandment and I was transferred to the regimental cells of the 2nd Battalion of the Royal Scots.

4th Battalion BW/
M.E.F.

Dearest Mum and Dad,

Some parents have a love for their children which is tainted with a type of pride, and so if the child disappoints them in its early youth, a feeling of bitterness is likely to be incurred. You my dears are complete and utter exceptions to this vile rule. I your son, have possibly given you more trouble and worry than almost any other of my age, and in return for my vile nature you only gave kindness generosity and deep affection. Now only do I realize that fact, and also I can see how my stupid brain has been clogged with limitless bravado and conceit. To blame you in any manner is wrong. True it is you spoiled me in a small way but if I had been half the character I thought I was it would have taken me but a few short months to realize how wrong I was and how right you were. Many people have children and the children begin by believing them and end by judging them. If I had only seen that you two are perfectly happy except when I used to cause innumerable rows in the house.

You denied yourselves almost everything to keep me at a decent school and have my brain trained along the lines of human life and decency. You struggled for me and I ignored your sacrifice. Believe me dears, now and now only, can I realize just what you did and how you had to bear my insults. To find two people as loving and as lovable as yourselves the world would have to be searched. No wonder Dad you are always popular amongst decent people wherever you travelled, no wonder Mum

people used to say to me, 'Your mother is the sweetest person I
have ever met'.

But look at their son. Or rather do not look at him. Through
my education I had an even chance at civilian life and in the army
quite an advantage, but this is how I end up, in the guard room.
Likely to click for a great punishment, and only because I was
too pigheaded to do the correct thing.

It is only fair to tell you everything. In the army we have
'paybooks' and these are the means by which a soldier is
identified. Naturally in a country such as this they are valuable to
any Jews who can lay their hands on them. Whilst I was in Egypt,
and when Y Company was being broken up six of the books
were left lying in a box of rubbish in a hut. These I shoved in my
kit and forgot all about it until we reached Palestine. Only then
the awful fact dawned on me that I could get into a terrible row
for having them. Had I not been such a coward I would have
taken and handed them in to the Company Office but I was
afraid that the people would start to wonder. I did not know
which way to turn. But on Easter Sunday I decided it was a case
of sink or bust. I knew that we were moving and I had not the
slightest intention of carrying them around any longer. Thus I
wrapped them up in a parcel and addressed them to you Mum
with instructions to burn them on arrival. One of the fellows
in my hut saw me pack them up and started to crib about it.
Whereupon with the usual style of loud-mouthed idiocy I
informed him I was going to sell them and if possible some rifles
as well. The fool believed me. Reported it to an officer
consequently. I was found in Haifa with the damned things in my
possession.

That is the complete story and now I must face the music, as
far as any defence goes I have not a leg to stand on, and if there is
a Court Martial, no officer would hope to make anything out of
it, he would not know the correct way to produce any sort of
defence. Do understand my dears, I *can* get at least four years for
this offence and men have been shot for going just a little further.

As yet the CO has not given any idea of his intentions, but I
think a Court Martial is unavoidable.

Now dears, it is up to you, do exactly as you choose. It seems
that I have caused you quite enough anguish and sorrow up to

now. I will write again in a couple of days time and tell you just how things pan out, but if I do get 'time' I don't think or expect you will wish to have anything to do with me. I cannot blame you only myself.

Your loving but hopeless son
John C.

A note on the letter in my father's hand, reads: 'Post Marked Field P.O. 25 April 1946'. The reader will note its lies.

Nowadays, if asked, I am inclined to characterize my behaviour with the paybooks as a mixture of masochistic spite and showing off. What might have happened if someone had come up to me in the street and offered to buy them, I do not care to think.

B Y 8 May, four days before the 4th Battalion held its last parade, I was charged with unlawful possession of the AB64s under the Defence (Emergency) Regulations for Palestine, a set of comprehensive powers designed to crush the insurgents, the equivalent of martial law. I pleaded guilty.

                                c/o The Provost Sergeant, Royal Scots
Dear Mum and Dad,
    I am increasing my knowledge of the 'great men', Shelley, Byron and Keats. But I cannot understand why James Elroy Flecker, my favourite poet, is not as well known. I am to be tried on May 27th.

Under the emergency regulations I would be judged summarily by a military court.

With me in the cells was a Glaswegian soldier called Gavin, due for court-martial on a charge of being absent without leave in Tel Aviv while in unauthorized possession of a military vehicle (his CO's new jeep), accompanied by a young woman by the name of Bebe wearing his glengarry with battledress jacket slung over her shoulders.

Gavin taught me the ballads of 'Kevin Barry', about an Irish patriot hanged for terrorism in the 1920s, and 'MacCafferty', in which a recruit to the Black Watch is hanged for shooting dead a captain who has taken a dislike to him. Gavin's day was spent sewing, letting fillets into the seams of his trousers and padding the shoulders of his jacket – retrieved from Bebe as the Military Police led him away. He was going to escape. The 2nd's cells had window bars set in wooden frames bolted to bricks. We worked out the bolts. When Gavin had heard about the paybooks he said I would get ten years. Better come with him. We'd take a 15 cwt truck, load it with tyres and spare parts, crash the camp gate and be in Lebanon by dawn. Bebe's father had a bar in Sidon. The truck, spares and tyres, would fetch around £(Palestinian) 3,000, enough for Bebe and him to start a bar in Beirut. 'The army won't look for us. They've got the Jews to deal with. In any case it's over for the English in Palestine.'

I was learning – slowly. The SAS, Popski's Private Army, or – bad as my immediate situation was – the life of a stranger in a strange land was not for me.

Gavin went through the window one midnight. I never saw or heard of him again.

FOUR officers sitting behind a wooden table passing sheets of paper to and fro while putting their heads together is what I remember of my trial.

This fits the instructions given in the *Military Courts' Manual* which says that, where pleas of guilty are concerned, the court hears the evidence and, after consultation, the President informs those brought before him of their sentences, which will be subject to confirmation, and whether or not these will be served 'with special treatment'.

The Manual adds: 'Members of the armed forces being sentenced to imprisonment are handed over to the Palestine Police for incarceration in one of the civil prisons. Special treatment is usually only granted to persons who by their social status, education and habits of life are accustomed to a superior mode of living.'

I got two years with special treatment.

When it was over, Ross came out of the building's sandbagged entrance with me. I asked him to write to my parents. We said goodbye and I was handed over to the Palestine Police in the form of a tall ombashi (corporal) carrying a loaded Sten gun. He motioned me into a jeep with the gun. We drove off, then stopped. The driver offered his companion and me cigarettes. We lit up. Then finished the journey to the Haifa lock-up.

> Lieutenant P. B. Ross,
> The Black Watch (Royal Highland Regiment)
> H.Q., 2nd British Infantry Brigade
> Middle East Forces
> 15.6.1946

Dear Mrs Logue,

Yesterday I attended the Military Court in Haifa where your son was tried for being in illegal possession of Army Pay Books.

I am indeed sorry to tell you that he was sentenced to two years imprisonment. Please do not think that this is as drastic as it sounds, for with remittance for good behaviour it will certainly not be longer than 16 months. He was awarded special treatment, which means that whilst he is out here he will be given his own quarters, together with other British troops, given British food, will be free to go to Church whenever he wishes, and will very probably be given a light office job to pass the time.

I hope you do not think I have taken a liberty in writing to you, but your son asked me to explain everything fully.

If there is anything I can possibly do to help you at this difficult time, please do not hesitate to let me know.

Yours sincerely,
Patrick Ross

I felt low. On getting Ross's letter my parents must have felt much worse. I sat in a small, triangular cell, crying. Not sobs. Just tears straight down my face. I thought of my parents going to bed at the end of the day on which they had received the news. I remembered their distress when they heard of Jack Musson's death. What could they say to one another that night, or next morning? As it turned out they did all they could to help me. Many letters to me, and to various authorities.

The cell faced on to the lock-up's yard. An elderly Palestinian was sweeping its flagstones with a long, straw-bristled hand-brush. After a time he came over and stood by the bars of my cell, smiling at me. Then he made the have-you-got-anything-to-smoke? sign – pursing, then moving the flat of his hand to and from his lips. There was a packet of Players in one of my best drill shirt's breast pockets. He took two, then vanished into the lock-up, returning with one of his alight, and a lit taper that he held through the bars for me to light up, the tears still running down my face, wetting the cigarette's paper.

My escorts returned. The back of my shirt had stuck to the black tar-like paint on the wall of my cell. Then I was driven along the perimeter of Haifa Bay to Acre Central Prison.

ONE of many strongholds raised on the site, modernized in the 1760s by an Ottoman despot known as Ahamad the Butcher, the fortress of Acre stands on a promontory overlooking the Mediterranean ten kilometres north of Haifa. What I knew of the place came from the days when I had seen *The Crusades* at the Southsea Odeon.

And there it was, the actual location, only, instead of battle-axing my way from an assault tower over the machicolations of its impregnable keep at Richard the Lionheart's side, I was being escorted in handcuffs and leg chains over the footbridge of the dry moat.

A disdainful sinjani (warder), his key chain so long it tapped against one of his gleaming boot heels, led me through the passage beneath the keep. I had assumed that Acre would be a silent place. I entered a sunlit pandemonium. The heart of the fortress was an extensive quadrangle bordered on three sides by vaulted cloisters, now used as cells. Along the fourth side, down which I was led towards the South Tower where those on special treatment were kept, was a high railing thronged by hundreds of Arab women talking, shouting, laughing at the tops of their voices, as they passed food, clean clothes, fruit and – though this was forbidden – packs of Ottomans, the popular cigarette, to their imprisoned menfolk. Acre held some six hundred Arab convicts and a few Jews (the terrorists we never saw), plus three British merchant seamen jailed for brawling in Haifa, and me.

My South Tower cell, one of ten set around a small courtyard, had glazed embrasures overlooking the moat towards the sea. I was given a meal of mutton stew with all the vegetables, fruit and bread I wanted. As at Prior, bells ruled the day. At 5.15 p.m. we were locked up.

The governor of Acre, Major Henry Grant, MC, said: 'A Sergeant Heggie of the Black Watch is bringing your books. If you have them with you, which you may, they will be stamped ACP and become part of the prison library.'

'Yes, sir.'

'Anything further?'

'My eye, sir.'

'Yes?'

'Just before my trial, sir, it seemed as if a shutter was covering half my left eye. The medical officer noticed it. It is still like that.'

He made a note. Then gave me the letters I had been sent care of the 4th and the Royal Scots.

I WAS set to work in the looms – four tall wooden frames in a vaulted hall that faced, on its barred side, into the Butcher's garden. Each frame had its team. Some threaded strips of coloured rag between its warps; others passed the shuttle between these cords. Some, the humblest, me among them, disentangled red and green strips from a mound of washed rag, then dragged them by the basketload to their loom.

Recruited in the Sudan, our sinjanis regarded us with genial contempt while they chain-smoked and chatted. Work went very, very slowly. Blankets and mattress ticking were our products. At the midday bell, stew, bread, fruit and water were brought to a table standing under the garden's vines. After thc meal, those with cigarettes smoked, the sinjanis ignoring them. The senior loomsters had wooden cigarette holders made from dowels pierced lengthwise with a hot wire, their mouthpieces carved from toothbrush handles. One of the sinjanis, an ex-soldier who had fought – for us – at the first battle of Tobruk, spoke rough English and made me his tutor.

I learnt that the Jewish insurgents were kept in the eastern part of the prison. They spoke only to each other. They were good fighters. There would never be peace for them.

Half the Palestinian Arabs were in for murder. There were some who, at the request of both families concerned, might never leave. If a murderer was released, a younger son from the victim's family would have to kill in turn. Perhaps when they were grey, they might be allowed home. It depended. God ruled all. And

what had I done? And why? Had the army dishonoured me?
Had I been overlooked? Had the Jews given me money? Was I a
Jew at heart? Did I hate Britain? Hard enough for me to explain
at this late date. Impossible to do so to this serious, likeable man.
How long was my sentence? Two years. 'Nothing,' he said,
'nothing. The Lord will guard you. He will welcome you. It is
nothing.'

PARTS of Acre were used as an asylum for the insane who had
fallen foul of the law or whose families could offer them no
refuge. They were treated amiably. They had the run of the moat.
A few would stand all day on the same spot, facing one of the
moat's stone sides. Some were naked save for blankets draped
over their heads. There were quarrels. Mostly they sat, or lay, or
wandered about. At five, the sinjanis rounded them up like sheep.
'They are', my sinjani said, 'God's very own.' When one died his
family would come for the corpse, or the prison would pay for it
to be buried in a potter's field.

Steve Heggie came and went. I had my books: Shakespeare,
Boswell, Wilde. I read and read.

The 4th had not been divided among other parts of the regiment. Its personnel were scattered as orderlies, drivers and runners through the Middle East. At the end of July I visited Haifa
general hospital, where a doctor looked at my eye. The gatemen
refused to allow our truck into the hospital's grounds. Out we
got, my ombashi toting his Sten, surrounded by curious passers-
by. Taking me for a political prisoner, perhaps, they pressed
money into my hands. 'Money – no! Cigarettes – yes!' commanded my ombashi. My eye was examined by two ex-European
Jewish eye specialists. On our way back to Acre we divided the
cigarettes between us: 'No search for you,' my ombashi said.
'OK?'

Later that week Major Grant told me that, when con-
firming my punishment, General Baring, GOC Palestine, had
directed that I should serve my sentence as a soldier. So I
would be transferred from Acre. Also, the hospital reported
that the retina of my left eye had become detached. This,
in the opinion of the Haifa specialists, resulted from the blow
of the sapling at Inverness. If the eye was to be saved, an

operation was required. This would be performed under army auspices.

'You will be transferred to Fifty-one Military Prison and Detention Barracks at Jerusalem. Goodbye.'

Glad as I was to be back in the army's hands, false as are most of the horror stories concerning British military prisons, the relaxed, mixed-race, unblaming, Muslim-Levantine ways of Acre had advantages when compared with the formal, minutely organized fellowship of 51 MPDB. Nevertheless, left in Acre, it is unlikely that the best would have been done to save my eye. And, likely as not, without the protection of Acre's British staff, my life there could easily have been far harder than it was.

In the cell I was to share with four others, my kit was tipped on to the floor and searched. From now on I must stand to attention, barking: 'Yes, Staff. No, Staff', as military-prison officers are called. Among them was an ex-4th Battalion man. We were both embarrassed.

Those who broke prison rules were given No. 1 or No. 2 Punishment Diet. PD1 meant one meal, plus so many ounces of bread, plus unlimited water, per day. PD2 the same, minus the meal. During either, you slept on 'biscuits' – three horsehair-stuffed squares laid on the floor. You had no reading matter save the Bible. Solitary confinement was the advantage of PD. Its disadvantage, for as many as you were given, you lost a day's remission. For refusing to break stones I got three of No. 1. Now and again the ex-4th Staff rolled a lighted cigarette under my door. My low opinion of the Bible as literature stems from those days. Perhaps it was the translation.

I became a cleaner. Having swept my corridor's floor and tidied out its empty cells I polished the brass valves of three fire extinguishers. These tasks had to last for four hours in the morning, two in the afternoon. The flourish of a duster among the scent of Duraglit kept everyone happy.

Occasionally I was detailed to clean one of the prison's offices, where the ashtrays provided a pocketful of cigarette ends, the desk drawers, a box of matches, the waste-paper baskets – though this was rare – a crumpled cigarette packet with one forgotten 'tailor-made' in its silver and tissue-paper lining.

In the cell the dog-ends would be opened, mixed, then rerolled in Bible-page rice-paper, matches split into four with a sliver of razor blade. Or we lit up from a tinderbox – an old boot-polish tin filled with burnt rag set smouldering by sparks flicked from a cigarette-lighter's flint.

> Ward 27, 12 British General Hospital
> Sarafand
> Palestine
> 26.8.'46

Dear Mum and Dad,

A most amazing occurrence has taken place. I am in hospital and for a lengthy period for my 'detached retina' operation. But I am free again. That is all important, free to write when I choose and to whom I choose. I gave the Commandant of the Detention Barracks my word that I was not going to escape! Thus now I am happy, happy and surrounded by white sheets, radios, nursing sisters, lovely books and everything that goes to make life worthwhile.

> 31.8.'46

. . . Tomorrow a new type of confinement. Confinement to my bed, this is done to accustom the patient to lying still and being a 'patient' patient. After that I shall have bandages placed over my eyes so that they may become rested and strain leave them. Then on Wednesday my operation. Lying in the next bed to mine is a lad who was suffering from the same complaint and he has described it to me. Until recently it was incurable but now the remedy has been discovered. It is absolutely painless, the only hardship while the operation is in progress is the heat which is unbearable and at the same time unavoidable. I shall be 'on the table' for roughly three and one-half hours; conscious all the time, the surgeon stops for a chat in the middle. The funny thing about it is that you can see the knife cutting the eyeball, and the electric needle grafting the disengaged part of the retina into its correct position. Of course the eyeball is out of the socket and you are looking at something you did not mean to at all. Sorry that is jumbled. He is twisting the eye and consequently your vision is being shifted without the wish of the patient. The bind of the whole matter is the aftermath. Six weeks of blindness and complete lack of motion on my part.

Do keep on trying to get Wavell's 'Other Mens Flowers' and Flecker, and if you would send it The Penguin New Writing . . .

What my fellow patient told me was true. With one eye on my cheek I could see the floor and the ceiling at the same time. It was hot under the lights, so beneath their overalls the theatre nurses wore bathing costumes.

No. 12 GH, MEF, 15.9.1946

Dear Mr Logue,

I writing this letter on behalf of your son John. As he cannot write to you I thought you might welcome a few lines from me. He has been busy composing poetry and has asked me to criticize it. I'm afraid I was pretty adamant about the standard despite my being only 2½ years his senior . . .

Yours sincerely,
Josephine Metcalf
Welfare Officer

Sometimes in the ward after lights out voices arose saying:

(Deep):	'Sister Anna, will carry the banner.'
(Shrill):	'I carried it last week.'
(Deep):	'You'll carry it this week, too.'
(Giggly):	'But I'm in a family way!'
(Flat):	'You're in every bastard's way.'
(Shrill)	'Mind my child!'
(Deep):	'Fuck your child.'
(Outraged):	'You'd fuck a child?'
(Flat):	'I'd fuck cheese.'
(Several):	'YOU CRAFTY FUCKER!'
(Shrill):	'I'll tell the vicar . . .'
(Pansy):	'I *am* the vicar.'
(Giggly):	'I'll tell the Pope!'
(Deep):	'Fuck the Pope.'
(Several):	'You'd fuck the *Pope*?'
(Several):	'I'd fuck the Pope with his hat on.'

Sister: 'Who said that?'

Sister was Irish.

Dead silence.

Sister: 'If I hear another word from Ward Twenty-seven I'll have the lot of you returned to your units on your crutches. Is that clear?'

A voice: 'Yes, Sister –'

'That's enough!'

Dead silence.

Sister: 'I'll find out who spoke in the morning.'

In October I wrote home: 'My operation was not a success, and as a direct consequence my left eye is as good as blind. "Operated on but not cured owing to a haemorrhage flooding the vitrius" is the official pronouncement. I have been downgraded from A4 to B4.'

In April, 51 MPDB was relocated to Fanâra, an Egyptian village close to the Great Bitter Lake. The train journey south was simply wonderful. The scrubby littoral was dressed with pink and white wild flowers. The Mediterranean glittered in the distance. We moved from window to corridor window to see both views. At sunset, I remember someone saying: 'This is the best hour of the day.' At night we slept by the track. You have never seen such stars. As big as your fist. As bright as sunlight on tin. Our spirits rose. Cigarettes appeared from nowhere.

We soldiers-under-sentence, SUS – our official style – did well from the move. Instead of living in a closed concrete and steel block set in the middle of a hostile city, we found ourselves in a large, tented compound, surrounded by concentration-camp-high barbed-wiring.

There were similar camps on either side of 51, save that their wiring was covered with hessian. Footwalks lay between us and them. Prison gossip alleged that one of them held ATS and NAAFI girls; the other, incorrigible Nazis convinced that Hitler's standards still flew over Europe, and that any day now the rumble of friendly Panzers would announce their liberation.

The prison had a Standard Unit Library. Between 1942 and 1944 the army, backed by the Treasury, organized a supply of 2,600,000 new books for the Army Education Scheme. Three thousand sets of the Unit Library were produced, each of 400 books, and distributed to every unit with a strength of five hundred or more. And a splendid 400 they were: *Wuthering Heights, Emma, Chambers Biographical Dictionary, Oldham's* (Shakespeare's) *First Folio* – with modernized spelling and punctuation – Helen Waddell's *Peter Abelard*, the *Oxford Book of English Verse, The Albatross Book of Verse* among them. George Sampson's *Cambridge History of English Literature* became my scripture.

ONE afternoon, three unusual-looking prisoners were admitted to 51. Overall, we SUS comprised true villains (a few), born troublemakers of one sort or another (not that many), and first offenders (the majority) – runaways, slovens, brawlers and muddleheads who had got into bother.

The three oddballs belonged to the RAF. One was a sturdy, round-faced, forty-year-old, with a ginger walrus moustache. The other two, blond and gangly. They were not like us. Nor were their sentences.

'Seven fucking years?' Taffy, our barrack-room lawyer (twelve months for stealing an ambulance full of medical supplies) declared: 'They're boasting.'

They were not. That night the forty-year-old, a conscripted electrician with five years overseas – i.e. no home leave – and a clean record, told us their story.

The war had been over for a year. Finding evidence that the slowness of their demobilization from the Sudan was a product of Westminster's need to protect its interests in this Anglo-Egyptian condominium, rather than anything to do with defeat of the Axis powers, two dozen airmen held a protest meeting in their NAAFI.

'We were skilled men,' he said. 'We sent and received cables. Without us, the planes couldn't fly. We were not political. It was just time we were sent home to our families and to find jobs. Instead, they charged us three with mutiny, promising us seven years apiece. After we'd helped to win the war. After VJ Day.'

They were on their way home under close arrest. Next day they were gone.

MY release, due at the end of the month, was discussed. 'There are four kinds of discharge for a private,' said Taffy. ' "Exemplary", meaning the army was sad to see you go. "Honourable", meaning you have done your best – neither of which applies to Chris, here, which leaves "Dishonourable" or "With Disgrace".' Opinion favoured 'With Disgrace'. Then Taffy produced his bombshell. 'Chris cannot hope for "With Disgrace",' he said. 'As with everyone sentenced to two years or more, he will be discharged with the little-known fifth kind – "With Ignominy".' My first encounter with the word. I guessed its weight. My heart swelled with pride.

'To be discharged "With Ignominy",' Taffy continued, 'means that he will get no demobilization leave, no free travel warrant to his place of abode, no free suit of civilian clothes, no gratuity of one week's pay for each month served with the colours, and he will have the word "ignominious" written *in red* by "Type of Discharge" in his paybook. Furthermore, as his sentence will not count as time served with the colours, he will have forfeited his original demobilization number, and therefore will be given a new, much larger number. It will be six months at least before he sees the white cliffs – if he keeps out of trouble, that is.' Taffy's last phrase was much heard in 51. Staffs and prisoners expected to meet one another again.

A week before my release there was a fight in the showers. Two soldiers attacked a third. I was the only other person in the showers. I heard grunts, cries and the thud of a body falling on to wet concrete. Grabbing up my clothes I ran out of the showers to look for a staff, desperately anxious to say I had nothing to do with it, nothing whatsoever, absolutely nothing to do with it. As loud as thunder, this fight brought home how much my imprisonment had hurt me. I was ready to say anything, about anyone, to keep out of trouble.

The fight went unreported and I became invisible. On 1 November I was taken from my duties and told to prepare myself for release. Almost everything Taffy said proved to be wrong. It was explained I would be taken to a transit camp for repatriation within 'twelve weeks'. The term 'with ignominy' was no longer used. I was B4. I would be discharged for medical reasons, and I would get what all other ranks got: suit, gratuity, etc. My tin kit-box was on the back of a 15 cwt truck. Out I went into the real world.

What bliss. The noise of the truck, the air on my face, the taste of a real cigarette – its butt then crushed underfoot – myself standing, holding the rollbars, singing 'Oh, Mr Porter'. I was no longer a soldier-under-sentence, just one of many hundreds arriving in transit from as far off as Iraq or the Sudan, soon to be shipped home. Their stories mentioned piles of radio transmitters, refrigerators, spare vehicle parts, lorries and ambulances now waste, not worth shipping, spread over airstrips to be crushed by tanks. Then the tanks tore up the airstrips with steel claws. Then the crews fired their tanks.

My twenty-first birthday came and went. Until our demobilization papers came, there was nothing to do except read, walk and talk. I bought twenty Tuinal capsules from a medical orderly as the poison for my escape outfit: 'They're new. Very strong.'

OUR troopship docked at Southampton in February 1948. After two years in bleaching sunlight we were struck by the crimson brickwork of the houses, by the intense greens surrounding our train. What fascinated us was the softness of the seats of our old, first-class carriage. We bounced up and down on our seats, then on each other's seats, then on the seats of the next compartment. Far from being rowdy, ours was a contented, scientific sort of bouncing.

At Aldershot we selected our free civilian outfits: shoes, socks, shirts (two), suit, tie, gloves, hat. They were folded into standard cartons and we carried them with us to the paymaster who issued our last week's pay and a travel warrant. Our gratuities (mine came to £180) would be paid via the Post Office. Some chaps changed in the lavatories at Aldershot station.

Two of us were going south. Him, a broad six-footer, to Romsey. Me, to Bournemouth. At Southampton Central we said goodbye. I was alone, ashamed of myself, unwilling to be in my parents' sight.

IT would have been best for the three of us if, after shedding tears together, I had gone over again, now face to face, the whys and the hows that had led to my imprisonment, seeking my parents' forgiveness through telling my story.

Though it was worth less than I got, I knew I had brought my sentence on myself. Yet I was not contrite. I refreshed the numbness I had developed immediately after my arrest, ignoring the contrast between my punishment and my parents' supportive kindness, unwilling to look at them in case I saw they had been marked by my disgrace.

So, when they came to the door, my mother first, drying her hands on her apron, my father behind her, his newspaper in his hand, I kept my eyes lowered, said my hellos offhandedly, kissed my mother's cheek with the corner of my mouth, shook my father's hand in an casual way, and by such behaviour indicated that questions about my recent past would be treated in the same way as when, teenaged, I had replied to a polite 'Where have you been today?' by saying: 'Oh, out . . . ' as I closed the door of my room.

Blessings were at hand. Hardly had I changed into some old clothes before Dad gave me my twenty-first birthday present: twenty one £1 notes. Then, on opening my cardboard box, we discovered that the lad from Romsey had gone off with my demob outfit, and I had been left with clothes suitable for someone twice my size. Molly was for my going back to change them, proposing herself as the companion most likely to guarantee I picked something decent, whereas my father, laughing, said that he would not hear of it 'as the army has had quite enough of old John'.

FROM my father's diary,
1 to 3 March 1948:

Gorgeous, warm and sunny. John to buy books in Bournemouth. Lunch – all together.

John to Central Library; for walk alone by sea in evening.

John and I sorting out boxes upstairs. He wrote to Mr Lindsay, present Headmaster of Portsmouth Grammar School, for interview regarding his university place.

During the months that followed I went from Bournemouth to London from London to Bournemouth, at least twenty times.

'John, still no job,' in Dad's diary, January 1949.

I DID not want a job. I would make do with as little money as possible. Coming in from a walk I heard Marius Goring read Coleridge's *Ancient Mariner* on the Third Programme. A masterpiece read by a master. Grand that the BBC had a Third Programme. I would go on the dole. With eighteen of my £21 I bought my first typewriter. I called almost daily at Bournemouth's reference library. Nothing came of my visit to Mr Lindsay.

When I could read no more, I walked by the sea or scanned the shelves of the poetry and drama sections of Bournemouth's five second-hand bookshops. So many books of weak poems! So many hopeless poets! This fate was not for *me*, or for *my* works – when they were written, if they were written, if they were published. My own volumes, handsomely produced, I saw as prominently displayed, downstairs, among the First Choice section of Cummins, the finest of the five shops. I discovered that certain books – first editions of T. S. Eliot or Ezra Pound, say – priced at 5/- in Boscombe, could, if offered to Cummins, fetch 7/6.

I HAD begun writing to Janet when I was in the army. She was my pen pal. By the time I reached Benyamina, I decided to bring matters to a head and wrote saying that my best friend had been killed in a motor-cycle accident. I had had no best friend. There had been no accident. Janet wrote back saying that she loved me. She was my girl. She would wait for me. When I was sent to prison, Janet did not waver. Then I was home, waiting to meet her at King's Cross.

The first thing I said when we reached Hilda's cottage on the Suburb and Janet and I took off our clothes, was: 'Oh, your breasts are so small.' We were shaking. Both virgins. I did not get erect. I had not washed my penis properly. I smelt. Later, I learnt the word *smegma*. Janet was ready to go on with our hapless lovemaking.

I became frantic, disgusted. If fucking was our right, I did not want that right, it was a burden. I turned to Hilda for comfort.

But what could Hilda do for this almost out-of-control, half-brother animal, tears running down his face, choking out: 'I can't do it.' Nothing in her life had fitted her to deal with someone in his present state. I reckon that Hilda – though I never would ask her – twenty-one years older than I was, knew as little of happy lovemaking as I did. In 1948, in Wordsworth Walk, fear and ignorance ruled.

It was a miserable time for Janet and me. I did not, and nor could Janet, know what I wanted. Again, years later, I asked myself, was I, at heart, both celibate and homosexual? Certainly it is true that unless given a strong lead, I am, sexually speaking, either hollowly insistent, or far too timid. Yet – though I have had homosexual friends – even in the mildest of ways, even in my mind, I cannot recall having desired, or having had to stifle a desire, for male flesh. Nor have I pined for homosexual love. Whereas I have lusted after, longed for and fantasized about both female flesh and female love. No matter that, when I have cried out for cunt, I have been given cunt. Yet when I went to eat it, I would retch, and when I went to enter it, I would fade.

For several months Janet and I went on as we began. I did not talk to myself about it. I went with fear in my heart to each meeting, at the same time as I insisted on those meetings. Quick enough to find reliable information when wanted, I read no books and asked no questions about sex from either the female or male point of view.

I RECOVER through denial. Or a change of scene. I thought of nothing other than myself. It never occurred to me to ask: What is Janet feeling? What does she think of me, of this? I did not want to face her sense of commitment. Perhaps my behaviour was a way of saying 'Go away' in order for me to avoid saying: 'This is a mess. I am in a mess. I need help. Experience.' Words that bind.

After three months I saw a local doctor who referred me to Dr Rowley at Sutton Emergency (Mental) Hospital.

Dr Rowley smoked a pipe. Keats was his favourite poet. He decided I should be something between an In and an Out patient. That is, provided I informed the ward sister, I was free to come and go. I received no medication. My favourite books were stacked on my locker. Most weekends I went up the Northern Line to stay with Hilda on the Suburb. Once a week I saw Dr Rowley. He must have diagnosed me as 'needing a rest, able to cope, but lost' – or psychiatric terms to that effect. He filled his pipe by turning it on one side and fingering the tobacco into its bowl from a transparent pouch while turning the pages of my case notes. He asked me this and that about my attitude to Janet. When I hedged, he did not press the matter. 'Ode to a Nightingale' was his best among Keats's best. I knew it. 'Recite it for me,' he said. In the middle of the fourth stanza my voice failed me. Looking out of the window of his office, he went on:

> 'Already with thee! tender is the night,
>   And haply the Queen-Moon is on her throne,
>   Cluster'd around by all her starry Fays . . . '

at which point I burst into tears, wailing: 'I will never write anything as good as that.'

'Don't worry too much,' Dr Rowley said, 'nobody else has.' Looking at my notes: 'You're twenty-two. Keats died from rotted lungs at twenty-six. At his rate you have four years to go. No time to waste. I'm discharging you at the end of next week.'

M Y mainstay at that time was my cousin, James Patrick Logue: Jimmy.

Jimmy Logue was a car dealer, a conservative anarchist, ferociously independent, uneducated, suspicious of the state, loathing the fact that somewhere, in some drawer, there was a birth certificate with his name on it. He carried a lot of money – several thousand pounds – in his pocket. He was a natural businessman, happy to buy and sell almost anything. Clever. Well liked. His territory: Edgware, Mill Hill, Finchley, Temple Fortune, the Suburb.

I admired Jimmy's wife, Jessica. Good legs, white high heels, twirly skirts, perfume, beret on a slant. She blew smoke rings and relished jokes. 'What will Jimmy do when he comes out of the Air Force?' Jessie once asked. And answered herself: 'This. Straight up to Warren Street. Buy a couple of second-hand cars. One to drive home. One to sell for the price of the two.'

I once saw Jimmy buy a house. We were driving around Mill

Hill when he spotted and took an instant liking to this house. It was a Sunday. There was no 'For Sale' sign. 'Come on, boy.' At the front door: 'Hello, my name's Jimmy Logue. I'd like to look around your house with a view to buying it. A very beautiful house, beautifully decorated, if I may say so.' We were in.

The occupants – a young woman and her mother – hadn't thought of selling. After twenty minutes and a cup of tea £5,000 was mentioned.

'How about four and a half?' Jimmy said, pouring himself a third cup.

It had to be five. The expense of moving. They'd have to rent . . .

'All right – four seven-five, and you can have it in cash,' Jimmy said, pulling a packet of banknotes from his inside breast pocket.

'Can I discuss it with my brother?' said the young woman.

'Very sensible,' replied Jimmy, putting the packet away. 'Let's settle it tomorrow evening, six-ish. OK?'

'What about searches, surveyors?' I asked, as we drove off.

'Bullshit.'

When we next met: 'You're a socialist, boy. You like giving away money that isn't yours. They wanted four-seven-five. Jessie wanted the house. As they moved out I put the money in their hands. Ted and Frank' – Ted, Jimmy's mechanic, and Frank, his paint sprayer, were both black – 'moved in for the night. That upset the neighbours, I can tell you. All Jews. Socialists, like you, boy.'

'How do you prove it's yours?'

'Jessie's in. Who's going to throw her out? You? Hitler and his mate Stalin? Two of a kind there, boy. The mother gave me some papers. They're in the garage safe. You read them. I haven't got time.'

Once a week, Jimmy sorted his letters. Most were binned. Some he superscribed 'O.K. J.' or 'No. J.' Then he stuck a Green Shield token stamp – '10,000 Gets a Washing Machine' – on their envelopes. 'Don't tell your father.' Jimmy admired my dad. Lastly, he'd take the letters he had set aside and, without opening them, stamp them with his special rubber stamp: RETURN TO SENDER. 'Never fails, boy. Sometimes they don't come back for years.' He didn't mention what they were. They were official-looking. Brown. Some marked URGENT.

Jimmy liked to drink in the Royal Oak, Temple Fortune. 'See him,' Jimmy once remarked, nodding at a man in a shabby over-coat who was tearing out pages from one of a pile of second-hand books on his table. 'That's John Gawsworth, a famous poet.'

Jimmy bought him a drink. Gawsworth explained he was compiling an anthology of love poems: 'I tear out the poems I like, write a note on the bottom, then send the whole thing in,' he said. 'Money for old rope.' I felt ashamed.

'Why not give him some of your poems?' Jimmy suggested as he drove me home to Hilda's cottage in Wordsworth Walk. 'He'd put them in.'

'I don't have any love poems.'

'Your being in love with your pen pal and when she turns up you go into hospital, sounds right for a poem to me. Give my best to Hilda.'

'Why not come in?'

'I can't stand family. Here.'

£10.

LONDON was sad. A place of war-damaged, unpainted houses, cellars filled with water, stairs and windows open to the sky, static-water tanks – big, four foot deep, iron rectangles brimming with black water intended to extinguish the fires started by the Luftwaffe's incendiary bombs – weed-covered bomb sites, mean 'caffs', miles apart from one another and almost always empty. There were sheep on Hampstead Heath, bound, I supposed, for grand restaurants. Very little in the shops.

Dr Rowley wished me good luck and goodbye. I had to get some money. My shoes had gone through.

I took a job as park keeper for Hendon Borough Council. My park was a long thin strip of grass with a brook as one of its boundaries and the back-garden hedges of four-bedroomed homes as the other.

I was clipping my side of the privet when, on the other, a fetching Indian girl of about twelve stood up on the pedals of her bike and said: 'Father asks if you would like to trim our side of the hedge.'

The front-door plate read 'Dr F. T. W. Patel/Dental Surgeon' followed by his letters. He gave me ten shillings. Two days later at about 8.15 a.m. – you start early in parks – Dr Patel knocked on the door of my hut and asked me if, as a severe cold was keeping his receptionist at home, and as there was no reply from her substitute's number, I would mind admitting the morning's patients until his wife, 'who is visiting her sister in Cricklewood,' got home?

Dressed in a white overall jacket, having studied the appointments book and scrubbed my hands, I was well into the part, opening, smiling, and somewhat *scraping*. 'Good morning, Mrs Bosomworthy, the doctor will be ready for you in a few moments . . .' when, at about 11.30, instead of receiving a Mr James Borradon, I opened the door to Mr Housego, Superintendent of Hendon Parks, who sacked me on the spot.

I was still lost. Not utterly as in my Bournemouth school days, because I knew more and, in a crude sort of way, I could write. But I was lost, none the less. I did nothing. And by doing nothing I had no defence against the hidden pressure of the world to find work. I walked up and down the King's Road and around Sloane Square hoping I might meet people like me.

At the time there was a celebrated bookseller, a Mr Robert Chris of Cecil Court, St Martin's Lane. He looked like Little John (Alan Hale) in *The Adventures of Robin Hood*. Sometimes he talked to me. I was keen on a short-story writer called Gerald Kersh. Mr Chris said Kersh was a regular customer of his. He would introduce me – if I happened to be there when his friend Kersh came in. Graham Greene was mentioned, too. Neither of them came in when I was there. When Mr Chris got fed up with me hanging around he produced a cardboard notice: DO NOT MISTAKE MY COURTESY FOR AN INVITATION TO STAY ALL DAY, and propped it up on the front of his desk.

One day, on leaving Chris's, I was tapped on the shoulder. Turning around I recognized one of my fellow prisoners from 51. Dirty, shivering, broken. I was dismayed. As if his touch reclaimed me for the prison. I fled.

In Bournemouth I had a friend whose father owned an ice-cream business. No older than me, he was getting married. He showed me over the flat where he and his wife were to live. I felt that, if I hinted at it, he would offer me a job. I did not know what to say. It was hard to show interest, wrong not to.

I began to read T. S. Eliot. This was special. Plainly outside the usual run. I went over and over Eliot's line describing a certain sort of evening sky: 'Like a patient etherized upon a table.' The metaphysical painters de Chirico and Carlo Carrà had painted Eliot's evening. I thought of waiting about in Russell Square until Eliot came out of Faber and Faber, the publishers where he worked. I would ask his advice. But I lacked the nerve.

As time went by I put aside my hope of finding a university place without much bitterness. Things might have been otherwise if my purely intellectual ambitions had gone deeper. I had understood that if, during those late forties early fifties days, you knew no one who knew how, in one way or another, university places were gained, much could be done by taking, and following, good advice, by writing intelligent letters, and by luck – knocking on the right door on the right day.

While shuttling between London and Bournemouth, I made one attempt in these directions, writing to, and being invited to visit, Professor Bonamy Dobrée, then Professor of English Literature at Leeds University. Dobrée had written – with G. E. Manwaring – a book I admired, *The Floating Republic*, a history of the naval mutinies at Spithead and the Nore in 1797.

I cannot recall how our meeting went. I had not prepared myself by discovering something more about Dobrée, or about the requirements of the university's English degree course. Nothing came of it. Leeds looked ghastly. Its university didn't fit my idea of such places at all, being no more than a scattering of large, nondescript, Victorian private houses.

Whatever I may have told myself, the truth was that I wanted to go to a university for social reasons. It was a door through which I knew I could escape from my circumstances. I was not ashamed of my family, or their friends. I would have been happy to introduce my father to anyone. Molly was well capable of looking after herself. But I knew that I needed to meet interesting, talented, clever, successful people. If this was to be managed, having the right social background was important. Being at university could provide such a background. Once that was achieved, access to cultivated people living in easy circumstances would follow. I did not want to change class, but to be class-free. An arty floater rather than a social climber

When we got to know each other, Bamber (Gascoigne) confessed: 'I was keen to go to King's College' – Cambridge – 'but my work wasn't up to scratch. So I applied to Magdalene, a college notorious to others for the supposed thickness of its undergraduates; in fact, a place at which I was happy and am proud to have attended.

'Despite Magdalene's reputation I was anxious about my interview – an important part of the admission process – with the Master, Sir Henry Willink. To be turned down by King's was one thing, by Magdalene, quite another. I did a lot of reading – the history of the college, the nature of its curriculum and so on. I was shown into a room where three men sat at a table, Sir Henry in the middle. After our introductions, Sir Henry said: "Tell me, Gascoigne, are you related to Sir Julian Gascoigne?" "Yes, sir. He is my uncle," I replied. "Then you'll be happy at Magdalene," he said. That was the end of the interview.'

I reckoned that if I 'got in' to a university I would be given a grant to live on. Everyone got a grant in those days. Which would remove the need of finding 'a proper job' for three years, at least. By which time I would know my way around. I would have contacts.

The idea of a university as the home of a body of scholars, of scholarship, and where, if you sought them, breadth of mind, humanist values, intellectual method, the ability to reason and to analyse, to think, could be learnt, did not occur to me.

And one thing more: 'university', for me, meant Oxford University. The architecture, the pictures, the undergraduate societies, the film club, the gardens, the not-too-earnest brilliance. Oxford did good things for people. It could do the same for me. Even Cambridge was a sort of second best. I was twenty-three.

In the second half of the fifties, part of my satisfaction of being liked by the likes of Lindsay Anderson and Ken Tynan came from their being Oxford boys. I had reinvented myself. I was 'in'. Now and again since then I have met those who assumed that I, too, had been an – not necessarily Oxford – undergraduate.

Whereupon it has been my pleasure to say, in a modest tone: 'Oh, no, I didn't go to a university.'

It was during these late fifties days I met some who considered that fate debarred those without higher education from writing – never mind composing verse – properly. They did not exactly say so. Yet their talk implied that their training had made them competent judges of new work, and had encouraged an acceptance of themselves as those who would bear the standards of literary excellence forward through time.

Forty years later I fancied there was a link between those fellows and a wish to stigmatize their certainties as 'élitist' by various 'lowlitists'. A depressing distinction born of vanity and resentment. Of course it is common for those (like me) who prefer Sophocles (in translation) to Boffocles (in the original) to share a smirk at the expense of the Boffoclesians glorying in their performers. And everybody knows that until the fifties British artists – poets included – came from the middle classes, helped out by the occasional aristo, well-to-do gent or taken-up-nobody. But since then those entering the world of the arts have arrived from all parts of the world, many from lower-middle-class and working-class backgrounds. To say nothing of women, blacks, ethnics, porpoises that sing and elephants that paint.

What I liked about Bamber, Ken and Lindsay, plus – once we were acquainted – Jocelyn Herbert, Xanthe Wakefield and Donald Carne-Ross – was that they went for any kind of art provided it was up to scratch.

BEFORE we went our separate army ways Patrick Brangwyn gave me his Portsmouth address. My card drew a card inviting me to stay.

The front door was opened by an elegant young woman with dark, wavy hair, wide-apart hazel eyes, and a daughter, Nonny, aged five, at her feet. Both laughing.

'You're Christopher, give me that' (my rucksack, I had hitch-hiked), she said in a clear, clear, gentle voice. 'I'm Audrey. Pat's wife. He's covering a football match in Fratton Park. You're to go over.'

It was raining. Patrick Brangwyn was among the few spectators.

'I'm working for the *Portsmouth Evening News*. We'll have to stay until the end to get the result.' We did not mention Oxford.

After tea, Patrick Brangwyn showed me his great find: 'A forgotten book. A masterwork,' he said, handing me a copy of:

CYCLOPS CHRISTIANUS;

OR,

AN ARGUMENT TO DISPROVE

THE

Supposed Antiquity

OF THE

STONEHENGE AND OTHER MEGALITHIC

ERECTIONS

IN ENGLAND AND BRITANNY.

BY

A. HERBERT,

LATE OF MERTON COLLEGE, AND OF THE INNER TEMPLE.

LONDON:
JOHN PETHERAM, 94, HIGH HOLBORN.
———
MDCCCXLIX.

---

in which, relying on evidence from certain ancient Welsh poems, Herbert showed that the renowned monument had been built during the thirteenth century.

After tea we took out our folders. Then, watched by Audrey, Nonny, Jane (in arms) and me, Patrick read Part One of his Herbert-inspired poem 'Nantwich the Smiter', beginning with a quotation from *Cyclops Christianus*:

Am I not exceeding blue?

I was impressed. Why didn't I have a theme like that?

Back in London, I took a job clerking for J. Arthur Rank. The advertisement had mentioned 'openings in the film industy'. My task was to record the movement of the prints Rank was distributing: 'N.17239, *Wicked Lady, The*, 10 reels. Ex-South Africa, London, 3.3.1949.' The people I worked with were respectable. Most were married or about to be married. Rank was a good employer. Their jobs were good jobs. They would last.

I stuck my job for three weeks. In the middle of the fourth week I decided that I had had enough. I would kill myself. I left my jacket hanging on the back of my chair and began to walk home from Oxford Street, going into each chemist I passed for a tube of codeine tablets. My Tuinals were in Bournemouth.

At the drinking fountain on the brow of Hampstead Heath I swallowed a tube's worth, then started down between the trees in the direction of Temple Fortune popping a tablet into my mouth every so often. By the time I got to the Suburb's Lutyens terraces I was light-headed, hallucinating a little, relieved I would not see Rank's offices again.

Hilda was away. Her cottage had a back entrance reached by a path between untrimmed hedges. As I walked down it a twig scratched my forearm. I did not notice a thing until I was in the kitchen and saw the blood running down the back of my hand. Thinking it unfair to stain the bedclothes, I wrapped a towel around my arm before I lay down and was asleep as soon as my head touched the pillow.

Next morning I woke, as usual, at 7 a.m. I felt dreadful. Repentant. My mouth and throat like brick. How painful for

Hilda, so kind to me, to have found me dead. I caught a train to Bournemouth.

M Y father was withdrawing from the world. In days gone by he liked to clip absurd stories from the newspapers. 'Listen to this, old John: "Mr Daniel Tong, the King's muffin maker, was fined thirty shillings at Chelsea Magistrates Court for covering his wife's marmalade jars with the remains of a top-secret report on the housing problem".'

T HERE was less of this. Sitting by the fire he would polish his bowls. Daily, as when a boy, I fetched his Players and *News Chronicle* from the corner shop. Mother spared me the gate-leg table from her guest bedroom.

To supplement their income – 'Your father's pension is worth less every day' – my mother took students as lodgers. Sent to her by an agency for Catholic families, these Spanish and French teenagers came to improve their English. They ate with my parents, their pronunciation being corrected by Molly. If girls, they were to be indoors by 8 p.m. No nonsense.

And still I had no money, or none to speak of, often not even the 30/- a week I allowed myself. I had been on the dole and on National Assistance. It was not that I wanted to have money. Simply that I could not do without it. I could not think of a job for myself. Anyway, I had a job. It just didn't produce, and probably would never produce, money.

Hilda saved me.

Retiring early from the Post Office, she had her cottage in Wordsworth Walk and a modest state pension. She pointed out that the loss of sight from my left eye while on military training entitled me to a disability pension. I thought my prison record would disqualify me. 'No,' Hilda said, 'it will not. Apply for it.'

My disability was assessed at 30 per cent, as a consequence of which I was awarded a pension of 13/6 per week – £30.36 a week today, 1998.

If I could earn small sums to add to this, then I could get by. A person of independent means. At home, although I cost my parents little, I contributed less. I had to get out. To get on. London offered nothing. Perhaps I should try Paris? Paris had a reputation of hospitality to artists, writers. For inspiration, I read Eliot. For instruction, Pound. Yeats for pleasure. Matters became clear. Either you did as well, as differently, as Eliot had done, or forget it. Become a film star, or a world leader.

And I made three close friends: Peter Clarke, Charles Fox and Paul Wallace.

'Do you remember our 1950 trip to Maiden Castle?' (the 2000 BC hill town near Dorchester) said Joyce Harper, Charles's companion. 'We sat down out of the wind to eat our sandwiches, and as you were reading us that poem of Hardy's about the seamstress who gets away with the murder of her brutal husband by sewing him into a mattress to suffocate while he's in a drunken sleep, a big collie dog came bounding up, snatched your sandwich out of your hand, and tore off with it. You were so cross. Charles had to look away.'

Charles the Amiable, the Discreet, the Stout, the Shy – with his low-pitched voice and big brown eyes above milky cheeks, so generous with his time, his knowledge, the founder of the Bournemouth Writers' Group, then working as sub-editor on the local paper, later as a London music critic, close to me until he died in 1991.

'Until three years ago,' Joyce said at the time of the sandwich incident, 'Charles paid some attention to politics. When they "banned" the *Daily Worker*, Charles, to my complete astonishment – after all, I had known him for several years – carried a placard. Actually carried a placard through the centre of Bournemouth, demanding – how ridiculous – for it to be "unbanned", or whatever the word is for opposite of "banning". Three months after the *Daily Worker* resumed publication Charles got a letter from the local Communist party – they got his name as a result of that placard business – practically ordering him to join a march to, as usual, *demand* that the Anarchist paper, the *Black Flag* – or some similarly unattractive title – be banned for *class treachery*. Whatever that means. And that, thank goodness, was the end of it. Politics has not been mentioned since.'

Peter Clarke – then a partner in his father's ticket-writing business – *Cold Cuts 3/- per lb*, penned or brushed on to a plastic shield – reminded me that we met on the steps of the Bourne-mouth Central Library. 'I had just taken out Pound's *Cantos* and was looking through it when you came up to me and said: "Pound, eh? Thank God. At last I've got someone to talk to in Bournemouth." Then you introduced yourself.'

'What else?'

'Hang on, hang on, I'm looking through it' – his 1949–51 diary – 'as fast as I can. Ah yes: "Chris has long hair, almost reaching to the back of his collar. When he smiled, beneath his large nose I noticed several of his teeth were missing. We walked along the cliffs to his parents' flat talking all the way. He has a small room. His bookcase contains a selection of Elizabethan dramatists and much modern poetry. He recited some of his own poetry. It has the imprint of Eliot. He criticized me for not having read the *Four Quartets*".'

I remember that walk. Looking down from the top of the East Cliff Road we saw that the words BAN THE BOMB had been painted in white along the width of the undercliff drive. It was the first such slogan either of us had seen.

'Who would have painted it?' I wondered.

'The Pacifists. They're quite strong in Bournemouth.'

'Are you a Pacifist?'

'Yes,' Peter said. 'I am. Not in a group.'

'You mean you'd let people like Hitler kill you rather than you killing him?'

'Yes,' he said. 'I suppose I would.'

'I'm not a Pacifist,' I said. 'I'm a militarist. I'll defend you with violence if it comes to it. Pacifism is just mystical.'

'Yes,' he said 'it *is* mystical. That is my last line of defence. I believe it is wrong to kill people. My stand is a lone stand.'

'I see,' I said, impressed in spite of myself.

'You know what people are like,' Peter said. 'They want to have a bomb. It makes them feel important and safe.'

'So you give up on the banning?'

'I don't expect to win.'

'If it looked like a big bomb war I'd spend my last days carving some Shakespeare in stone,' I said.

'What bit?'

'Clarence's speech about going under the sea.'

'That's a very long speech,' Peter said.

'Are you coming to the Writers' Group meeting?'

'No,' he said. 'I'm a reader, not a writer.'

'I bet you could write if you tried. Why not try? I'll tell you if it's any good or not.'

'I'm sure you would.'

In fact, Peter, as well as a reader, was a collector. Minor English poets, his rage. A skilful buyer: 'I don't like to pay more than a shilling' – 5p in 1999 money – 'a volume.' In 1949 he had 500 poetry books of this kind.

THE Writers' Group met at Charles's house. He introduced me to his mother. Mrs Fox put her hand around the living-room door, I shook it. I did not see her face. That was that. Our one meeting in thirty years.

Although there were chairs, it was not easy to find a place to sit in Charles's large room for he – you would never have known it to look at him, always collar-and-tied – lived in disorder. His room was awash with gramophone records balanced on magazines balanced on (two) gramophones, all overlooked by bowed bookshelves, and, ah, yes, there – suddenly wanted – Beddoes' *Poems* – Charles on one foot leaning up, across, his pen between his teeth, finger-tipping his Beddoes out, oops, and – caught (just) – book, pen and Charles safely back on, not quite, yes, on the floor, ankle deep among the items we had removed from our chairs on arrival, paging through for the quotation.

Critically minded, Charles disliked making critical comments. Obliqueness made him prize, buy, and – always well after the occasion provoking the gift – present his literary friends with copies of *The Stuffed Owl*, a collection of bad poetry edited by D. B. Wyndham Lewis and Charles Lee. Nothing better to charm a gloomy heart than Charles beginning a selection of readings from the book with Dryden's couplet on the Earl of Musgrave's translation of Ovid:

> How will sweet Ovid's ghost be pleased to hear
> His fame augmented by a British peer.

Then moving to a passage from 'The Fight in the Cave' by the Australian politician-poet Adam Lindsay Gordon (1833–70)

– who, by the way, has a massive bust in Poets' Corner – covering
the arrest of a bushranger:

> FLASH! flash! bang! bang! and we blazed away,
>   And the grey roof reddened and rang;
> Flash! flash! and I felt his bullet fly
>   The tip of my ear. Flash! bang!
> Bang! flash! and my pistol arm fell broke;
>   I struck with my left hand then –
> Struck at a corpse through a cloud of smoke –
>   I had shot him dead in his den!

While even the most intense bout of self-pity collapsed on
hearing lines from *Science Revealed; a Poem, descriptive of the
Works of Creation and the Truth of Scripture Record,* by George
Everleigh (*fl.* 1863) the businessman poet:

> Thus, if a Government agrees to give,
> Whenever Public Companies are formed,
> To each a dividend – say, six per cent
> Per annum for a certain fixèd time,
> And for security inspects accounts –
> Then, of the profits which each yieldeth more
> Than the same dividend of six per cent,
> Two-thirds the Government itself shall claim,
> The other third remaining to afford
> The Company an extra dividend.

PETER Clarke, Charles Fox, Christopher Logue, Paul Wallace.
We were interested in serious writing. Comic, not comical.
Entertaining, not entertainment. We had no wish to claim that,
because of what we read, we were better than those who read
trash. We did not consider ourselves superior to our parents. We
told ourselves that the things we valued in good writing – exalt-
ation of the spirit, insight into the lives and minds of others, good
humour, the power to attack wrong, exposure to the differences
between our own and other times, the constant challenge of high
standards set by those who had gone before us – were benefits
that might come to others in other ways, but our particular needs
were literature, painting, music, all as part of our daily, ordinary,

everyday lives, even though the rest of the world gave not a farthing for them.

As well, we agreed that poetry must be beautiful – to hear and to read – and witty, and interesting, and say useful, unusual things, and exhilarate. And that the work of poets who do not produce such effects would be forgotten.

These thoughts, so obviously the case, left me worried and downhearted. Would I ever be able to produce such qualities? Years later, when a reviewer said of my poems 'Mr Logue should learn that it is not enough to be interesting,' I felt, 'well, at least I've got that far.'

And, of course, we loved books. Books were the thing. Portable, durable, inexpensive – a marvel of technology needing no intermediates save spectacles; that can be exceptionally beautiful, and may become valuable. Above all – free-spirited, subversive, difficult to police.

THE Wallaces lived in seclusion at the end of Dover Road, an unadopted lane half a mile inland from the Westbourne Chines. Their house, a substantial residence, was surrounded by large rhododendron bushes through which pine and cedar trees as high as fifty feet rose into the quiet air. Tranquillity, lightly scented by the tang of resin, pervaded cliff-top Westbourne.

Until the door to his study closed behind us, Paul and I spoke in hushed tones. Saville, his elder brother, suffered from profound deafness. He passed his time playing chess, sometimes against Paul, mostly against himself, never leaving the house. Paul's mother, like Charles's, I met once only, Paul saying as he opened the door of her sitting room an inch or two: 'Mother, Christopher – I believe I have mentioned him – is here.' Who to my 'Good afternoon, Mrs Wallace,' replied: 'Good afternoon, young man. We are so pleased Paul has made a new friend in the neighbourhood. Westbourne people are so reserved.'

Though the house was provided with fine furniture, Paul's study was monastic. A plain table under his window; on it, open, the work – perhaps a classroom Horace – he was studying, a Woolworth's exercise book beside the Horace. Two wooden chairs. 'Let me fetch you a cushion.'

Then we would talk, him explaining how, for example, it had taken him years to 'think my way out of the guilt for everything, for nothing, aroused by my Christian indoctrination. Gibbon was my master. Then the Roman poet Lucretius – a great poet – the equal of Ovid, but, unlike Ovid, never popular.' Such things voiced shyly, always softly, as if he was alone.

Among other qualities I admired Paul for his readiness to enlarge on what he meant.

'First you use *myth*, then you say *fiction*?'

'Myth for me,' he answered, 'means Greek myth. Nothing else. At its lowest, a set of fantastic anecdotes about an extended family with supernatural powers. Whereas fiction is Dickens, real stuff from a real world. He mixes those worlds. There is also what appears to be your sort of thing: *Paradise Lost*, Titania/ Oberon, fables, beliefs, unrealities. The world of poetry. Shakespeare mixes all worlds. No wonder he is loved. So poetic. So sane.

'Perhaps the shop girl reading trash knows everything that is in *Emma* without reading *Emma*. We are modern – that is to say humanistic, sentimental. I am content to pay taxes for an Education Act that enables her to read *True Romances*. Her taxes go towards the spectacles enabling me to read Horace. Horace is a better writer than the people who compose *True Romances* – as I am sure she would agree. The point is – her point and mine – that the betterness on which we all agree is unimportant. Literature is an amusement to get you from womb to tomb.'

With Paul I discussed my moving to Paris. He saw my nervousness. 'I'm going to be there in September. We could meet. It might make things easier.'

That almost settled it. I began to economize. My pension was renewed. A monthly magazine called the *Bournemouth Critic* took several short pieces by me, paying as much for each as Rank had for a week's clerking.

Through this sort of work, plus the selling of a book or two, I saved. Most of my life has been so managed – bits and bobs assembled round small regular payments: my pension, my cheque from *Private Eye*, my stalls – of which latter more later. Eventually, the bits and bobs grew larger. Never mind: bits and bobs they were.

A literary magazine called *Nine* appeared. Edited by a young poet, Peter Russell, *Nine* aimed to publish the work of poets and critics yet to make their name whose standards met those laid down by Ezra Pound. In the magazine's first number – for which I wrote off – Russell's newcomers included a critic named Donald Carne-Ross.

This lot seemed the lot to be in with. Though I had written nothing good enough for *Nine* to publish, I thought it unlikely that the magazine had a South Coast sales representative. If I applied for this position, I might – as sales leapt in Bournemouth and Portsmouth – be invited to meet some of the contributors, or even the editor.

A week after my letter of application I received a parcel containing twenty copies of the second issue and a note from Russell appointing me the magazine's representative for the whole of southern England. Of each copy sold, I was to keep one-third of the cover price.

I bought an invoice book. Charles and Peter bought copies of *Nine*. Paul bought two copies. He did not comment on the contents. At the end of a long conversation, Cummins took one copy on sale or return. The other bookshops declined to stock it.

Then, miraculously, a new second-hand bookshop called Francis's opened in Boscombe. It was elegantly fitted: polished-oak parquet flooring; long, deep, varnished shelves; tables, choice items laid thereon, standing on Eastern rugs

As for the owner, Francis, he was too good to be true. He didn't look like a second-hand bookseller – whose clothes are, for the most part, undistinguished. Francis dressed like a London car salesman – the sort of fellow glimpsed through the windows of Jack Barclay's of Berkeley Square – brown suede shoes, well pressed lightweight grey flannel trousers, silver-buttoned blazer complete with embroidered breast-pocket club badge, white shirt, regimental tie. He was about forty-five, with a pink complexion, a wide, cheerful mouth, and dark hair which he smoothed from time to time, coughing the while, his other hand over his mouth.

'Well, old chap,' he said, looking me up and down, 'give me half a dozen copies for a start.'

'Half a dozen – are you sure?' I said.

'Why not? Must support the poets.'

I got out my invoice book.

'Let's not bother with sale or return,' he said. 'I'll give you a cheque.'

He put two copies in the window. I told Peter and Charles. From now on we agreed to buy everything essential – collected works, et cetera – from Francis.

Francis was a chain smoker. He had a large silver cigarette case. 'One for you?' Out it came, tap-tap-tap on its curved silver surface.

Kipling was his favourite poet. Walking his parquet, a quick draw – Kensitas his brand – smoke out through the nose, 'herumph, herumph' – hand over mouth – then, after smoothing his hair, a rendition of 'Fuzzy-Wuzzy', powerful, exact, with a contented snarl on the lines – particularly the sixth.

> We took our chanst among the Kyber 'ills,
>   The Boers knocked us silly at a mile,
> The Burman give us Irriwaddy chills,
>   An' a Zulu *impi* dished us up in style:
> But all we ever got from such as they
>   Was pop to what the Fuzzy made us swaller;
> We 'eld our bloomin' own, the papers say,
>   But man for man the Fuzzy knocked us 'oller.

Few people entered his shop. 'I bought the *Thousand and One Nights*, full text, four volumes, much reduced, from Francis's,' Peter said. 'He told me that an unsuspecting father bought it for his daughter's birthday and returned it next day.'

Two years later, on the first day of my first trip home from Paris, I walked round to see Francis. The shop was To Let. Its fittings stripped. I always read 'Fuzzy-Wuzzy' aloud *à la* Francis. It goes down a treat.

MY mother's next student was to be a boy. French, twenty-one, Georges Barthès de Ruyter was the son of a Paris wine merchant. Georges' English was good. He wanted to sharpen it. As a reward for being among the first five of his year at the École Normale Supérieur – one of the best schools in France – his father presented him with a car to bring to England. Georges found our grammar hilarious.

'Why do you call the verb *to be*, *to be* not *to am*, or *to are*? What do I find in my book under *to be*? *Am*, *are*, *is*, *was*, *were*, *being*, *been*, when all I need is *is*, *was*, and *will be*.'

He and I drove to marvellous places: Stourhead, Stonehenge, the Chesil Bank, Kimmeridge – its beach overgrown with swags of seaweed smelling of iodine, its bay dominated by a ruined tower, two iron cannons buried in the grass by its foundation. I told him of my Paris plan.

'That is right for you. Paris is not expensive. You get a good big meal – with wine – for three shillings. A small hotel room costs four pounds a month. Many hotels let rooms by the month. When you are ready, write to my mother. You will stay with us until you are established.'

That settled it.

I told my parents I wanted to live in Paris. Dad said he would find £50 to start me off. As Georges was leaving for home, he said: 'Did you hear of the Frenchman who believed that to know English properly you must live in England? The first thing he saw at Victoria Station was a sign saying "Cavalcade Pronounced Success" – so he shot himself. See you soon.' It was April 1951.

VIS-À-VIS *Nine*: Paul said he could spend no more time on it; Peter thought it was unpleasant:

'On the one hand it contains a long essay on a bad poet called Croxhall. Have you ever heard of Croxhall? No. Only Peter Russell and I have heard of him – 1691 to 1750, hopeless. On the other there is a scurrilous review of Auden's new book. I'm not buying it again.'

I wrote to Russell returning four copies and a postal order for the sixteen copies sold: the ten already mentioned, the other six to me. Russell was pleased. He invited me to visit him.

Pretending I had other things to do there I hitch-hiked to London. I was nervous. Apart from my meeting with John Gawsworth, this was my first contact with the literary world. I arrived at *Nine*'s address an hour early.

There was no doorbell marked 'Russell'. Had he moved in the past ten days and forgotten to let me know? I checked the street name. Duke Street. No doubt of it. A postman came by. 'I'm looking for a Peter Russell. He should be here,' I said, pointing to the door. 'Nar Russells,' he said. 'There must be,' I said, producing a piece of paper with *Nine*'s address. 'That's Duke Street, Marylebone, this 'un's St James's.'

It was a fast, thirty-minute walk.

Russell doesn't change. A large man with a benevolent smile, looking like a cross between Professor Joad, the radio philosopher, and Doc, the leader of Disney's Seven Dwarfs, the last time I saw him was in Harry's Bar in Venice, in the early seventies. He had been teaching English poetry in Teheran. Then the mullahs came to power, confiscated his library, and kicked him out.

His study was four times the size of my room and lined from floor to ceiling with expensive books. In one corner there was a radiogram fitted with a huge papier-mâché horn. I had never been in a house where art was taken with such – to me – wealthy seriousness. 'This is hopeless,' I told myself, 'he'll see through me the moment I open my mouth. He won't bother with autodidacts. I know nothing about anything.'

We had coffee and biscuits. Though we should have had something to say to each other, particularly about Pound on whose work Russell was an expert, we failed to get a conversation started. As I left he invited me to a reading from Pound's *Pisan Cantos* he was to give later that day.

He had an audience of twenty. The event made my trip worthwhile. Although I had practised repeating the *Cantos* aloud, partly to learn how to handle the spacing of the verse, partly to realize the overall, musical flow of the work, I had never heard them read by someone else – Charles declining, Paul cool, Peter too shy. Russell's performance was professional, able to pass an audition, his voice soft, carrying the non-musical elements of the verse forward, clearly, without hesitation, clarifying, for me, what had been obscurities. As well, I was pleased to find that my own attempts had been, crudely, in line with his.

'Will I ever,' I asked Paul, 'have a house of my own filled with books and music as Russell's is?'

I N May my parents decided that Molly should have a fortnight's holiday, Dad staying with Hilda while she was away. They would go up to London, settle Dad into Wordsworth Walk, then she and Aunt Margaret would leave for Dublin.

I sat with Dad while Molly packed their cases. He reminded me that the £50 to take me to Paris was waiting. He would draw it out of the building society when mother and he returned to Bournemouth. The taxi was at the door. I carried his case downstairs, where we shook hands, he, as was his wont, smiling, his head to one side.

Paul, Charles and I planned an outing. We would meet in Swanage and walk to St Alban's Head. 'Swanage street furniture is worth a look,' Charles said. 'The lampposts are stamped *Property of Bradford City Council,* the manhole covers say *Scarborough Works Department.*' Vain of my sense of direction, I left the bus at Corfe to make the rest of the journey across country on foot. Peter's diary says:

> Charles reports C lost while hiking to Swanage. Had to ask some visitors the way. Fifteen minutes later the same group met Charles who, unbeknownst, was following C's path. 'They were very excited,' Charles told me. 'We have just seen a person who looks like John the Baptist,' they said. 'Was he missing two teeth?' I said. 'Yes, that's him,' they replied. 'Then it's only my friend Christopher on his way to see the manhole covers of Swanage,' Charles said. Whereupon they hurried away. C has had his hair cut. He is to leave for Paris in September.

My mother was not due to return from Dublin until the first week of June. Then I received a message from a neighbour who was on the telephone to say she was back early because Dad was ill. I should go to London immediately.

There were screens around his hospital bed. He had shrunk. His voice, though faint, was still his own light, mildly satirical, friendly voice. He had no specific illness. 'He developed a cold,' Hilda said. 'Then everything seemed to come at once. Dropsy, liver failure, you see how yellow he is.' Molly sat on one side of his bed, Hilda on the other, each holding one of his hands. I sat on the end of his bed for an hour. We did not speak. Eventually, I said I would go.

'Goodbye, Dad.'

'Goodbye, old John.'

There was a priest in the corridor. 'He had the sacraments, then fell asleep and died an hour after you left,' mother said. He was eighty-one.

I did not find it surprising that in the thirty years she lived after his death my mother seldom mentioned my father to me. Just the occasional: 'What a nice man he was. So honest. So polite with everyone. If only you could be just a little more like him.' She would not have found their love a fit subject for words. She missed him, always. Not bitterly. His photograph – looking very fine, him in a stiff collar, his tie elegantly tied – never wanted a posy. She died with his prayerbook in her hands.

I SAT on the bus trying to remember everything about him. His love of Ireland, of musical evenings. Firm that the value of administrative work should be recognized. Singing me to sleep. 'Lily of Laguna'. Me conducting. Him at the end of my bed –

> 'She's my lay-dee love,
> She is my love, my dai-see-dove . . .'

'Singing in Handel's "Hallelujah Chorus" was the grandest moment of my life,' he said.

Since my childhood, we had not been close. I had worried and disappointed him. But he never gave up on me. At the back of my mind, he was always there, rubbing my stomach as I sat on the lavatory with my first gut-cramping cold, ready to sharpen my pencils, laugh at my boasts, telling me not to be afraid, to look people in the eye, that if I got into a fight – 'which I don't recommend, for you're not as like our Jim as you think' – I was to make sure to keep my head up, that to lie was low, was cowardly, and that those who lied to you would lie about you.

I decided I had to get away from my mother. To avoid being stuck with her. Now there was no one between us. Dad's death had made me 'the man of the house'. At least it had in my own mind. I cringed at the thought. My mother and I could never live quietly in the same house. Either we would quarrel, or come to an understanding through talk. I wanted neither. And neither, perhaps, did she.

I WROTE to Mme Barthès. Paul would meet me in Paris. Molly drew out my £50.

'Don't you worry about me. Your father and I managed to save. I have the flat and my students. You must do whatever it is that makes you happy.'

'He went to France and left his mother to starve,' Aunt Gladys said.

'Well,' Mother said, 'that's your aunt Gladys. She suffered agonies from constipation.'

1951–1956

PARIS

THE Barthès de Ruyters' apartment was on rue Legendre, Paris 16. Having introduced me to his mother, Georges led the way up the back stairs to their *chambres des bonnes*, tried the taps of that to be mine, said dinner was at eight-fifteen, and disappeared.

To the right my window looked out at the top of the Arc de Triomphe; to the left the Tour Eiffel, illuminated in the dusk. 'This is the place for me,' I said as I smoothed out my best trousers. 'This is definitely the place for me.'

Descending the back stairs at twelve minutes past eight I realized I had not noticed on which floor of the nine-storey building the de Ruyters lived. There was only one solution – to the bottom and round to the front door.

There, as it began to rain, I met my first French concierge, a middle-aged woman who came out of her *loge* and stared at me through the glassed-in ironwork of the residents' entrance, while I varied my most respectful smile by mouthing 'de Ruyters' pointing first at my chest and then at the lobby's ceiling.

I was late. It was a supper party. Linen. Crystal. Silver. Candles. A Renoir nude on the wall. Eleven people at table; one, a man with a magnificent head of silver grey hair wearing a tricolour sash. '*Notre Député*,' Madame Barthès explained.

Monsieur Barthès introduced me as '*Monsieur Christophe, un poète Anglais*, a friend of my son Georges, who has, naturally, come to live in France,' then seated me on Madame's left.

Georges' father was short, tubby, bald, with a broad red mouth.

I had never had a meal like it. I managed the soup (my first croûtons), copied Madame's use of the three drinking glasses, and sipped my wine (another first).

My challenge came with the entrée: two frying-pan-sized steaks, each an inch thick, seared, and surrounded by what looked like a pool of hot blood, before which M. Barthès rose, then cut into portions. Down the table came the plates, mine bearing one of the larger cuts.

My anxiety was lessened by the sight of M. Barthès. Satisfied that his table was replete, he cut his own helping into smaller pieces, set his knife and fork aside, and then (breaking the pattern occasionally with a fork-load of runner beans) popped the pieces into his mouth with his fingers. This was delicately done: a finger bowl to his left, by it a pile of napkins, off which, after each mouthful – his cufflinks glittering – having dipped his fingertips in the bowl, he would take a fold and dry them, dab his lips, then drop the cloth into a wicker basket beside his chair.

Suddenly I was drunk. I had been drinking wine to help the meat down. The room was revolving. Then Georges was there, leading me out of the dining room, back up the stairs, to my attic.

NEXT day Georges made his tyres screech as we came across place de la Concorde on to the quai des Tuileries. When we stopped at the pont du Carousel he said: '*Le voilà!*', continuing – as the standards supporting the lamps, one at each corner of the bridge, began to telescope upwards through the dusk: 'The height necessary for their beams to meet in the middle of the span would be unsightly by day.'

We drove on. The city was alive. Full of light. People looked good. So different from London. London had been bombed. Paris had not. The war was over – we had won it. Why had nothing in London changed? Colour was absent. There was something more than the pain of the recent past to this disparity. Being occupied and half-starved could not have been easy for the French. Perhaps it was true: the English lacked *joie de vivre*.

Nowadays (1998) London is as bright as Paris, brighter maybe. Then, the sophisticated richness of Paris came as a slap.

PAUL arrived. We met underneath a vast advertising placard, that declared: MAURICE THOREZ VA BIEN. Thorez was the leader of the French Communist party. 'A comforting announcement,' Paul said.

If I didn't want to return home I had to find a cheap, by-the-month, Latin Quarter hotel room, and a way of earning some money.

There was a third requirement. In 1951 visitors to France were obliged to leave the country every twelve weeks. To remain there, you crossed, then recrossed the nearest frontier, getting a new entry date stamped on your passport. Or you applied for a *carte de séjour*, though, if you did, the police wanted proof you had money enough to live in France without working. 'For while one Frenchman remains unemployed no foreigner can work here,' Drago Kostió, a friend of Paul's, an amiable Yugoslav working at the Voice of America's Paris studio, told me.

'Do not despair,' he continued. 'You might register yourself as an external student at the Sorbonne. You pay £10, you receive a *carte d'étudiant*. Or apply to the School of Arts and Crafts. Their *cartes* cost a mere three thousand francs.' (£3) 'You must have a *carte*. One *carte* leads to the other *cartes*. Meantime, as a friend of Paul's, therefore a friend of mine, I advise you to confer with Oklahoma.'

Paul was leaving for Bournemouth the next day. He saw the anxiety on my face. Would I be able to stay? To go back to England was unthinkable. Every scrap of information about Paris was precious and immediately followed up. Agreements to meet at, say, an hotel room, were accompanied by a hand-drawn map supplementing the right co-ordinates on the *Plan de Paris par Arrondissement*: 'Press the bell, cross the courtyard, take the right-hand-corner staircase, sixth *étage*, my name is on the third door.'

I heard there was a sunny room going for £6 a month at the hotel on place de la Contrescarpe. The place is charming. Broad pavements. Cafés. Self-contained. The room had gone. You had to be quick. Better to know the person moving out. Or be introduced to an hotel's *propriétaire* by one of its foreign residents.

On the afternoon before Paul left for Bournemouth, Georges drove him and me out to Versailles. I thought of nothing except finding a room. Here were hundreds of empty rooms. Paul had only stopped off at Paris to meet me when on his way home from a walking tour in the Vaucluse. His French – self-taught – was textbook stiff, but good, while mine was non-existent. We had our last cup of coffee together near the Gare Saint-Lazare. I didn't have much to say.

UNTIL I met Oklahoma and Mary Jane James, his companion, the only Americans I had known were the black US soldiers waiting at Southbourne for D-Day.

When Mary Jane opened their hotel room door, her and Oklahoma's appearance gave me the feeling that I knew where I was, i.e. in a film, set in mid-west America. As thin as James Stewart, Oklahoma was taller. Mary Jane was tall, too, with a stern, handsome face; a young frontierswoman, used to handling a rifle. Drago had spoken to them on my behalf.

Theirs was a square room, fifteen feet by fifteen, with three floor-to-ceiling windows overlooking the rue Servandoni, an alcove kitchen and a large double bed. As well as the guitar in Oklahoma's hand, I found he owned two saxophones, a (portable) harmonium, several banjos, a violin, a Welsh harp, and a piano accordion. These, Mary explained, Oklahoma – he was on the GI Bill of Rights, a US post-military service grant for Second World War veterans – had bought at Paris street markets, repaired, learnt to play. 'Then he gives them to his cousin, Lyle. That's Lyle over there . . .'

'Hi.'

'. . . who takes them over to a French shopkeeper on the Right Bank.'

Lyle, too, was on the Bill. He had flown B38s in the war and came from Tulsa: 'Don't go there.'

Then they got on to my case. First, the job.

'He must visit the agencies' – UNO etc. – 'and get his name on their waiting lists.'

'Right.'

'NATO is hiring English-speaking chauffeurs,' said Lyle.

I admitted I couldn't drive.

A pause.

Mary Jane said: 'He'd best try for the messengers. Lyle can introduce him to Bob – his cousin, ex-US Navy, on the Bill – 'at UNO.' And to me: 'None of the agencies trust the French and the French distrust everybody. Bob's wife, Dolores, who works for the CIA –'

'Only as a secretary.'

'– says the French employ twenty-five thousand phone tappers known as *les Gardes des Oreilles*.'

'Messenging's easy,' said Lyle. 'Just ridin' around in limos with Top Secret envelopes chained to your wrist. Two hundred dollars a month.'

'You need clearance to be a messenger,' Oklahoma said.

I explained I had been in prison.

A pause.

Then Beryl, Lyle's companion, an English girl from Nottingham working as a nurse in the American Hospital at Neuilly, arrived.

'The only thing for him,' Beryl said, 'is Berlitz.' Meaning the Berlitz School of Languages.

Everyone felt sorry for me.

'The Dutch girl in my hotel – the Poitou – is homesick. Give her what's left of her month's rent and Madame Tonture, who owns it, will let you have her room for the same.'

I was in! A room, the chance of a job. I felt so good I decided to walk to the rue Legendre from Saint-Germain, down rue Bonaparte to the Seine, over the pont des Arts, a glance at Notre-Dame, down the steps and along the Right Bank quais until the Tuileries were above, then up and through their statuary to place de la Concorde.

Apart from its deep-set, steep-sided, many-bridged river, and from the rapid, wide, light grey and leaf-green, open urbanity through which it flowed, what struck me when walking by day in Paris was the way the women dressed. I learnt the meaning of the word *chic*. It was not a question of cash. As far as cash went, the difference between London and Paris was small. It was a question of idea. You were meant to look. To appraise.

There was a young man living in the Latin Quarter who believed himself to be Napoleon and did in fact look like Bonaparte when he was studying at École Militaire in 1784. He wore a two-cornered black hat over his long auburn hair, a black cloak edged with red, and he clutched what looked like a pace-stick as he sped through the streets adjacent to pont Neuf, always close to the wall, staring at the rest of us with contempt on his fine, olive face.

I envied the way the young men and women of the Quarter walked, the arm of one thrown casually across the shoulders of the other – not necessarily a sexual thing, as often not a gesture of friendship. I had never had a woman friend.

Throughout my adult life, I have been drawn to women. Equally I have disliked physical intimacy. I did not like being touched. Women or men, it made no difference. I hated it when my mother spat on, then rubbed her handkerchief across my face to remove a smear of chocolate, or washed my face with a stale flannel.

'You were impossible,' Isobel said. 'It was clear you fancied me. You could hardly keep your eyes off me the first time we met, though I'm skinny, not your natural type. But do what I could – I agree it wasn't that much – I couldn't get you to start making love, then let nature take over. Or you would start, then stop and start talking. Sometimes we went on like that for half the night. Next day we were both exhausted. Some people reckoned we had been screwing like crazy from sunset to sunrise. Some hope.

'The most annoying thing was your insisting that what you really and truly wanted was a girl-friend who was also your *friend* in the ordinary way. A friend you fucked. Or the other way round. Someone who would make you want to make love. Someone you started off with for sex's sake, who then became a dear, true friend. But there was always "something in the way", when in fact there was nothing in the way that wasn't between your own ears.

'You had your fair share of chances. Do you know what Letia told me? "We slept in each other's beds for six months without my learning he had false teeth."

'Then that dumpy rich-girl-pretending-to-be-a-model, Belle, came along.'

'She wasn't dumpy.'

'She was. I had a good look at her the one time we met. Anyway, the reason you had such a fine time of it between her legs and not between Letia's or mine was mostly because she was always on the point of going away to some remote part of the world – if you did actually have such a fine time.

'Letia thought she was dumpy, too.'

ONE day, walking to rue Legendre from the Quarter, I came up from the quai des Tuileries on to place de la Concorde, hundreds of student demonstrators with placards declaring the innocence of the American atom spies Julius and Ethel Rosenberg were driven past me by a line of cloaked policemen. 'Watch those cloaks,' Oklahoma advised, 'their seams are loaded with shot.'

The Hotel Poitou, 32 rue de Seine, belonged to Monsieur and Madame Claude-Louis Tonture. I agreed to give Anka – the Dutch girl – the balance of the rent she had paid for one of the Poitou's smaller rooms. 'Monsieur Tonture', she told me, 'runs a coal business with his brother, Boniface, in the hotel's back yard. Both of them were gassed in the First World War. They are heavy drinkers. *Never* give him your rent.'

As we tiptoed past the Poitou's curtained *loge*, an outburst of coughing, broken by the phrase '*Chauffage en plus!*' followed us up the stairs to the first floor.

Anka's room, £3 a month, was ten feet long by four feet wide with a red tile floor. Her bag, packed, was on the two-foot-wide bed. A hook on the back of the door, a bowl and ewer – 'The tap is on the stairs. One floor up' – a tin bidet, the first I had seen, and a curtain for the window forming the room's fourth side, were its furniture.

'Cooking in the rooms is not permitted,' Anka explained. 'The lights go off at 9.30 p.m. Music of any kind is forbidden. Madame Tonture is very religious. To her, all music, except church music, is wrong.' She looked anxious, as if I might change my mind. When I gave her the money in return for the key, she said 'I'll leave you my dustpan and brush,' took her bag and went.

I sat on the bed, incredibly happy. The Ministry of Defence had agreed to pay my pension in francs, via the British Embassy. I had to earn a little more to secure my room. Never mind about food, laundry, and so forth. The important thing was, I would not have to go back.

Madame Barthès made me an omelette, runny on the inside, easy as that, salad dressing mixed as she did so. After the meal she insisted I wipe my plate with a piece of bread. 'A habit from the occupation. A bad time. Avoid it in conversation. Hatreds were born. You understand?' As I walked I had noticed, set into walls, often with a bunch of flowers left beneath them, plaques that read: 'Here such and such a young man was shot by the Germans.' Then the date, 1942 or 1943.

Madame Barthès drove me to the Poitou.

'I will not leave you here. It is too bad. Too bad. Where is your running water? Let me see the lavatory ... Ah! A hole. Nothing but a hole. If your mother hears of this, I will be humiliated. This is not how Madame Logue looked after my son.' I promised to call on her soon. Because I did not learn to speak French I was ashamed to do so. We never met again.

THE Berlitz School of Languages was permitted to employ foreigners as its Method stipulated that pupils be taught by native speakers. Near avenue de l'Opéra, the school consisted of a hall, an office, and twenty-five cubicles.

Mr Watson was the school's inspector. On the wall of his office was a photograph of James Joyce, captioned: 'One of our ex-teachers'. There was a loudspeaker on his table. If Mr Watson liked the look of you, and provided you spoke clear English, after a week's unpaid training in the use of the Berlitz books (Book One, Lesson 1. At the Airport. Pupil: 'Where is the check-in?' Teacher: 'On your left.' Pupil: 'Am I overweight?' Teacher: 'Let us see.') you were hired.

The lessons, some communal, mostly one-to-one, were held in the cubicles. Teachers were forbidden to speak any language other than their own. On the wall of each cubicle was a boxed microphone allowing Mr Watson to listen in, and, if necessary, to interrupt, any lesson during which he heard French being spoken.

A lesson took fifty-five minutes, the pupil paying 450 francs, the teacher getting 200 – in cash. Thousand-franc notes decorated with a portrait of Richelieu were known as '*cardinals*'; those of a hundred francs, picturing Rimbaud, as '*rêves*'.

Face-to-face teaching is hard work. The bell rang. You went to the cubicle with Book One, say (for which you, like your pupil, had paid) at the ready. It was not unknown for a pupil, usually keen, wanting English for business reasons, to enter the cubicle and find their teacher not, as Mr Watson recommended '... with "an alert, welcoming smile" on your face ...' but slumped over the desk, asleep.

Nessie Dunsmuir – the poet W. S. Graham's companion – my fellow teacher at the Paris Berlitz, said that after teaching for five hours in a row she slept through a whole lesson, waking to the time-up bell, and began: 'At the Airport . . .' to an empty chair.

'Mr Watson did not sack me,' Nessie said. 'He never sacked anyone. He was kind. He knew it was inadvisable to let me work that long at a stretch. But he knew I needed the money. Most of his teachers were doing it to get a *carte de séjour*.'

In retrospect, I came to bless the place. There was a blonde girl teacher called Patsy who in our lunch hour used to translate Jacques Prévert's poems as she recited them:

> 'Our Father, who art in Heaven,
> Stay there . . .'

And I fell in love with one of my pupils, Mme Marguerite Anan. And there was the cash, the flexible hours. And when I came out in the evening, tired though I was, turning into avenue de l'Opéra, my spirits rose. It was so well lit, so busy. Outbursts of hooting from the traffic, the shops full of good things, the effort made to look smart, to be lively. And all at once – crossing the rue de Rivoli, entering the place du Carrousel of the Louvre – darkness, quietude, the river. Then over the pont des Arts into the Quarter. Where the girls were inventing rough-chic: bitten fingernails, black liner around the eyes, white cheeks, long greasy hair.

At the Poitou, the larger room next to mine was occupied by Elmer Hazin, a painter-to-be from St Louis, studying art history on the Bill. Elmer's room was full of canvases.

'There are twenty-eight thousand artists in Paris,' he said. 'I am not yet among the two per cent who earn enough from their art to eat. There must be many more poets – smaller outlay. Sugar?'

Madame Tonture allowed her guests to make coffee in their rooms. As the Poitou lacked power points, you bought – usually from someone who was leaving – a cup, a spirit stove, a hand mill and a small saucepan.

'Poets are worse off than painters,' Elmer continued. 'They have nothing to sell. Look at this' – showing me a painting of a lawnmower – 'it's no good. I put black lines around everything like Picasso. Only my black lines are no good.'

Before introducing me to his friend, Gaït, we went to the

market at the carrefour de Buci. I had not dreamt that there could be such a variety of food. Everyone was buying small portions. Elmer bought six different portions – three of pâté, three of cheese – each neatly double-wrapped, the packet sealed with well-designed paper labels. There were twenty abundant, busy shops that, in retrospect, made Fortnum and Mason look like Jimmy James's supermarket in Westbourne Grove.

'People like us survive here because of our numbers,' Elmer said. 'What we have, we spend with the locals. The trouble is we dislike each other. Always sleeping with each others' husbands or wives. You're a homosexual if you don't. "That Elmer Hazin's a fag." I'm not. I masturbate. I have a clean whore when Uncle Sam's cheque arrives. When the cheques stop I'll go home, become a dentist like my father, marry a decent Jewish girl, have a couple of kids and thirty years of good, healthy sexual inter-course, then die. Read Céline. You haven't read Céline? The best French writer since Proust. He'd have put Proust and me into a gas chamber.'

A HUNDRED yards from the Poitou was The English Book-shop, owned by a Frenchwoman, Gaït Frogé, a quiet, well-read Bretonne speaking fluent English, inclined to reserve, noticing you, not minding if you didn't notice her, a fair judge of character, and, to those who became the magazine *Merlin's* crowd, a friend.

Gaït's hair was chestnut coloured, her eyes large, brown, and rather mournful. For three years I used her shop as my address. Sometimes there was no one at the desk. Then the curtain draped behind it swung aside and Gaït appeared, always fashionably dressed, handing me my letters, with: 'One for you, and will you be seeing Alex?' – Alexander Trocchi, the editor of *Merlin*. 'There are two for him – and I would like a word in his ear later today.'

When Elmer and I entered the shop a tall black-haired man dressed in a brown two-piece suit was reading aloud. Gaït was encouraging the reader with a smile at the same time as, without looking at them, she turned the pages of the book on her desk. The man was reading in Latin. Catullus, as it turned out:

'Flavi, delicias tuas Catullo . . .'

Then he hurried out of the shop, snapping shut his book as he went.

Later that week, at a programme of Surrealist films, I met the reader, one Philip Oxman, the son of a wealthy salesman from Washington, a medievalist, writing a treatise on Nicholas of Causa: '1401 to 1464, anticipated Copernicus' proof of heliocentricity but predicted the world would end on the second Thursday of September, 1743'.

Philip was a godsend. I was fascinated by things medieval. Among my books, the essay on falconry by Frederick II, *De arte venandi cum avibus*.

'If I came over to your place, Philip,' I said, 'would you translate a few pages of *De arte* for me?'

Place, rather than room, for Philip – a scholarship from Chicago University, an allowance from his father – occupied one of the many apartments into which Raymond Duncan, the brother of Isadora, had divided his *hôtel particulier*, a few doors away from The English Bookshop.

Only the rich, or those who had bought in the 1890s, owned *hôtels particuliers* in central Paris. Duncan's – in 1951 he must have been in his eighties – was vast. A pair of shops selling his booklets and the products of his studio flanked the archway leading to its courtyard.

Duncan grew his silver grey hair down to his shoulders, wove and wore smocks of heavy brown wool, fastened by wooden, golf-ball sized bobbles incised with occult signs. Snow or shine he walked the Quarter in home-made sandals, wore no socks, '. . . and, I am told,' said Gaït, 'nothing under his robe'. Duncan considered Gaït a rival, an upstart, and he would stream past her shop with never a glance.

At the back of his courtyard was a large room called the Akademika Duncan. It had a stage on which he performed original chants and dances to a tambourine. Pamphlets giving the words and music of the chants, with diagrams of his dance steps, were on sale in the archway shops. After the performance, members of the audience would be offered a bowl of vegetarian soup and a cob of home-baked bread.

I began to see a lot of Philip. Besides his friendliness I was drawn to, and alarmed by, his interest in personality.

He spoke of me to me, to me of himself, as if we were specimens.

'It is the way you talk that interests me, Christopher. You are good, but not as good as you think, at telling stories. Louis de Wet' – a painter, a friend to both of us – 'is better than you at stories. What you have is linguistic self-confidence. You make a good point. You see a thing, then wrap it up in serviceable words. Often as not, you are wrong. No matter. What you have said, right or wrong, I see. And you have good taste. You and de Wet are burdened by good taste. You – not de Wet –miss many things and, like me, you have trouble with women. Our troubles with women are not the same sort of troubles, mind you. I'll leave that for another day.'

We would breakfast at the Café La Palette opposite the Poitou. The proprietor, M. Teaux, was M. Tonture's competitor. Like many of the Quarter's small café owners, M. Teaux sold fuel – wood, coal, paraffin – to his neighbours.

M. Teaux had a handsome daughter, Martine. She served those occupying the comfortable red and yellow wicker chairs of her father's terrace. Plenty of men, Philip included, longed to take Martine out.

In the inner room of La Palette was a billiard table. At the table, at all hours of the day, every day, stood Roger – we never learnt his surname – cue in hand, potting a ball every so often. Otherwise he never took his eye off Martine. His origins and means of livelihood were both mysterious. It was clear that Martine was his. He would marry her. M. Teaux approved. Martine was satisfied. That was the end of the matter. Roger watched. Martine served.

Pushing his black-rimmed glasses on to the brow of his scholarly face, rubbing both eyes with the thumb and centre finger while stirring his *grande crème*, Philip maintained: 'Don't tell me we're not excluded from their world, or that you, like me, don't feel envious of them – Martine, Roger. Understand something about Americans like me. I was a bright student. Now I look at what I wrote six years ago and I think: Am I a phoney?'

'You're not.'

'Listen. Actually *listen* for once. Be kind enough not to give me that middle-class British bullshit about introspection being bad for art. What I mean is: Am I thinking what I am thinking not because I am genuinely interested in what I am thinking about, but only to discover what I am?'

'Do you mean that though you think that things like personal freedom are beyond price and decent people feel a sense of responsibility towards other people – in fact, you don't give a damn about either, so long as you can do what you like?'

'I sit here thinking about Martine's cunt. If I am not thinking about her cunt, I am thinking about some other woman's cunt. I think about Nicholas of Causa to take my mind off cunt.'

Rue de Seine did not get going before 9 a.m. The street sweepers were busy, the hydrants on, the water carrying litter to the drains.

'Now, in your worst moments – you grant you have such moments? – you never had that sort of discussion with yourself Right?'

'Um . . .'

'What you say to yourself in those moments is: If what I do is good, good. If not, not. *C'est tout.*'

'Neither of us is like Martine and Roger. He is her farmer. She is his cow. They will have a lot of fucks. A family. Not a bit like us. Not phoney.'

I⸢T⸣ was Philip who introduced me to Alexander Trocchi. One winter morning Philip and I decided to walk via rue Saint-André-des-Arts, and the boulevard Saint Michel to see if George Whitman – of whom more later – had any translations in his shop from the work of Bertolt Brecht, a new name in the Quarter.

'I met an interesting Scotsman called Trocchi at Gaït's,' Philip said 'Let's see if he's in.' We bought slices of apple tart and detoured by Picasso's studio in rue des Grands-Augustins.

'You began telling me about this woman you're in love with. One of your pupils at Berlitz.'

'Um. . .'

'Well, assuming – which in your case is quite a lot – that you do actually want to sleep with her – fuck her, that is – are you worried about the length of your penis?'

'I have never considered the matter.'

'Crap. I am six foot two and you are five foot seven. Popular belief says your penis is smaller than mine: long legs, long cocks.'

'I thought it was noses.'

'Exactly.'

'As a matter of interest I have heard that the largest known example of the European penis was/is that of Barbatus Hanna, a sergeant in the Austro-Hungarian army, his exemplary organ pickled after he fell in 1866 at the battle of Sadowa, 23.7 cm, detumescent, an astonishing item that formed part of the Institut für Sexualwissenschaft's "Means of Love" exhibition.'

'Was there a postcard of it?'

'That is typically English. Getting out of a subject you find frightening with a joke. You have a poor sex life. Probably, masturbation aside, no sex life. Neither do I. It is a defect. Own up.'

Aside from the Christian Brothers, until meeting Philip I had no contact with deliberateness of mind. I was to meet it again in John Phillips Marquand, Austryn Wainhouse, Richard Seaver, and disguised as 'Don't-mind-me-I'm-only-kidding' in George Plimpton. It was, moreover, American deliberation. It said: 'I accept you for what you are. I will give you what help I can. You must rely on yourself to keep up.' A grave, serious quality when contrasted to English ironizing and self-deprecation. Whatever Philip thought related to this – in him – virtuous gravity. Indeed, it preceded his thought, or, as de Wet believed, inspired it.

After I had bought something of Brecht's, Philip and I called on Trocchi. Patrick Bowles – soon to be one of the Merlinites – has described Alex's hotel.

It was in the darkest depths of the Latin Quarter. It really was dark. Only the rooms overlooking the street had real windows, but most were lost in the tiny burrowing staircases, with a small token window on an airshaft, like Trocchi's. One could put one's head through but not, I think, one's shoulders.

The hotel was in rue de la Huchette. Its guests were mostly poor Algerians, then, as now, the least of the least as far as Paris is concerned. A cover of Le Canard Enchaîné showed an Algerian pedlar saying: 'Madam, it is me, not the carpet, that smells.'

1 My father, John Dominic Logue, in 1905, aged thirty-four, not long after he had disbanded his team of cross-country runners and in their stead had organized a local, north London, cricket eleven.

2 My mother, Florence Mabel Chapman, *c.* 1913, aged twenty-five, ten years before she married my father: 'I was not sure about marrying. I had my suitors. But your grandmother and I got along so happily. And there was plenty of room at home.'

4 Margaret Logue, my father's sister, a schoolmistress who never married. When I was five she taught me to read and write.

3 Hilda Logue, *c.* 1924, my step-sister, aged nineteen. Hilda's mother, my father's first wife, died in 1920.

5 Myself, *c.* 1932.

PRIOR PARK COLLEGE, BATH.

McGarvey   Twist   P Morgan   Pardoe   Wingate

Daly Bro.Phelan Bro Blake   :COLL·PRIOR·PARK: Bro Boyle   Bro Hayes
JUNIOR SCHOOL,   Bro Forde   June 1937

Hagan   Baker   Logue   MC

DEO·DUCE 1830 DEO·LUCE

6 Brother Ford of the Irish Christian Brothers, headmaster of Prior Park
College, Bath, with me at his feet. This illustration comes from a larger photograph showing Prior's junior school in 1937. Perhaps I was so placed as one
needing special attention.

7 The Bournemouth friends, *c*. 1950: Paul Wallace, Charles Fox, Peter Clarke, Christopher Logue. 'Books were our thing. Portable, durable, inexpensive – a marvel of technology needing no intermediates save spectacles . . .'

8 Patrick Bowles (Beckett's translator), George Plimpton (editor of the *Paris Review*), Jane Lougee (proprietor of *Merlin* magazine), her cat Fuki, and myself outside Gaït Frogé's, the English Bookshop in rue de Seine, Paris, *c.* 1954.

9 Maurice Girodias, the imperial pornocrat, proprietor of the Olympia Press, in the indoor garden of his nightclub, La Grande Séverine: 'Christopher, you are not writing pornography to amuse yourself. Olympia's customers are men seeking sexual relief in one of the most normal of ways. All mammals, including humans, masturbate. Children should be taught how to masturbate. To condemn masturbation is to encourage rape.'

10 Alexander Trocchi, the editor of *Merlin* and the author of *Cain's Book*, in Majorca to supervise the printing of *Merlin* No. 3 in 1953.

11 Austryn Wainhouse,
novelist, editor, publisher and
translator (of de Sade), by
Pierre Klossowski.

12 The novelist William
Gardiner Smith, Maria
Luchana, Countess of
Zobregón, and myself in the
Café Tournon, *c.* 1956.

Alex was sitting on his bed, his typewriter on a crate in front of him. Rising, he apologized for his circumstances and offered us his Gitanes. He had a charming, intimate, educated Scottish voice, seldom raised, ready to laugh. We began talking about poetry, me quoting Pound, Philip, Wallace Stevens, Alex, Eliot. Then he remarked: 'You have to admit there's reason in Eliot's art even if you disagree with what he says.'

MY first three months in France were almost up. I had not been at Berlitz long enough to apply for a *carte de séjour*. Elmer stressed: 'The Tontures registered you with the police. One morning at 5 a.m. the Sûreté will knock on your door. If the entry stamp on your passport is more than twelve weeks old you will be told to leave within twenty-four hours. You may get a mark in your passport meaning: no admittance to France for a year.'

'You had better go to Amsterdam and stay with my friend, Gerrit Kouwanaar,' Simon Vinknoog, a Dutch poet living in Paris, said.

Amsterdam was bitterly cold. The canals were frozen. Gerrit, his wife and I were so poor we had to stay in bed to keep warm.

When I returned to Paris my bottom left teeth began to ache. Twice a day from the tin that had once held my escape outfit I took a capsule of Tuinal, mixed its powder with oil of cloves, and rubbed the paste on the gum by the bad teeth. By Saturday evening the gum was untouchable, so I swallowed the capsule and went to sleep. Early on Sunday my swollen face woke me. Around nine I went over to Philip who looked at me, dressed, then telephoned his dentist friend from La Palette, Beit Kiewicz. On the bus to the surgery Philip said: 'Beit is a French Pole. He fixed the teeth of those who fought in the Maquis during the war. He will expect to get on with it.'

'*Voilà, Anglais – en chaise,*' Dr Kiewicz said. I opened my mouth and began to recite Yeats's poem 'Easter 1916' to myself. If, I reckoned, I could get as far as the line 'Hearts with one purpose alone' without running out of the room, I could face the needle, the cross-beaked pliers, the wrench as the molar left its socket.

After a short inspection Dr Kiewicz said: '*Bon. On y va,*' and led the way to his Renault.

'We are going to a hospital,' Philip said. 'He has to extract two molars.'

At the hospital Dr Kiewicz left us in a corridor with stools along one of its walls occupied by patients in blue canvas pyjamas. Without moving, one of the men began to piss. Philip and I watched the puddle forming on the floor. My teeth had stopped aching.

I said: 'This is a lunatic asylum, isn't it?'

Philip nodded. 'It's the only place open for operations on Sundays.'

Moments later, two orderlies came down the passage and hustled me through a set of rubber doors into a three-table operating theatre, where, as they stripped me to the waist, lifted me, then clipped my wrists and ankles to the nearest table, I saw Dr Kiewicz in green rubber gloves, who said:

'*Lumière et gaz,*' and then: '*Au revoir, Anglais,*' as one of the orderlies settled the hissing mask on to my face.

After the extractions, when I mentioned the clips, Philip said: 'Holy shit, a castration nightmare.'

Dr Kiewicz said I was fit to leave: 'Preferably not to a cold room.' Philip had called Trocchi's girlfriend, Jane. 'She says there may be a problem about your staying. Anyway, I'm to bring you over.'

JANE Lougee had a studio apartment at Auteuil on the west of Paris. She came to the door wearing a raincoat over her nightie, said: 'Shush!', nodded goodbye to Philip, and led me upstairs.

Jane had the sort of looks that made both sexes turn. Black hair, oval eyes, oval face, firm, well-defined lips under a straight nose and above a discreetly curved chin. This Sunday her appearance was altered by her skin being light yellow instead, as I learnt, of its usual china white.

At the top of the stairs was the studio. In its middle, on the eight-foot-by-eight-foot bed into which Jane jumped, lay Alex, a brighter shade of yellow than Jane. They were recovering from a mild bout of hepatitis A. Alex said: 'You'd better get into bed, old man'. Which I did, and fell asleep.

Next morning, Jane, the fittest of us, went shopping. Hardly was she out of the door when the lady who owned the apartment to which the studio was attached paid a surprise visit to her presentable young American tenant, to find two naked men, one yellow, in bed together.

Alex told me about his father.

'Our house had doors front and back. His rule was: adults used the front door, children and tradesmen the back. His great fear was that he would drop dead in the street. In public. Towards the end of his life going out was a risk.

'He had a secret grief. He told me about it in an angry, mistrustful way, almost as if he didn't know why he had come out with it. In 1940, when Italy entered the war on Hitler's side, the police rounded up many Italian-Glaswegians and deported them to Canada on a prison ship called the *Andorra Star* that the German navy torpedoed with a loss of twelve hundred lives, some of them his close friends, young and old.'

I confessed I was unsure of what I wished for myself. My certainties turned around what I wanted to avoid: a job, boredom, living vocationless. It was better to be like Philip: school, university, a subject.

Alex vowed: 'I wanted to be idle. When the question of what I was going to do when I grew up came up, my mind went blank. I'd say: I'm going to be God.'

We talked about writing.

'What notions you have, old man,' he said – meaning my conviction of the power of literature to bring social change. 'The only thing to be said in their favour is that you are not getting them across.' Then, after I had dismissed logic as a spot-the-contradiction word game concocted by ancient windbags as a way of winning arguments: 'Very well, old man. That is your opinion. It will not be said that Alexander Trocchi invited a friend to lift his head on to the block, but nor is it appropriate to keep so fine a communications centre in the sand. True, the chief use of logical discourse is highlighting fallacy. To spot the lie in fair, or wicked, words is as useful, yet not so well rewarded, as it is to invent King Kong. What's more, evil men fear those who can do it.'

Our talk made me realize how long it had been since my last conversation with anyone save myself about the actual business of writing, of making things clear in words, of bringing new powers into existence.

Happy as I was with such talk, Alex saying that Jane intended to publish a magazine devoted to new, experimental writing, which he would edit, made me even happier.

Jane's landlady said she would require the studio at the end of the present quarter. I returned to the Poitou and Berlitz.

Jane was twenty-five when we met. Already married and divorced, the daughter of an independent banker from Limerick, Maine, she wore long skirts, gold-thonged sandals, and, with her easy grace, was a treat to notice: holding an elastic band between her teeth as she gathered her hair into a tail, then toss/snapped it through the band, before settling back in her chair to brandy and coffee on the terrace of the Old Navy café, a Gitane in her cigarette holder, her Siamese cat on her lap

Established in Auteuil by mid-1951, Jane had planned to start a literary magazine with a man from Chicago called Victor.

'He was to be the publisher, I was the secretary,' Jane said. 'I had two hundred dollars a month from my father. Then Victor disappeared and Alex said: "Why don't you be the publisher? I'll be your editor. Madame wants us out – OK, we'll get a room in the Quarter. The balance of the rent you're paying here can go on the magazine. Money will not be our problem. That will be getting good texts."

'Alex was the most attractive man I had ever met,' Jane said. 'He had a lot of energy to spare, as you did. His energy was focused. Yours was not. So I said yes. My father will give me some extra money. He won't like it, but he will. And Alex and I fell in love, and you – with your teeth out – were our first guest. Alex inspired the magazine. You named it.

'You were besotted with Ezra Pound, falconry and that Marguerite you met through Berlitz. It was difficult to see why she took up with you. She was so *chic*. Always perfectly made up. Her accessories cost more than you could earn in years.

'In the Cluny Museum you found a tapestry of a young woman with a falcon on her wrist. You knew that the hawks women hunted with were called merlins and that merlins were reckoned as faster and more courageous than tercels, their males. That's where the name *Merlin* came from.'

Jane's kind was new to me. I loved her casual determination, her willingness, once decided, to take what she had and spend it on doing what she believed was worthwhile – in this case, publishing a magazine for people like me to be seen in. There was a friendly coolness to whatever she did or said. Smiling, offering you her Gitanes, a drink.

In April 1952 Shirley Wales the Canadian engraver lent me her bicycle while she visited Tunisia.

Finished at Berlitz, I cycled to Auteuil where the first issue of *Merlin* was being assembled. I learned world-famous names: Bodoni, Garamond, Baskerville. New terms: upper case, lower case, set to centre, range left.

Knowing these terms helped me to understand the correspondence between the way verse appears on the page and its musical expressiveness, printed verse being a sort of a score as well as a text. These terms allowed me to describe what I tried out on my typewriter. I spent whole lunch hours talking about it to Marguerite in terrible French, her helping me find the right term in her dictionary, never complaining that it was for me to teach her English, not her, me, French printers' terms.

Marguerite was twenty-one, hoping to be a couturier's model. She was a pleasure to teach. We were ready for an affair. A good thing for us both. The trouble began when I persuaded us to be in love. How odd we must have looked sitting in the cold on a bench in the Tuileries, Marguerite dressed as if to be photographed, me in a duffel coat and crumpled cords, bent over a dictionary, the two of us now and then exchanging a kiss.

Imprimerie Mazarine – across the road from the site of the theatre where Molière's widow directed her husband's plays – was our printer. Each issue would cost £430 to produce – this when a woman's two-piece suit cost £5. Arthur Fogg Lougee, proprietor of the Casco Bank and Trust Company, was coming to Paris with the money for Number 1. An American banker crossing the Atlantic with the money to publish his daughter's literary magazine? Unbelievable.

Besides Gaït, the Quarter had a second – and in time more celebrated – English-language bookseller: the Bostonian, George Whitman. George resembled Daumier's Don Quixote. Tall, skinny, with a faraway look in his light blue eyes, he wore a plaid waistcoat, and had a liking for richly embroidered ties.

It was his habit to break off a conversation in mid-sentence, take up a book, dust it, begin to read it, and forget you, wandering away, book in hand, to disappear through the curtains at the back of his shop, Librairie Mistral, rue de la Bûcherie, Paris cinquième, facing the south transept of Notre-Dame.

Not that George neglected those in his company. Likely enough, a few moments after leaving you, he reappeared carrying a trayful of steaming yoghurt jars. And: 'Tea, tea, tea for all who like it,' he would announce – which most people did, for the Mistral was more than a bookshop.

'My father, Walt, not *the*, of course' – though George, fifty in 1951, was disinclined to reject a family connection – 'was a nomadic teacher-cum-science-writer, from Salem, Massachusetts, who lectured, with my mother and me as part of his audience, in China, Turkey and Russia.'

George served with the Merchant Marine during the Second World War, and arrived in Paris – on the Bill – in 1946. 'Then', he stressed, 'everything was in super-short supply, including books. With my Bill's textbook allowance I began buying volumes in English from the booksellers along the *quais*. When I got back from my lectures on French civilization, my room in the Hôtel Suez, windowless, on-the-airshaft, five dollars a week, was full of people reading. Then they began staying for dinner. When I got a slightly larger room, they started to sleep on the floor. Then I inherited some money and bought 37 rue de la Bûcherie from an Algerian grocer.'

By 1951, as well as the shop, George managed a lending library of 4,000 books. One of its upstairs rooms had become a reading room, its windows overlooking Notre-Dame, another, lined with bunks, a place for penniless writers to sleep, and on Sundays, tea and cakes for all, and every day the Librairie was open from 10 a.m. to midnight.

'My philosophy is sharing, my love is literature, my home, like-minded company,' I hear him say. Librairie Mistral became *Merlin*'s first editorial address. The last time I saw him, George, I calculate, was some eighty-seven or eighty-eight years old, rather dusty, and when we shook hands he vanished in a cloud of it, sending several customers – a word he would not deign to use – coughing on to the pavement.

The magazine's subscription form said:

MERLIN will appear 4 times a year on the 15th of May, September, December and February. Single issues $0.60, 3s. 6d. Frs. 250. Life subscriptions (2 copies of each issue) $50.00, 20 gns, Frs. 20,000.

PATRICK Bowles, soon to be Samuel Beckett's translator, became my friend. Employed as an assistant teacher at a school in Le Havre, Patrick bicycled to Paris – 220 kilometres each way – at the weekends, his *lycée* arranging that he had no classes on Friday afternoon or Monday morning. Neither of us had money to spare. In cold weather we went to a slot-in-the-wall café and ordered two *vins chauds*. When they were half finished the proprietor, without complaint, would *réchauffer* them. To eat – one meal a day was enough – we visited Le Restaurant Jean, a church-hall sized dining room feeding workers and students. Deep bowls of barley soup plus bread (amount unlimited), F.50 (2/-, now 10p). Steak (horse) and *frites:* F.150. Non-stop talk throughout of poetry and other serious topics, Patrick by instinct humane, ambitious.

'My novel will occupy three volumes. I will walk into Jonathan Cape and place it on the table, beautifully typed, in green binders.' He never wrote it.

We did not think of ourselves as poor. We were young, fit, strong. If, when you got up, you had enough money to get you through the day – F.1,000 – that was plenty. In any case, most people are poor. Better to be as we were than to waste time in the company those who want to make money must keep.

As writers, the Merlinites wanted more than literary fame. Alex put it clearly.

'Art in writing is not enough. There must be philosophy in the art. An evident stance. A moral stance from which the reader sees you see, and, perhaps, becomes converted to your coherent reasons. Unreasonable maybe? Coherent nonetheless. Eliot has it – reactionary though it is. Pound has it – mad though it is. Yeats pretends to have it. Patriotism is as near as he gets.'

There was a proselytizer in Alex. True or false, the story that, seven years later, by which time he was a wanted heroin addict, Alex carried a shoulder pulpit from which, to avoid arrest by the New York police, he delivered street-corner sermons, fits.

'I want my reader hardly to know my book has started,' Patrick said. 'To slide into it by accident, as it were. But to emerge changed.' Then we would mount our bikes and ride out to Auteuil.

We all agreed: literature had moral, as well as aesthetic power. It could do harm as well as good. Poets, novelists, dramatists and critics were responsible people. Unable to avoid certain issues. These convictions came, partly, from something that was in the air of Paris at the time, a mood generated by the work of Sartre, Camus, de Beauvoir, Brecht and Eluard.

Similar convictions were to surface in London four years later, but in that case it involved the rejection of a victorious past whose preoccupations no longer sustained the moral demands of the present. Each place offered a different manifestation of the same seriousness: in Paris, brilliantly described in *The Left Bank*, by Herbert Lottman, it was a matter of creating watertight philosophical-political systems on which to act; in London, of confrontation, rejection, and satire.

ONE evening as I returned from Berlitz, Mme Tonture handed me a letter franked *Sûreté Nationale*. 'De la part de la Police Secrète,' she said in a mournful voice.

I met Elmer on the stairs. 'If they wanted you, they'd come for you,' he said. 'It's your *carte*.' I must report, carrying this letter, to the Vestibule of the Dépôt de la Préfecture de Police, Île de la Cité.

Early (as usual), I viewed the figures representing Truth, Law, Eloquence and Clemency decorating the façade of the

Correctional Court. Then I was led upstairs, along a corridor, down a circular stairway, over a glassed-in bridge, through two sets of swing doors, into a lift, out, through a glass door to a waiting room, bare but for a wooden bench supporting a young woman, a child on each side of her, looking straight ahead.

After ten minutes, a policeman put his head around the door and called them in. After an hour, the same policeman called for, then led me into a large office full of men – secret policemen, I assumed – laughing, talking, smoking, on the telephone, reading newspapers, looking about, some with their legs up on their desks. Mine, when I had been seated, said:

'Bonjour, Monsieur Logue. You work at the Berlitz school?' looking at his papers.

'Yes, Monsieur.'

'Why do you want to live in France?'

'I am a writer. France is hospitable to artists. I would like to live where some of the writers I admire have lived.'

'And they are?'

'James Joyce, Ezra Pound.'

'Hemingway?'

'Less.'

'How long are you hoping to remain in France?'

'Five years. I'm not sure.'

'Are you a member of a political party?'

'No.'

'No politics?'

'I'm of the Left.'

'Naturally.'

'You have French friends?'

I gave M. de Ruyter's name.

'What do you write?'

'Poetry.'

'Published?'

At Alex's recommendation Princess Caetani, publisher and editor of the literary magazine *Botteghe Oscure*, had accepted some poems of mine, one of them, 'To my Father', my best so far. Issued in Rome, *Botteghe* came out in French, German, Italian and English. I had a copy of it – including my work – in my shoulder bag. The police approved.

'Quatre langues, si?' paging through. 'François' – his neighbour – 'nous avons un poète ici.' I had realized France was a country where writers counted. The appellation *homme de lettres* carried weight. Sartre, Camus and Co. were a force.

The inspector signed my card. For five years I was free to live in France coming and going as I pleased. Thirty-eight years expired, the card remains in my possession. One never knows.

'Bonjour, Monsieur Logue. Keep out of our way.'

The proofs of *Merlin* 1 arrived. I looked at my untitled poem. It was clear what the words said; less clear was how they related to anything other than my wish to write poetry. When I read it aloud, it was worse.

Yet it was not a failure. Looking at it again the other day – 1998 – I was struck by what seemed to be a semi-Poundian account of a group of ancient oarsmen setting out from nowhere to nowhere. Goodness only knows where it came from. My reading, I suppose. There is something of Eliot in its disjointedness. And, although it is most unlikely that anyone but me would say so, there is a touch of *War Music* about it. The best poem in *Merlin* 1 was 'The Monkey' by William Burford. A really good poem. I wonder what became of him.

Jane, Alex and I went to Imprimerie Mazarine with the contents of *Merlin* 1. It was my first visit to a printing works. What excitement. The noise of the machines. The little red suckers whipping printed sheets from forme to tray. The smells of oil and ink.

Before long, the proprietor was showing us his works' latest *truc*, a 'gun' that made possible printing two colours in one impression – for almost no extra charge. Instantly, Jane saw a two-colour cover, while I saw the first capital letter of my poem printed in red. Alex saw £50 being added to *Merlin's* bill and said so.

JANE held a party for the magazine's publication. Copies were handed round. The cover was plain white with MERLIN in specially drawn capitals along the top. Completely impractical. Dirty in a moment. Who could tell what was inside?

But beautiful. We contributors signed each other's copies. Champagne was served. Jane introduced her father to the contributors. Patrick asked Arthur Fogg to sign his copy.

'When I was your age, Mr Bowles,' Mr Lougee said as he signed, 'I had a thousand dollars in the bank and had never visited a cinema.'

'So you became a banker?'

'A local banker.'

'A banker, nonetheless. One of those who rule the world, sir.'

'Mr Bowles, I have more trouble from those I think you mean, the so-called national banks, than you will ever know. If I treated my depositors as those gentlemen treat me, nothing beyond my own money would be left at the Casco Bank by the week's end. Those people are an arm of the state, sir. I don't mean my State, the State of Maine. They are the next worst of people after their friends, the liberal politicians.'

'Are you a supporter of Senator McCarthy, sir?'

'No, Mr Bowles, I am not. The Senator for Wisconsin shields himself with Stalin's crimes and twists minds by twisting words. No doubt there are home-bred Communist agents in the United States of America, my country. I do not fear them. I am American. Thomas Jefferson and George Washington are my men. I stand against privilege. Including, sir, kings, queens, bishops, the sort of people you English cling to. You like crooking the knee. I have no time for fancy words. Do you use fancy words in here, Mr Bowles?' – holding up the magazine he had just paid to produce.

'Never,' said Pat, truthfully. 'And by the way, sir, I am South African.'

I hope he didn't ask me the same question. I had *halcyon, chyle, Trezibond* (mis-spelt for Trebizond) in mine – and had only just missed out *bezel*.

'What do you count as a fancy word, Mr Lougee?' I said.

'*Progress* is a fancy. *Efficiency* is a fancy. Immodest, power-hungry words. Curse words, in my book.'

Marguerite was among the guests. Bold with her English. Friendly. Very smart. When the party was over Marguerite and I walked by the Seine. She was puzzled by my making so little effort to get her into bed.

I said I had heard of a well-paid job in Rome. With the United Nations. Editing professional texts into readable

English. When I asked her to come with me, she explained that to get a passport she needed her husband's permission. She would think of the best way to bring the matter up. The whole family were going to Deauville for their summer holidays.

Alex and Jane were living in the Hôtel Verneuil. £20 a month. A big room. Cooking allowed. Alex was broad-shouldered, easy on his feet, with a gliding walk. He dressed in green or grey cords, sandals, check socks, a windcheater. When he drew himself up to look each way before dodging the traffic, his six-foot-two surprised. There was something of the shepherd about him, a collie-like way of getting Jane, Philip and me across a boulevard on to the terrace of a busy café, still discussing the contents of the next issue as he ordered our drinks, paying for them if he had money, or with someone else's money, laughing in his good-tempered way: 'Oh, the rascal, the terrible rascal' – over, for instance, one of the magazine's vanished distributors.

He was keen on a philosopher called Alfred Korzybski. We were on our way to George's bookshop to see if he had anything by Korzybski – 'A mad empiricist,' according to Philip – Alex saying that if he had his life over again he would be a mathematician because in mathematics you couldn't wriggle out of things. 'Nothing is left to chance. X plus y equals x plus y. That's it. That's why people say they don't like maths. The truth is they don't like being proved wrong.'

Going down the rue Saint-André-des-Arts we passed a chap with a shield-shaped face and bright red lips standing by an upright piano. Hearing our talk, he apologized for his interruption, then asked if we could help him get the piano into his hotel room. It took an hour.

Spread across his table were transparent sheets of hand-inked, extremely complicated, perfectly drafted music ready to be engraved as a score. Superb, intellectual draftsmanship, something to be admired. The young man was Alexander Goehr; the engraver's copy, of a work by his teacher, Pierre Boulez.

George had nothing on Korzybski.

'Do you think that chap Goehr would set some lyrics if I wrote them? Wedekind, Brecht-like stuff,' I asked Alex as we sat looking at the Préfecture de Police.

'Not a chance,' Alex said. 'Unpopular composers hate words. When they need something for their singers, that's to say, people trained to be a living musical instrument, they get someone to supply a line of vowels set in some – very simple – grammatical order. Their style of singer can't sing consonants.'

'Vaughan-Williams and Britten can set good words properly. As clear as Cole Porter or Harold Arlen.'

'Perhaps you should approach one of them, then.'

'The poems Schubert set go for nothing.

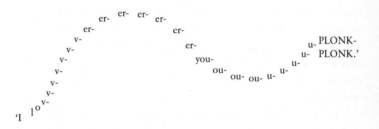

Fantastic applause. "Divine melisma!" Cryings-out for more. "Now I can die happy." Poor old Goethe.'

I WROTE to Pound at his asylum, St Elizabeth's, Washington DC, and was proud of his reply to my first, respectful, letter. Others, which I was keen to show Alex, followed. I took them with me to the Verneuil. Handing them back Alex said: 'They are gibberish with a dash of sense. I'm sorry. I can't be bothered with him. Do you really have a job in Rome, old man?'

'I have a contact at FAO.' The United Nations Food and Agricultural Organization.

'If you get it, how much will it pay?'

'A hundred and fifty dollars a month.'

'I don't understand. Marguerite is here in Paris. She's taken with you. You have Jane, Bowles, Philip, me and *Merlin*. In Rome you know nobody. You don't speak a word of Italian. You cannot write directly to Marguerite. She will find writing to you very difficult.'

'Are you saying you won't be our go-between?'

'You know we will. Just don't forget you decided to go away from her and us.'

'Caetani might help me.'

Princess Caetani, née Biddle – 'Of the Philadelphia Biddles,' Jane said, 'millions from railroads' – was the wife of Prince Caetani, scion of a noble Roman family. She held literary court at Palazzo Caetani. An amusing woman: 'I'm surprised to be here. We made a last-minute dash to miss the train.' The Princess paid a dollar a line for verse, a munificent sum.

'Caetani is a patron with a dozen famous writers at her feet. She won't turn you away. On the other hand – why should she do more than give you a drink?' Alex said. I did not tell him that I had, finally, managed to spoil my chances with Marguerite. No sooner was she on holiday with her family in Deauville than I pestered her with letters. How could she go away? I was distraught without her. Why didn't she write to me? My life was horrible. At some risk, she returned to Paris. After an hour of my walking up and down my room describing how I was going to go to Rome and then send for her, Marguerite said: 'Nothing is going to happen unless you make it happen,' and returned to Deauville.

I ARRIVED in Rome with £20 and found a room near the Ponte Sisto.

Outside my room was a telephone, its dial secured by a little padlock, the key – one of a bunch – attached to the crucifix of my landlady's rosary. My landlady drank. She spent hours shouting into the telephone. Then she would slam the handset down and pace the corridor. I had no one to call. The retired general – I have forgotten his name, given to me by Pound – was not in the directory. There was no job at FAO. Reception there told me that the man who might have hired me had gone to open a local publications department in New Guinea. I ignored a letter from Mr Watson advising me that my Paris job was gone unless I made contact.

Rome in the early 1950s was no place for a penniless foreign writer speaking no Italian. The sensible thing to do would have been to see the sights and return to Paris. I wrote to Alex to say what marvellous accommodation I had found. What Elmer

Hazin had said was true: unlike Rome Paris had accepted the sort of person I was because Paris always had.

I called at the Palazzo Caetani. The doorman said the Principessa was away until October. I left my name and address. Consciously, for the first time, I began to suffer from loneliness. I knew no one. I was more or less without money. My refuges were the American library and the library of the British Council. The former was near the Via Veneto, a wealthy street, its terraces full of happy people. I walked along it quickly. My hair was long, greasy. Perhaps I resembled that poor mad fellow who sped through the Quarter thinking he was the young Bonaparte. Once, soon after dusk, I saw Pope Pius XII. Brightly lit, dressed in white and gold and wearing granny glasses, he sat on a red-upholstered armchair in the back of a limousine giving his sign to the passers-by.

The British Council library was located at the top of a dark staircase of what had once been a palazzo. I sat in the library from ten to one, at which point I went out for a sandwich, then from two to four, when I returned to my room. It is difficult to be without money, and alone. You are ground down. You stop thinking. Paralysis sets in. To complete a simple task requires a vast effort, and, when completed, if completed, it gives no satisfaction. A weight gathers behind your eyes. Things you found valuable lose their worth. Your own things, specifically. Useless to tell yourself, 'Well' – naming a favourite poet or painter – 'their work seems pointless to me today, too' – remembering that similar lows have passed off after a night's sleep or a visit to a friend. In a flash, you sense that when you wake up next day, instead of being restored, you will at once be possessed by that low weightiness, and that there is no one to visit, or, if there is, you have visited them too often, and, really, they have only been seeing you as a favour to an old friend. And to tell the truth, they can hardly wait to get this boring visitor out of the house. And, need I say, you, too, are thinking, he is keen to get rid of me. And why not? And what on earth am I going to do with myself when I leave his house, except walk along the road bordering the Tiber until I reach the Ponte Sisto?

Then there is the question of money. Counting it out on

the bedspread. Separating it into days – sandwiches, cigarettes, postage.

My letters overflowed with a self-pity, that some, seeing me, may well have thought justified.

Rome: September 1952

Dear Jane,

Do you think you could ask Alex to ring Marguerite up and tell her that I have had no letter for nine days? I am sort of paralysed against action of any sort.

Rome: September 1952

Jane, my pet,

Marguerite still has not written – WHAT on God's name has happened? I am shaking with fear that I must come starved and depressed to Paris – God I will KILL THE WOMAN.

Rome: October 1952

Dear Alex,

Thanks for the two letters. I am thinking of abandoning writing altogether. Come back to Paris now? I would be at M's disposal for her to execute as she chooses. Here I can at least execute myself. I feel on the verge of catastrophe. Oh god my poor Mother!

THEN matters improved.

I was in a trattoria near the Spanish Steps, wondering how long I could make my coffee last, when a voice behind me said: 'I, too, have fallen from a great height.'

This came from W. S. Graham – 'I answer to Sydney' – the Scottish poet, who had tracked me down through Caetani's doorman.

Eight years my senior, with sharp grey eyes and a pile of reddish-brown curls, Sydney looked like a sailor. In Rome for six months, he had improved his circumstances by moving in with the young Danish woman who rented the rooms above his own, paid for by Caetani, now sublet for cash. Eliot was his publisher. 'He loves gossip,' Sydney said. 'He told me that Hemingway went to the lavatory in Pound's Paris hotel and pulled the chain so hard the cistern came off the wall and knocked him out. Then he claimed his bruises were from defeating three Lascars in a street fight. Cheer up. Tomorrow we will visit Keats in the English cemetery.'

T HE bus stopped by the Pyramid of Cestius. We bought sandwiches at the cemetery gate. Inside, it was quiet, planted with pine trees, birds twittering on high. Keats's grave was just a mound. Shelley's stone some way away. Sydney had a flask of red wine and two paper cups. I had a guidebook containing Hardy's poem 'At the Pyramid of Cestius near the Graves of Shelley and Keats':

> Who, then, was Cestius,
>   And what is he to me? –
> Amid thick thoughts and memories multitudinous
>   One thought alone brings he.
>
> I can recall no word
>   Of anything he did;
> For me he is a man who died and was interred
>   To leave a pyramid
>   Whose purpose was exprest
>   Not with its first design,
> Nor till, far down in Time, beside it found their rest
>   Two countrymen of mine . . .

We ate our sandwiches and drank the wine. On the bus back Sydney said: 'They were not my countrymen.'

Later, he said: 'You must publish a book. A poet without a book is no poet at all. Spouting is for those who can judge by ear. Not many nowadays. "There's my book," you say – "that's where my words are." '

A book with my name on it appeared in my mind's eye. I brought my folders over to Sydney's place.

'This one's no good,' Sydney said – throwing it into the wastepaper basket.

'I spent a lot of time on that.'

'Then you wasted your time. This is better. Yes. Put it over there . . . Read this one out.' I did.

'Now do you see what's wrong with it?' I knew what he was going to say. 'It starts well enough. Then it starts to wobble. The meaning gets a bit ho-hum. Then just here' – pointing – 'it picks up again. Therefore' – folding the page – 'miss out the middle and in she goes.'

So my first collection, *Wand and Quadrant*, was assembled and sent, with a covering note from Sydney, to Eliot. At most, it had three poems worth printing. Eliot returned it with a friendly letter. When I got angry with him, some years later, I threw the letter away. The message was: keep going, work harder, read more.

Sydney received some extra money. 'For reasons of health,' he said, 'we shall visit a brothel.'

Its plain door opened on to narrow wooden stairs. Through a window at their top, Sydney bought two numbered tickets for £2 each. Reception was a room of sixty by thirty feet, smelling of disinfectant, occupied by benchfuls of men reading newspapers and smoking. One of the room's long walls had a set of doors. We took our places on the bottom bench; me rather uneasy.

Facing us was a high desk behind which sat a grey-haired woman dressed in black, also smoking, reading a magazine. The door nearest the desk opened and through it a female voice called: 'Maria!' whereupon, without looking up, the woman at the desk said: 'Number 42, door 3.' Number 42 put his slip on the desk and made his way through the third door. Then we all moved up.

My heart began to thump. Sydney, reading the international edition of the *Herald Tribune*, was no help. When the waiter from a nearby café came in for orders, he asked for a beer. After about ten minutes I plucked up my courage and told Sydney I would wait outside.

Rome: October 1952
Dear Jane and Alex,
I am arriving 10.15 a.m. Gare de Lyon Thursday.

Sydney put me on the train.

Spring 1996. Faber and Faber's new books catalogue arrives. On page 25, with a photograph of him still looking like a sailor, there is an announcement of W. S. Graham's *Selected Poems*, next to those of mine. He died in Cornwall thirteen years ago.

On the way back to Paris I thought of my book, not of Marguerite.

Alex met me.

To save money he and Jane had moved out of the Verneuil and into a storeroom at 8 rue du Sabot, a step from Place Saint-Germain. It was large, dry – and free. Arthur Fogg Lougee had decided not to back further issues of *Merlin*. From time to time he sent his daughter food parcels: chocolate, tinned fruit, a ham, a king-size fruit cake.

Merlin earnt nothing to speak of. Alex sent the second number, Autumn 1952, to be printed on credit. It included an essay, 'Samuel Beckett: an Introduction' by one Richard Seaver, which began:

> Samuel Beckett, an Irish writer long established in France, has recently published two novels which, although they defy all commentary, merit the attention of anyone interested in this century's literature. The position of Mr Beckett is quite unique.

There was no money to meet the printer's bill. Dick Seaver, together with another American, Austryn Wainhouse, saved the magazine.

Dick came to Paris in 1951. Dark-haired, quick-witted, determined, idealistic and shrewd, with firm, delicate movements, he was engaged to be married to a French violinist, Jeanette – as he was, and remains. He intended to become – as he has – a distinguished, independent, New York publisher. Lost in my own affairs, I did not see what was plain to Dick: the burden of raising money for *Merlin*, as well as the editing of it, was taking too much of Alex's time.

'I used to walk past *Les Éditions de Minuit*, Jérôme Lindon's publishing house started under the German occupation as an outlet for writers the Nazis would not tolerate,' Dick said. 'Through the window I saw these books, *Molloy* and *Malone* by Samuel Beckett, an Irishman who wrote in French. I had heard a version of his play *En Attendant Godot* when it was broadcast. I bought and read both books. I felt my mind expanding. Beckett was every young publisher's dream come true. A big, unknown fish. A week earlier Patrick Bowles had introduced me to Alex. Next time we met, Alex said: "Who in France is the most important younger living writer?" Forgetting that Beckett was hardly young – forty-six – I began to expound his genius. "Stop talking, man!" Alex said. "Write it down. Do a piece for *Merlin* on Beckett." '

'I saw Alex fretting,' Jane said. 'His novel *Young Adam* was rejected by publisher after publisher. We owed Imprimerie Mazarine £500. Until Girodias and his Olympia Press appeared, Dick was our support. We could not have continued without him. We – Alex and I – gave English lessons. You had your pension.' Which I collected once a month from the British Embassy. £5 in francs. In the early fifties, people married on £10 a week. This, and giving lessons, got me by.

'Lessons, plus my allowance, would not pay Mazarine's bill,' Jane said. 'To earn money for *Merlin* Dick took a teaching job at the US Army's Chaumont base two hundred miles south of Paris. He and Jeanette married. We planned issues 3 and 4 of *Merlin* by post.

'Dick wrote to us:

Meanwhile Jeanette and I are eating into the money we put aside. Nevertheless, I can plan on putting up another F.100,000 above and beyond whatever you have had to use to live on. Let's get number 4 out and see where we go from there. I fully understand your temptation to let the whole project drop. I am the first (after you) to deplore the inroads *Merlin* has made on your writing. The amount of money I seem to be coming off with is pitifully small for the sacrifice involved. Let's count on a break and work as we can to make the break.'

THESE words of Dick's bear out those he wrote twenty years later:

During those *Merlin* years I was as close to Trocchi as I have ever been to any friend or colleague. We worked together closely, and always in harmony.

'Of course I will help you publish *Wand and Quadrant*, old man,' Alex said to me. 'Get an estimate from Mazarine. Print a subscription form for a numbered edition on special paper at a price to cover the cost. Start collecting subscriptions.'

He had not changed his view about Marguerite. She had begun to work as a model for Marcel Rochas. 'She is interested in a love affair. That or nothing. Start the affair, or you will lose her. And you risk an unpleasant ending. Neither of you coming out of it well in your own eyes. And it will be your fault, old man.'

At my pleading, Alex agreed to invite Marguerite to have coffee with him in the Sabot storeroom. I was to hide in the storeroom's deep cupboard. In their conversation, Alex would try to get her to say what she thought about me.

'I am doing a bad thing,' Alex said. 'Give me your word you will never mention it to anyone else, anyone at all – including Jane.'

'I promise.'

'And regardless of what you hear you are not to emerge from the cupboard until I have taken her to Saint-Germain.'

'Yes.'

Marguerite accepted Alex's invitation.

When she knocked at the storeroom's door, I stepped into the cupboard – more of a closet, really – and closed its curtain. Peeping around the edge I saw she was wearing a swingy, Picasso-inspired knitwear coat over soft, dark yellow trousers. The tiny buckle brooch gathering her black hair matched the silver clips on her black, patent-leather shoes.

The interview revealed nothing. Marguerite was wary, Alex – for once – abashed. Of course she liked me. Of course she wanted to go on seeing me. Christopher is being silly. Then they left.

Anxious, determined to keep my word and stay put for the stipulated time, then dash to Place Saint-Germain for a sham-chance meeting, I did not hear the visitor who tiptoed into the storeroom seconds after Marguerite and Alex left. Then, who-ever it was stuck a hand under the curtain and started to feel around my feet. Then the hand found what it sought: the tin containing Arthur Fogg's latest fruit cake. Then its pair came forward, and together they removed the tin.

Longing for my reunion with Marguerite, I whipped the curtain back and the thief – a poet friend of Jane's called Ronald Clouder – caught in the very act of tearing away a massive lump of fruit cake, dropped the lump and stared saucer-eyed at me as I shot by.

It was getting dark. Alex and Marguerite were at the taxi rank. Annoyed by my appearance, Alex disappeared.

Marguerite and I walked towards the Palais du Luxembourg, me saying how much I loved her, how I wanted to live with her etc., etc.

Outside the main gates of the Palais two policemen were strolling past two plumed, breastplated Garde Républicaine sentries when Marguerite turned to me and said: 'You are a bore. *Un casse-pieds*.' Without thinking, infuriated by this truth, I slapped her face hard enough to send one of her earrings skittering across the pavement.

I expected to be arrested. I would be thrown out of France. But the policemen turned away. When I turned back towards her, Marguerite had gone. We never saw or spoke to each other again.

As with Philip, I met Austryn Wainhouse, *Merlin*'s co-saviour – with his doubting smile, his east coast American voice, at his feet a large, neatly organized briefcase – in Gaït's bookshop.

One day in December 1952, Austryn received a *pneumatique* (hand-written letter-forms transmitted by suction tube throughout central Paris) from Alex – whom he had never met – summoning him to George Whitman's bookshop.

'Alex', Austryn said, 'was dressed in a raincoat, the collar pulled up, over its rim his long nose set between two very blue, winning eyes. Bundles of *Merlin* 2 were stacked on the floor. He asked for my opinion of it. No cover was ever so austere. An uncompromising editorial called for the rejection of petrified verbal categories. I liked it.

'"I understand you have some texts?" Alex began. "Translations of the Marquis de Sade. Let me tell you my scheme."

'Which was', Austryn said, 'to finance *Merlin* by publishing Sade in English. If translations of Sade existed, few knew of them. From Philip, Alex heard I had translated Sade's *Bedroom Philosophers*, a dialogue on the connection between sexual pleasure and pain. The *Philosophers* would be the first volume to be published under the imprint Collection Merlin, the proposed book-producing side of the magazine.

'I explained that Sade's works were banned in France. If a French citizen published Sade they would be prosecuted. As foreigners, Alex and I would get preferential treatment: immediate expulsion. What *Merlin* needed was a Frenchman unafraid of his own government. Someone to publish Sade because Sade was an important writer. Such a one would become *Merlin*'s gérant, or French partner. He must have a liking for confrontation, a taste for prosecution.'

On leaving Gaït's, Austryn took me to the Café de Tournon, near the Palais du Luxembourg, a middle-sized establishment with a one-table-deep terrace, red banquettes inside, chess, reading and writing encouraged – owned by M. and Mme Alazard.

'There has never been more interest in Sade in France than there is now,' said Austryn – him in his belted trench mac, briefcase in hand, me in my duffel coat and green felt hat – as we made our way along the rue du Four. 'Sade is on the outermost edge of literature, as good as outside it. During the war a clandestine press came into existence – Les Éditions de Minuit, for instance – whose function, duty, almost, was to publish what the Nazis forbade. That determination has been switched to literature.' Austryn was a born executive, never so happy as when drawing up a plan. 'And, as it happens, I know the very *gérant* for us.' Charles, the Tournon's waiter – saving every franc he could to open a café of his own – brought us coffee.

In the same week as he met Alex, Austryn had received a letter from a Monsieur Girodias suggesting that they meet 'for business reasons' at the Café des Deux Magots at place Saint-Germain.

'Girodias', Austryn recounted, 'was dressed in a dark suit with a dark tie. Thirtyish. Very sober. He shook hands with his left hand, for his right was in a bandage. He mentioned his liver. His constitution. The colour of his urine. When he asked me in his perfect English how I was,' Austryn said, 'it seemed like an appeal for me to consider his own frail health. His voice was low. I had to strain to catch what he said.'

Maurice Girodias was the son of a French mother and of Jack Kahane, a Mancunian dandy, himself the publisher of Henry Miller, Anaïs Nin, Radclyffe Hall, Lawrence Durrell and James Joyce.

Far from being in poor condition, or any kind of a victim, Maurice was a bold, litigious fantasist; combative, clever, unscrupulous, sensual; without doubt the most interesting independent publisher of his day. And, in his fashion, idealistic. Convinced that, if all forms of sexual censorship were removed, human problems would wither away.

Muffie Wainhouse, Austryn's wife, in whom, when she became his secretary, Maurice confided, told me: 'He is a born gambler – not just with money. During the war – he was a British-Jewish national, remember – he never left Paris. He had access to paper at a time when the Germans controlled its distribution.'

'You mean he collaborated?'

'Mm ... He was lucky. He had Resistance connections, as well – or so he says. He must have done. He didn't hide. When the war was over no one hated him. The underground needed paper, too. He came out of the war a rich man. In fact, it was only after the war that he lost money.'

'After Girodias had ordered me an expensive brandy and mineral water for himself,' Austryn continued, 'he got down to business. "I understand you have translated *La Philosophie dans le boudoir*, Mr Wainhouse," he said. "I am interested in seeing your work." I went to my hotel and fetched the manuscript of which he read the first two pages. Then, saying how sorry he was that the sum was so modest, offered me £150 for it.

' "I am going to open a publishing firm called the Olympia Press," he confided. "My speciality will be books that others dare not issue. No one in my field has such a wealth of experience. As a child I sat on Radclyffe Hall's knee. Olympia's first titles will be Henry Miller's *Nexus* and the Sade/Wainhouse *Philosophy*." I asked him if the second title would be appearing before too long. "Oh," he said, "there can be no delay." '

Austryn told Maurice he had certain friends, fine writers with bilingual skills. A meeting might be to everyone's advantage.

The meeting, the first of two, between Maurice, Alex, Austryn, Jane, Patrick, Dick and me, occurred in Dick and Jeanette's flat above the storeroom. Maurice, his hand still bandaged, sat down in Dick's chair and offered his Gitanes to the bed-load of writers who were, via the Olympia Press, to help him make, and watch him spend, a substantial fortune. Everyone lit up.

Maurice agreed that all those present must work together. 'As serious literary artists,' he said, 'you intend to produce and, through *Merlin*, propagate new forms of writing.' He, as a publisher, intended to print and distribute books in English whose content would confront the censorious western world.

'I expect', Maurice said, 'to be prosecuted by the police. These prosecutions will be the mark of my success. Your position as foreigners makes it inadvisable for you to share the risks. Fortunately, the same need not be said of the rewards. You must devote yourselves to the novel, to poetry, to the drama. The tedious business of dealing with printers and distributors – these are not the sort of things on which creative writers should waste their time.'

Was *Merlin* in debt? It was. Would Jane like him to be the magazine's publisher – its next two issues guaranteed? She would. Very well, he had underwritten other literary publications. And were there no books we wished to publish? Austryn had mentioned something about a Collection Merlin? Dick was interested in that curious foreigner, Samuel Beckett? Everything was possible.

Before leaving, Maurice explained there was a contribution to the future of the Olympia Press he would like us to make. It had to do with English texts. 'Let me be candid,' he said. 'I require simple stories of a wholly pornographic kind. Character draw-ing, social context are of no importance. Disadvantages even. I want constant, heavy, serious fucking.'

These books would, naturally, be published under a separate imprint, the Traveller's Companion Library; only the creative texts belonged with the Olympia Press or Collection Merlin. Unlike creative work, though, the pornographic texts would be paid for. £200 per 150 printed pages. £200 per reprint. World rights to him. Translations from any language, £100. £100 per reprint. He would provide pseudonyms. He looked forward to seeing us: 'You will find me in the rue Jacob.'

THROUGH Jérôme Lindon, Dick discovered that Beckett had an unpublished novel, *Watt*, written in English, and wrote to Beckett asking if he could read the manuscript with a view to publishing an extract from it in *Merlin*.

'One evening a few days after I posted my letter,' Dick said, 'I answered a knock on the door to a tall, handsome man with a neat crest of grey hair who said: "Beckett". (Pause.) "*Watt*." (Pause.) Then handed me a typewritten manuscript bound in black patent leather and was gone before I could say thank you.'

By next evening we were all at Dick's flat. Jeanette served coffee. Since Beckett had become news among us, our literary talk centred on him. Now seven or eight of us sat on Jeanette's and Dick's bed, going quiet when Dick produced the manuscript and began to read the passages Beckett had marked as suitable for publication.

Watt had little to say on the subject of the second closing period in Mr Knott's house. Here he moved, to and fro, from the door to the window, from the window to the door; from the window to the door, from the door to the window; from the fire to the bed, from the bed to the fire; from the bed to the fire, from the fire to the bed; from the door to the fire, from the fire to the door; from the fire to the door, from the door to the fire; from the window to the bed, from the bed to the window . . .

At which point it was agreed that Dick should go back to the beginning of the book and read it through. Progress was slow because, at first, the text was so comical. Everyone wanted to read. Patrick was the best: deadpan, following the punctuation.

As we read on, the writing unsettled us, became frightening and funny by turns; comedy at its most extreme. We found the use of English astonishing. Rhythmically fine-tuned. A first of its kind. Beautiful.

For us, it was as it must have been for those who came across the work of Picasso and Duchamp in the 1910s. Or the poetry of Eliot in the twenties. An aesthetically encouraging shock. As is usual when one comes into contact with something good, we felt good. Alex proposed we publish the whole thing. *Watt* becoming Collection Merlin's first title.

'ARE you going to write one of Girodias's dirty books?' Patrick wanted to know.

'I haven't been asked.'

'He asked everybody. For a year you have been talking about artistic integrity. You admired Joyce's watchwords, "silence, exile and cunning", the three things he required in order to write freely. Also, Brecht's singularity of political purpose. And right now, Beckett's purity of vision.'

'The kind of book Girodias is talking about does no harm.'

'You might argue they do good. Yours will not be an attempt to make a work of art.'

'You mean it will be bad writing.'

'Yes. And bad because – again, correct me if I am wrong – you have nothing whatsoever of interest to say about sex. And sex is an important topic. If you had something of importance to say about it, that is not what Girodias wants. He wants trash.'

'Not necessarily.'

'Necessarily. Old man, if you want to write about sex, write about how falling in love makes you miserable and gives trouble to your friends. Girodias will not want that book.'

I TALKED to Alex about *Wand and Quadrant*. I had retyped the text prepared in Rome, adding hand-lettered dropped capitals at the beginning of several poems and the signs of the zodiac (indented) to the verses of the untitled poem. I was not sure why. They looked interesting. Very Poundian. I hoped Austryn did not ask why they were there.

The question was: would Collection Merlin publish *Wand and Quadrant* after *Watt* came out? Yes, Alex said.

'Alex . . .'

'Yes, old man?'

'Have you begun a book for Maurice?'

'I have.'

'What's it called?'

'*Young Adam.*'

'The name of your novel.'

'Ten publishers have turned *Young Adam* down. I am going to dirty it up. Why waste it? We need the money.'

Jane said that Alex and Maurice had started to see a lot of each other.

Having read *Watt*, Maurice began to think of his promise to publish it as a favour to us rather than an advantage to him.

'He was nervous when I called at rue Jacob,' Austryn said. 'His urine has a bad colour. He thought *Watt* had one fairly indecent scene in the first chapter. As for the addenda at the back, headed: *The following precious and illuminating material should be carefully studied. Only fatigue and disgust prevented its incorporation*, Maurice said: "Then why incorporate it?" When I told him *Watt* was a masterpiece, a work for tomorrow, he said he would wait until tomorrow before making up his mind to bring it out.'

There was the question of who should translate Beckett's novels *Molloy* and *Malone* for Collection Merlin. Dick had attempted a story of Beckett's. 'It was difficult,' he said. 'My French is good. I thought Patrick might have more success. He sent Beckett a few trial pages. Beckett read them and said: "Bowles isn't a translator. He's a writer. That's what I want."' Patrick noted:

A knock on the door this morning at 11 a.m. while I was preparing a second cup of coffee announced Samuel Beckett who had climbed six flight of stairs (to my tiny attic room in the Cité Vaneau) but did not look daunted by them. He came and sat on the bed while I fiddled, prepared myself, my affairs, explained that I had just woken, which was not true. I woke at ten and would have been quite capable of working, at my own work, indeed I was looking forward to it, and he was the only person for whom I'd have interrupted or, for that morning, abandoned it without hesitation: however, for him to take all the trouble to come out was more than overwhelming, it was actually moving; so many of the slightest acts and gestures meaningless or unnoticeable in many people seem with him to move one, to evoke so readily one's – or my, at any rate – sympathy. He sat on the bed and read the manuscripts I gave him. I gave them to him largely because I didn't know what else to do. We went down to a café.

'It was slow, painstaking work,' Patrick said. 'Wrung and thrashed and hammered out. It took us fifteen months. For less than 240 pages. If it had been a 240-page poem no one would have been surprised that it took more than a year. Yet although the techniques of prose and verse are different, the intensity of concentration is the same. Or it should be.'

LIKE Beckett's unflinching vision, almost as if our discovery of his work was prophetic, my first knowledge of what is now called the Holocaust came from the Winter 1953 issue of *Merlin*.

I knew that dreadful things had been done. My father and me at the Dachau film. Stories from Poland. From Russia. Then, courtesy of *Les Temps Modernes*, in whose pages it had appeared in French, Austryn and Dick translated two extracts from a Declaration made by Dr Miklos Nyiszli, a Hungarian, which began:

I, the undersigned, Dr Nyiszli, Miklos, physician, former prisoner of the KZ. Number 8450, declare that this work, which relates the darkest days in the History of Mankind, was drawn up by me in strict accordance with reality, and without the slightest exaggeration, in my capacity as an eyewitness and involuntary participant in the work of the Auschwitz crematoria into whose fires millions of fathers, mothers and children disappeared.

As chief physician of the Auschwitz crematoria I drafted numerous affidavits of dissection and forensic medicine findings which I signed with my own tattoo number. I sent these documents by mail, countersigned by my superior, Dr Mengele, to the Berlin-Dahlem address of the 'Institut für Rassenbiologische und anthropologische Forschungen', one of the most qualified medical research centres of the Third Reich.

It should still be possible to find them today in the archives of this Research Institute.

Merlin published these extracts under the title *SS Obersturm-führer Doktor Mengele*. They explained, in detail, what happened in the death camps. It is possible that they were the first publication of Dr Nyiszli's Declaration in English.

A LEX and I sat on the terrace of the Old Navy with the manuscript of the Nyiszli translation on our table. Neither of us could think of anything to say. Alex said: 'This changes everything.' And I thought: That's right.

Then the French poet Daniel Mauroc joined us. He had read Dr Nyiszli's Declaration in *Les Temps Modernes*. Mauroc was homosexual.

'There's another piece to be written about the German homosexuals. The Nazis made them wear a pink triangle. Then they killed them. It will be a difficult piece to write because they killed almost everyone. The same goes for the gypsies.'

S UBSCRIPTIONS to *Wand and Quadrant* were going slowly. Of the forms I posted, only Jimmy Logue's – 'Three copies but don't bother to send them' – had been returned. The book would cost £150 to print. I had subscriptions worth £50. Then my luck changed.

I was friends with a tall blonde English girl called Jean Crouch who had decided to spend a year in the Quarter 'before settling down'.

'I was quite interested in you at the time,' Jean told me in 1995. 'You were slightly smelly. Your teeth were in a terrible state. Things soon put right. You had no eyes for me at all. You sang "Black Is the Colour of My True Love's Hair" in quite a pleasant voice. Then you told me how I was nothing to look at in comparison to Marguerite, though that was over, or to Kri, a Brazilian girl you had just fallen in love with.'

Jean and I were sitting on the terrace of the Café Monaco, me showing her the manuscript of my book while complaining I was still short of the £100 Alex had insisted was found before production could be started, when a large redheaded girl with an

American accent at the next table leant over and said: 'Show me that.'

Jean handed it over. The girl began to read it. After five minutes she handed the manuscript back and said: 'How much do you need to get this stuff printed?'

'Fifty pounds,' I said, not wanting to push my luck.

'Don't you mean a hundred?' said Jean.

'How much is that in dollars?' the girl asked.

Bill Boyce, a racing-car driver from Wyoming, was reading the *International Herald Tribune* along the terrace. He gave us the daily rate.

'You've got it,' said the redhead. 'Give me an address. You get the money in exchange for the manuscript. OK?'

'You mean he's to leave the manuscript at his address, and when you deliver the money it's yours?' Jean said.

'That's what I mean,' said the redhead.

I was so nervous I knocked my glass of wine over the manuscript, saying as I dried it with Jean's tissues: 'Never mind. I have another copy.'

'This one's mine,' said the redhead. 'As is. Now I must go.'

Jean gave her Gaït's address.

'Do you think she means it?' I said.

'Yes,' Jean said. 'And make sure Gaït gets her name and the name of her hotel. Her suit cost more than my entire wardrobe.'

AUSTRYN and I visited the office of Olympia Press. I had submitted a proposal for a dirty book to be called *The Abominable Circus*. It was to feature a troupe of sexual gold-medallists performing singly, in pairs, trios, quartets, or even larger combinations, on horse and/or elephant back, up on the highwire; swinging from the trapeze or while being fired from cannons. Their pan-European adventures were to be set in the seventeenth century. Loved by the public, they were to be pursued from fair to fair by the Papal Secret Police.

Maurice looked pale. He wore a dark grey suit, a blue shirt, a dark blue tie. There was a new second-hand sofa in front of his trestle-table desk, a new paraffin heater to his right.

'Please sit down,' he whispered. 'You both look so well. How lucky you are to enjoy perfect health. My wife has a cold. I feel a cold coming on. Now – your pages, Austryn.' Austryn slid the folder containing his pages across the table, and, while Maurice counted them, we all lit up.

'Lisa,' Maurice said, taking a bottle out of his pocket without looking up (Lisa, his secretary, sat at a second table beyond the paraffin heater), 'a glass of slightly warmed water, please.'

Maurice paid £1 per page. He liked to receive ten pages every other day. 'I must have ten books in print by Christmas.'

While he read Austryn's pages Maurice unscrewed the bottle cap, rolled a green-black capsule out on to the table, recapped the bottle while leafing the pages, then slipped the nostrum, plus a tiny sip of water, between his teeth, and said without looking up: 'Very good. A nice touch. Convincing.'

Big men carrying plain cartons came and went. Lisa signed the delivery notes. A tense five minutes.

When he had finished, Maurice put his hand into his trousers pocket and took out a sheaf of once-folded banknotes, saying, 'Let's see what we have here. It was ten pages, Austryn?'

'Twelve pages, Maurice.'

'Don't mind my asking. I have the weekend to think of.'

The banknotes were held in a gold-plated paper clip.

'Well' – selecting two of 1,000 francs, one of 10,000 francs – 'there you are' – sliding them across the table – 'let's meet again on Tuesday.'

As Austryn accepted, Maurice looked at me and said: 'I know you have no money at all, Christopher, but this' – sliding my proposal towards me – 'will never do.

'You are not writing pornography to amuse yourself. Olympia's customers are men seeking sexual relief in one of the most normal of ways. All mammals, including humans, masturbate. Children should be taught how to masturbate. To condemn masturbation is to encourage rape. But few adults want to laugh while they do it. And even fewer want to be laughed at for doing it. Did you know, according to yesterday's London *Daily Telegraph*' – Maurice was a loyal *Telegraph* reader – 'that Boccaccio is going to be prosecuted in Swindon, Wiltshire? This in 1953. Consult Alex. I want one full encounter of at least five pages for every ten pages. I don't mind a joke or two. But nothing snobby.'

MY backer from the Café Monaco left the dollars and took the manuscript. I did not get her address or her name. Three weeks later the actual printed edition was delivered to Gaït's. It looked good. I had lunch with Alex and Austryn. We turned its pages. Alex asked me if I was pleased. I was. After lunch Austryn and I sent off review copies. Until he mentioned the need of such copies, I had not considered them. Beyond its printing, I had no grasp of how a book, any book, never mind a book of verse, was published. When I was alone, my heart sank. I knew by now that it was not half as good a book as I would have liked it to have been. It would not make anyone say: 'Wow. . .' as some must have when they read *Songs of Innocence* or *Prufrock and Other Observations*.

After talking the matter through with Alex, I started on my dirty book, *Lust*. Slightly ashamed of what I was up to, I told myself it was going to be a left-wing dirty book. Which is not a bad idea. Except that *Lust* was nothing of the kind.

I wrote ten pages a day, half sexually aroused, for twenty days, taking a fortnight's break – which Maurice referred to as 'a nervous breakdown' – in the middle. I do not recommend the task. Or the book.

Calling at Olympia's offices: 'I am far from well today,' Maurice revealed. 'You forget, Christopher, that I am fifteen years older than any of you, my writers. I have begun dyeing my hair. The police take grey hair as a sign of weakness. It excites their love of punishment.

'Let's see what we have here. . .' turning over my new pages. 'Um . . . Not the best, but censorable. A fairly candid appeal to low instincts . . .'

When he had paid me, I said: 'I have an idea for a book. An anthology of limericks.'

'Um.'

'Most limericks are obscene in a funny way. Everybody likes them.'

'Do women like them? I know there is a big market for female pornography. The difficulty is – how to tap it? Tell me a limerick.'

> 'Said the Nabob of Trincomalee:
> "Young man, do you fart when you pee?"

> I replied with some wit:
> "Do you belch when you shit?" –
> I think that was one up for me.'

Maurice did not laugh. He took a sip of Perrier water, then said: 'Are there any collections already on sale?'

'Norman Douglas published one in the 1930s.'

'Why don't I reprint his?'

'You could.'

'Give me a ten-page sample. Four per page.'

He decided my *nom de plume* for *Lust* would be Count Palmiro Vicarion. He used the same name on the *Limericks*, with which in 1955 he, and I, had a small succes. This was followed two years later by the Count's *Book of Bawdy Ballads*.

GAÏT had an American friend called Halley. Halley commuted between Paris and London, where she had two boyfriends. One, Anthony Hill, the constructivist artist, said of her: 'I didn't last long, I can tell you. In one side of the bed, out the other.' The other was Terence, now Sir Terence, Conran. Halley brought him to Paris. 'This is Terence, he's in furniture,' she said.

Except for his height, Terence looked about nine years old. He could not keep still. He walked around Gaït's apartment peering out of the window, picking things up, looking at them, putting them down: 'Hum' (meaning, rotten); 'Ummm' (meaning, not bad). Then he sat down for half a minute. Then he got up, looked at Halley and said: 'Let's go shopping.'

Terence was the first man I heard suggest such a thing. So far as I was concerned, shopping was a waste of time – bookshopping excepted.

'We went to all the ironmongers in Paris,' Halley boasted. 'He was mad about some ladles in the Bon Marché. It took an hour to find out who the suppliers were. We had to buy a dictionary to look the words up.'

This was/is Terence. Very bossy, but visionary. William Morris's dictum: *Have nothing in your house that is not useful and beautiful*, was his guide. He wanted you, that is to say, everyone, to have a sense of design. He would not have found it odd to say that good design was moral, bad, immoral.

'I hadn't heard from Halley for about thirty years,' Anthony said. 'Then she phoned up. "Hi, I'm just around the corner from you. Can you tell me where the nearest laundromat is?"'

LOOKING at the packages containing *Wand and Quadrant* depressed me. What on earth was I to do with 600 books?

'You must sell them, Christopher,' Gaït said.

'Well,' Muffie reckoned, 'let's look on the bright side. For £150 you have received 600 books, worth, if sold – minus the subscriber/complimentary copies – at least £1,000.'

'I have never sold anything in my life.'

'Have you ever bought anything?'

'Don't laugh.'

'I mean have you ever bought anything for no particular reason, just because you fancied it, suddenly, out of the blue?'

The truth was I felt toffee-nosed about selling. One of the copies George Whitman lent out was returned with 'Drivel' written in a neat hand on the bottom right-hand corner of each page. Another had: 'See you in the Royal at 15.30, Jennifer,' scrawled across the title page in lipstick.

I was no good as a salesman. Holding a copy, I would approach English-speaking visitors at café tables.

'Excuse me. Would you like to buy my book?'

'What's it about?'

'It's a book of poems.'

'What are they about?'

Even as it irritated me, I felt that this was a fair question.

'Some are about being in love. Some are about sailing to an unknown country with the help of ancient stars.'

'Are there modern stars?' (Pause) 'All right, we'll have one. After all, we're in Paris.'

As soon as I made, if I made, two sales I hastened to the Tournon feeling every inch a left-wing poet concerned with the world's wrongs. I sent Pound a copy. In return, came my one hand-written letter from him. It said: 'Not bad. I can read quite a bit of it.' High praise. Whatever else he was, where verse was concerned, Pound was no liar.

It was some years before I read the texts of the radio broadcasts Pound made to the American soldiers who were fighting in Italy in 1943 and 1944. They were worse than I had guessed. Full of anti-Semitic ravings. If a Jewish-American serviceman had shot him dead – fair enough. By the time of my letter from him (I have it still) I had read Dr Nyiszli's *Declaration*. Pound was a fighter for the kind of literary art I admired, an experimental idea of beauty. And at the same time, he was advocating a perverse delusion realized through a criminal ideology.

Literary commentators who try to justify, or apologize for, racist – in Pound's case – views by appealing to the poet's undoubted gifts soil themselves. In verse (as elsewhere) beauty will serve any view and give it a glamour. We should not be afraid to call it whorish.

IT is lowering to recount behaviour one is ashamed of. For more than thirty years I went, either overexcitedly or coldly evasive, from one affair to another.

Jane, an undergraduate, irritated by my insistence that she spend a weekend with me in London, breaking contact when, having done so, I merely played at making love. Down to Oxford I went with a look of despair on my face, and got into her room. I was found asleep on her bed by another, proper, lover, who picked me up, knocked me down, and threw me out.

Emily – my friend for over a year – when almost by chance we began to kiss and cuddle, her suggesting: 'Let's go on.' And me wanting no more than the kiss, the cuddle.

Emily and I remained friends. My first woman friend.

Monica, well-off, the mother of two young children, her husband a doctor. We stayed in Ghent for a few days. We had met in Amsterdam, where she lived. A fortnight later, she arrived at the door of my room in Paris, declaring she had left her husband and her children for me. My resentful and panicky response was to lug her suitcase down the stairs and along the street to an hotel. And then, in a darkened doorway, Monica pleading with me to give her a chance – to which all I could say was no, goodbye, leaving her in tears.

And Philip, pushing me into serious words on the subject: 'Do stop treating women as if they were made of glass. You have not ruined anyone's life by failing to stand by them. You are both over twenty-one. You are not committed. She is not your mother. Is it the fear of failure to make love in what you believe to be an acceptable way? Or that your so-called failure becomes a matter of gossip? So you masturbate to kill desire. That's normal enough. To leave it at that, that's infantile.'

Mark you, in more cases than one I got my comeuppance, a well-placed clout to the ego by a young woman as much in a mist as I was.

'When I think of the way our generation behaved towards each other,' Nell murmured in her self-surprised way. 'Quite outrageous. And nobody seemed to mind. It was a sort of fate. You just took it, and moved on.'

Then, too, in retrospect I see myself indulging in weeks, sometimes months, of beady-eyed frownings, stalkings off into the night. Accusing others of my own deceits, independent fellow suddenly turned into clinging vine. Then just as suddenly out of the wood, chattering way away as if there had never been a Marguerite or a Jane or an Emily or a Monica, their letters, their memory, abandoned, the people they had introduced me to avoided.

Isobel, clever, disconsolate, soon to marry Rascomb, a mutual friend, still my friend, said: 'We saw each other almost daily. But I knew when we met that you had not thought about me in the meantime. You didn't want to think about me, Isobel – five-seven, shoe size four, no money, no education, no self-confidence, too fond of drink. Just very good-looking – in your eyes.'

Grace – in 1965, in London – without my asking – though I let her – moved in with me. When I spent all day elsewhere and slept on the floor at night, Grace took an overdose. All I felt was anger that I should be so bothered with this irritating behaviour, and fear that I could somehow be blamed for her desperation. Even for a moment, I was unwilling to bear another's burden. I called Isobel who got Grace into hospital while I went away for a fortnight.

As mentioned, during 1953–4 I fell in love with Kri, a Brazilian girl who was living with her mother pending their return to São Paulo. Kri was eighteen.

For three weeks after we had fallen in love Kri and I met each morning at nine, then wandered about the city until ten at night, when I took her home. We decided she would remain in Paris. We would find a studio.

Inez, Kri's cousin, was giving up her job at UNESCO. Kri reckoned to get it. When her father sent for them, Kri told her mother that she would be staying with me in Paris. I would not hear of it. We promised each other that she would come back in three months' time. Then she was gone. Followed (need I say) by a stream of letters from me.

This time there were no replies. Inez explained that as soon as she was back in her own world, 'so much friendlier than here', Kri's plans for a life in Paris with me would have vanished. She must study. Brazil needed ten thousand Kris. She came from a responsible, leftish, bourgeois family. She could not ignore either her family obligations or her country's plight. The message was: if you love her, don't bother her. I took it badly, shuffling into a dejected, continuously suicidal frame of mind, varied by demands on myself to find a job, to save enough money to go to Brazil.

From time to time since my teenage I had threatened myself with death. For the most part, these occasions were outbursts of self-pity, goings to the bottom of the garden to eat worms. Now, though, thoughts of suicide began to fill my days. Whereas in the past I had to summon up such a consideration, presently I had to dismiss it, and, like other preoccupations temporarily dismissed, the moment my mental sentries dozed, back it came.

Jean Crouch had been lent a house in Knightsbridge. I went back to London to stay with her. Halley had told Terence of my job/Brazil plan. Terence took charge. He decided I should apply for a copywriter's job at J. Walter Thompson, the advertising agency. 'Don't worry. I will introduce you to Ward. He runs various important accounts there,' Terence said.

Ward took me to a bar patronized by the JWT people. He was a friendly, blue-eyed bull of a man, a chain smoker, now with a large whisky in the same hand as his cigarette: 'What's yours? Move up, Daisy – had your hair done, I see. Meet Chris. You may be typing his copy before long. . .' If I filled in the application form and passed the agency's written test, after an interview with the personnel manager I would become a trainee copywriter.

For the interview Terence dressed me in one of his suits. Drainpipe trousers. Red braces. Dark tie. Pins. The trousers hitched up.

'Don't move. Give me another pin. Now walk to the door,' said Terence, head on one side. Then getting up: 'That will do. Don't let me down.'

Trouble came with the personnel manager:

'I see you joined up in May 1944 and were discharged in February 1948.'

'Yes.'

'Why so late? Those serving from May '44 were due for discharge by mid-'47?'

The answer being that time spent in prison did not count as time served.

'Then I cannot recommend your being employed by the Agency.'

I walked back to Jean's, delivered the suit to Terence's – thankful he was out – and hitch-hiked to Bournemouth.

'YOU were in a bad state,' Peter Clarke recalled. 'I was used to you being emotional about almost anything. Now you had gone political. You came out with hours of Marxist ravings. How you were prepared to fight in the streets, that the country was in the hands of criminals, then saying, very quietly, that you were miserable, you did not know what to do. Goodness me, you were boring about Marx.

' "Have you read the Communist Manifesto?"

' "No."

' "Read it, man! Read it! Read Engels, and above all read Lenin's *State and Revolution.*"

' "Can you recommend something more up to date?"

' "Mao Tse-Tung. A poet of genius."

'I remember laughing over this last year (1994) when, in an aside, you confessed that all you ever read of any of these authors was three pages of Marx in *The Handbook of Marxism*, whereas I, impressed by your insistence that we should "prepare ourselves philosophically for the struggle to come", bought Marx's *Collected Works*, six volumes for thirteen shillings, and read three of them, taking notes as you had said.'

'One afternoon,' Peter remembered, 'we went to see a double bill: *Bicycle Thieves*, marvellous, and *La Ronde*, which I never saw because you begged me to leave the cinema. We spent a miserable hour in an almost empty public house. "I can't bear to be alone," you said. I recalled your talk of suicide not long after we first met. You were in a similar sort of mood, with this difference: it did not shift as your moods always did. I did not like to bring the subject of suicide up. It crossed my mind, all the same. It depressed me.

'Normally you liked being alone. You came to see me when you felt like company. After three or four hours you'd say: "Well, I'm off. See you later," then go.

' "Let's go round and see Charles", I suggested. "Charles is like a rock. I always go and see Charles when I am depressed."

'It had turned foggy. You were silent. As we walked, I told you about an ex-girlfriend of mine, Susan. When we stopped seeing each other she got engaged to a chap called Gifford. A month later he was in the Sunday papers accused of murdering both his parents before throwing their bodies over a cliff

'Charles was in. When you mentioned my story about Gifford, Charles – not one for dramatic gestures – sprang to his feet, and declared: "Miles Gifford! A double murderer! I played cricket with him, the minor county eleven! It's in Wisden. '48 or '49. I'll find it," reaching up for and bringing half a dozen more Wisdens down on to the plate of cheese and tomato sandwiches his mother had just handed around the edge of the door.'

A DAY or two before I returned to Paris my brain took on a life of its own and began to race, emitting a stream of images and of voices as if it, or a part of it, having gone mad, was distinct from my body, seeing and gabbling of its own accord. Though it has never happened to me, I do not doubt those who say that when they have found themselves on the verge of sudden, unexpected death, their past lives have flashed before their minds. This fractured, babbling film, projected inside my head, was akin to their experiences. Had the noise it – I – was making risen to a shriek, the part of me that was still blank and silent would have been swamped. And that could have meant I had gone mad.

Not long ago the painter Tracey Emin remarked that sometimes her body started to scream: 'It's terrible when it happens, but when it goes away it's like a loss and you want it to come back again.'

For me, it was my brain. I do not want it to come back again. I went down on to my knees with my head between my hands and stared as hard as I could at the pattern in the linoleum. Slowly, after a long, hard, physical effort, my brain reregistered. Incredibly relieved, I stood up covered with sweat, my knees shaking. In the mirror I saw that my hair had gone straight. It remained straight for two days.

ON reaching Paris I avoided Alex. Seeing him would bring out my suicide plan. And once it was out, the will to do it would be endangered. Or he might lose patience and say: 'Right, old man, you run along and kill yourself. Jane and I are going for supper.' Or if I told Austryn he might say: 'Very well, then. We will get you a pistol, a ticket to Washington, and you can shoot Senator McCarthy, then turn the barrel on yourself.' Or Dick: 'When René Crevel gassed himself he was found with a note pinned to his jacket bearing the word: "Disgusted". Your comment?'

Why delay? Swallow the Tuinal right now. Why wait to hire a rowing boat in a Mediterranean resort, as I had been planning, and then take my capsules when out of sight of land? Unattractive as was the idea of poisoning myself in a cheap hotel room, the killing was getting closer. Under a train? Over an edge?

When I lost my reading glasses and did not – never mind immediately – bother to replace them, I realized with a jolt how serious my intentions were.

Thoughts of Kri did not enter my head. If, by magic, she had reappeared, I am sure I would have been dismayed.

I spent my time sitting in unfamiliar cafés, or talking to Philip's friend, the painter Louis de Wet, who, when that unhappy time had passed, became my friend, admired by me at the outset, more so today.

Others – none of them have asked for his comments – have misrepresented Louis, describing him as a Mephistopheles who helped me on my way to self-destruction. Louis was, and is, forthright, unflinching, kind, sensitive. As I hoped, he took me and my plan – Perpignan was the town I had settled on – seriously. He argued with me. He recommended patience. When he asked: 'What does Trocchi have to say?' I lied to him, implying that Alex was bored with me. He asked me to consider the effect my suicide would have on my mother. When I said: 'Here is an opportunity for you to kill someone and get away with it. I will write a suicide note. You can push me off a cliff,' he did not find it funny, saying: 'You are not the only one with difficulties. My father is a policeman. A white South African policeman. He never cared for me, his son. I was living away, at university. When I came home my father asked: "Well, my lord, what are you going to do now?" I told him I was going to Paris to be a painter. "If you go to that Sodium and Gomorrah you will be lost. And if you follow the profession of Picassio I will never speak to you again." He never has.'

I F asked, I would have been hard put to explain why I proposed to mete out such a terrible punishment as suicide to myself. In a general way, ignorance of what death means to the mature living might be said to have something to do with it. As would, I suppose, a hidden fury occasioned by my believing myself to be unlovable; bad, even. After all, the bad have to do something bad in order to be bad, and killing is a serious thing. This fury was intensified, perhaps, by the knowledge that I had provoked, if not love, at least an active liking. I drove away, or ran away from, or bored, or dodged, those who had returned my feelings.

Then there was my mother. My death would hurt her. Well, then, I would have proven myself a bad person, with something so unattractive in himself the only escape was through death.

P ERPIGNAN was a poor choice. The sea was seven miles from the town. When my train arrived, it was getting dark. Along the road, giant palm trees, a fountain, music. Pleasant smells in the air.

In the morning I took the single-track tram to Canet Plage, the nearest beach. I had imagined a lonely shore with a dory for me to row away. Had there been such a boat, the sea was too rough for one pair of hands to pass the breakers. There were children tearing about, having the time of their lives. I sat down with my back against the breakwater and took my tin out of my shoulder bag. Yes, there were my Tuinals. Then Alex came along, sat down beside me, and I began to weep.

Louis had told Austryn where I had gone. Austryn and George Plimpton gave Alex plenty of money.

From the beach, Alex took me to the railway station where he bought two first-class couchettes plus first-class seats on the overnight train to Paris, reserving a table as well in the dining car. Then he telephoned Jane.

We passed the day at the local Turkish baths. I had little to say for myself. I kept repeating: 'I am so sorry. I am so ashamed.' And Alex: 'Say no more. What is there to be ashamed of? What is there to feel sorry for? You are alive, old man.'

The food on the SNCF's *grandes lignes* was cooked and served with style. Alex ordered fine wine of both colours. As we ate the tears ran down my cheeks. The food was so delicious, the movement of the train so comforting, our fellow diners so hand-some, I wished this moment would last for ever.

Jane was waiting for us at Gare d'Austerlitz. 'You looked dreadful, white,' she said. 'Alex was exhausted. I had never seen Alex so tired.'

To this day, I have been afraid to ask either Austryn or Louis what happened between them before Louis told Alex where I had gone. I have never drawn near to suicide again. When Austryn was visiting London recently (1996), we spoke of my trip to Perpignan for the first time.

'You had been in London looking for work. You came to our hotel room and told Muffie that you could not bear to live any more. She thought you were in danger. We were both very fond of you. As was Patrick. As was Alex.

'My brother had just died. Throughout his adult life he had sought dangerous tasks – trimming sequoia tree tops, being buried in Nevada desert cellars to observe the impact of rocket warheads. Then he got what he wanted. The boat he was sailing alone overturned. He drowned.

'I stood outside your hotel all night for three nights running. One morning you had gone. At first, Louis – to whom I went – refused to say where you had gone. He told Alex when I fetched him. When Alex brought you back from Perpignan, he, Dick, Patrick and I clubbed together to provide you with an income of £20 a month. And, well, in next to no time you were your usual rude self. Laughing away as if there was no past, working away at your sonnets that you sent to the *Times Literary Supplement*. And when I asked you why you didn't submit them to *Merlin* you said in an airy way that it was "time I enlarged my readership".'

I COMPLETED my dirty book: then started work on the anthologies.

Perhaps I was too embarrassed to face Alex, or he was tired of me. Either way, I saw less of him. By now he had written two dirty books for Maurice. I disapproved. Not of their contents; of Alex wasting time on hackwork. He dismissed my remarks. He had brains, energy and luck. 'I can do it, old man. You'll see. You'll see. Stop looking down your nose.'

I thought he was wrong. More, it was clear that he had lost interest in a direct relationship between fine writing and politics.

'Chris,' he said, 'I told you my father's *Andorra Star* story. For a while I thought I might make something out of it. I checked the facts. Everyone of Italian extraction in Glasgow knew the truth. Then I saw I couldn't. I did not know how to begin. The disaster had nothing to do with my life. What I write has to come from me, through me, be of my time and place, if it is to have authenticity *for* me.'

'Homer never went to Troy, Dante to Hell, or Shakespeare to Venice,' I said.

'I am the chap you know, old man. Speak to me about me.'

One day when Patrick and I were walking along boulevard Saint-Michel we ran into Alex and Maurice leaving an expensive restaurant. 'They are each other's customers,' Patrick noted.

'Give Maurice his due.'

'The censors are his friends. In 1401 they banned the Bible in English and hanged people for reading it in English. Can you see Girodias publishing an English Bible in 1401? He is a trouble-maker. He dislikes experimental literature.'

'You can hardly call the Bible experimental literature.' We went into Gaït's.

'Do you mind hanging on while I go to the bank?' she said.

'The English Bible *was* experimental. And it was revolutionary. You are no more interested in experimental literature than Maurice.'

'Patrick, get politics into your writing. If that's not experimental, what is?'

A man came in and asked for a copy of *White Thighs*, one of Alex's pornographic novels. I served him while Patrick stated: 'You can hardly expect me to make an exhaustive statement of my position here and now.'

The man wanted to know if *White Thighs* was any good.

'It's a masterpiece,' I assured him. 'At the frontier of erotic adventure.'

'I am not *a priori* loyal to anything,' Patrick continued. 'Person, group, nationality. I do not act from friendship for its own sake. I would not support a bad poem of yours. That is my position.'

The *White Thighs* man only had a F.5,000 note.

'Why not have *The Debauched Hospodar* as well?' I said. *The Hospodar* was a translation by Alex of a pornographic novel by Apollinaire.

He flicked through *The Hospodar* and decided against it.

'Then you'll have to wait until the owner comes back,' I said, adding: 'You can't expect us to have change for a large note.' Then to Patrick: 'How can there be experimental writing that is "above politics"?'

'Are your love poems political – or experimental?'

The *White Thighs* man decided not to buy anything and left.

BACK from the bank Gaït handed me a letter from Alan Pryce-Jones, editor of the *Times Literary Supplement*, saying he accepted my sonnets for publication. My heart leapt. Here was someone who knew about writing, who did not know me from Adam, who was going to print a *whole column* of my work in the best place for new verse to be seen in London. When the Times Newspapers cheque for £14 arrived, I kept it for days.

Then a letter came from the BBC's Third Programme saying that they would like to broadcast the sonnets. My work to be broadcast on the Third! That was something. On the network that had inspired and encouraged me when, how long ago it seemed, I came home from Suez in 1948. In the strange way they have, things were turning in my favour.

A NEW literary magazine appeared in Paris, published from rue Garancière, a prestigious address around the corner from the Tournon. Rumour had it as the work of a few wealthy New Yorkers, not serious chaps, a lightweight affair, like its title, the *Paris Review*. Anyway, who on earth were they going to publish? Give it a couple of issues at the most. It was edited by one George Ames Plimpton.

Austryn, who had been at school with George, doubted his abilities as an editor, saying: 'You will find the *Paris Review*'s editor, his assistant editors, and his contributing editors, etc. on holiday with the bulls at Pamplona, fishing off the coast of Celebes, drifting from penthouse to penthouse in New York, not in the bookshops and cafés of the Quarter.' I saw Alex thinking what I was thinking: Not bad – drifting from one New York penthouse to another.

The rivalry between the magazines did not last; some of us were published in both, their editors became friends.

George was/is romantic, mad on Hemingway, socially adventurous. 'Let's *go* there, let's just *go* there, we'll see what they're like' – whether it happened to be the world's flea-circus chariot-racing championships, or the possibility of wangling an invitation for drinks at the Duchess of Windsor's.

M Y first sight of George was him clambering from an open-topped car outside the Tournon, draped with a long scarf, hat whacked on the back of his head, a skinny six foot-fourer managing to get one leg tangled up with the lead of a dog being taken on its daily, righting himself, apologizing to the dog's owner, and, as he lurched over to our terrace table, dumping a pile of manuscripts under my nose and Alfred Chester's (that marvellous, undervalued writer), before ordering us and himself a drink, asking if we knew the result of the Marciano/Walcott fight.

George concealed his professional determination. He knew what he wanted from his magazine: that it should last. It was he who proposed its soon-to-be-valued 'Art of Fiction' – interviews with celebrated novelists. The *Review's* 150th issue is just out. *Merlin*'s seventh was its last.

'Why don't you interview me, George?' Alfred wanted to know.

'But, Alfred,' George said, 'you're not famous, and I am interested in fame.'

Alfred had a pink, freckled, ginger owl of a face, and a soft, squeaky voice. He was small, with tiny, delicate hands, though the first thing I and, I suppose, everyone else noticed was his wig: orange brown with an oily sheen, sitting unwanted on the top of his head.

'And as far as you, George, are concerned, I'll stay that way,' Alfred said. Then to me. 'George here – in case he hasn't told you already – has currently rejected a story of mine for his, let's face it, not very distinguished *Paris Review* – couldn't you think of a better, even slightly better, title than that, George? – on the grounds that the main character in my story is *too oozy*. What kind of criticism is that, George? *Too oozy* – it's me you're talking about, not the story. George thinks I am ugly.'

'I most certainly do not,' declared George.

'And the other reason for George's ongoing rejection of my oozy story was that George didn't dare carry my thumbnail biography: *Alfred Chester is an impenitent atheistic Jew, a heavy drinker, continually smoking nicotine – with or without marijuana – a pill-popping hairless albino homosexual who cannot keep a lover and an American citizen of exemplary right-wing views.*'

George said: 'What about that other story?'

'"Rapunzel, Rapunzel"? You won't like it.'

'I might,' George offered, hurt.

'I can't read it to you here. It's too noisy.'

As we walked to place Saint-Sulpice and a quiet café, George maintained: 'Don't be surprised if people cross the road when they see us coming. I bear a strong resemblance to Alger Hiss.'

Alfred read 'Rapunzel, Rapunzel' very softly, a relaxed, intelligent reading, his squeakiness working in the story's favour.

When Gwendolyn left the house she turned at once in the direction of Market Square; having taken a triple dose of Forgetfulness Drops, she was certain she would get there. Since death's imminence had been announced to her, she rarely went on specific errands, but when she did, if she were not numbed with Forgetfulness Drops, she almost never reached her destination, for adventure usually fell to her. Others called it disorderly conduct or, more severely, wickedness. Her favourite adventure was to enter a crowded grocery and insist on immediate service, luring the clerks to her with smiles and promises of money; she would then go round the shop, pointing to random tins and packages.

'Four of those,' she would say. 'And six of these. I want twelve one-hundred a thousand of those.' And when the clerks frowned she passed several large bills between her hands and smiled. 'O never mind. Ten will do.'

'I'd like to publish that,' George said.

It was through Alfred that I found the house in London where I lived for twenty-eight years. ' My friends the Sullivans are moving house,' he said. 'Their place would suit you.' Born in 1928, he died alone, in Jerusalem, in 1971.

'I CAME to Paris for an adventure year. 1951. Now it's '55. I have a good job. One day I'll go back. Not yet awhile,' was how the novelist William Gardiner Smith, my first black friend, working on the American desk at Agence France-Presse, explained his arrival in Paris from Philadelphia. Most days when he finished at AFP, Bill came to the Tournon for a Tuborg.

'A favourite saying of my mother's was: "Always take sensible precautions",' Bill tendered. 'I take after her. Trouble is, if you're an American black, you can't.

'I grew up in a quiet part of Philly – blacks, Hispanos, low-income whites. Some rivalry. Touches of colour about it. Nothing too serious. One morning – me around ten – on a not too busy sidewalk, I was about to pass this middle-aged white guy who, instead of swinging slightly to one side as one does when passing, smashed his elbow into my shoulder, so I spun, just keeping my feet, thinking "Excuse *me*", and then, out of nowhere, this same guy launched himself into a stream of racial insults.

'At first, I didn't understand they were aimed at me – except they obviously were. Incredulity was my reaction. I had never, never dreamed I could excite hatred – for that's what it was. He hated me because I was milk-chocolate coloured. Except he didn't hate me. He didn't know a thing about me. So far as he was conerned, "me" didn't exist. Just this black thing in his line of vision.

'I was very frightened. One of our neighbours had been taken to an institution. He escaped, and came back shouting out words like that white man did. He was crazy. But the white man wasn't crazy. In the end he shut up – just like that – looked around himself, and walked on.

'When I got home I began crying. My mother said the world was full of crazy people. I had better take precautions. My step-father said: "Did anyone passing say anything to that man?" "No, sir."

'Nothing like it has ever happened to me again. But from then on I knew it could happen anywhere, at any time, *in my own country*. It was wild power. Outside the law. Outside order. And when I met with it, it was like I was caught in an invisible rip tide. There was nothing I could do.

'Other thoughts followed on. I began to look for prejudice. "He's one, she's one," if a white jumped a line I was in.

'Worse still, maybe there was something wrong with blacks. Perhaps my brain *was* smaller than a white brain? Being a writer, I felt I had to fight these thoughts. I didn't want to write about racism. Then phrases like: "You must fight for your people. You must stand with your brothers and sisters," began coming at me.

'When I asked myself if I felt any kinship with my supposed people, my brothers by colour, the answer was "Not particularly." By the time I was drafted I knew enough about my brother blacks to know that if ever they did come to power, watch your ass, sonny – white or black.

'I'm not like Richard Wright. Not a protest writer. I want to write about other things. Protest of a sort is bound to come into it.'

For the most part Muffie kept her own counsel. Now she said: 'What Bill says about discovering he was black is like discovering you're a woman. A funny sort of a thing that isn't a man. Your life is cut out for you. I'm glad I'm not a black woman married to a black man.'

Bill introduced me to Richard Wright, author of *Native Son*, and to Ollie Harrington, Oliver Wendell Harrington, the satirical cartoonist, the son of a black American father and a Polish–Jewish mother, named after my own father's favourite American author, Oliver Wendell Holmes, a man strong in the fight for emancipation.

Bill and I had been to the public baths for a shower. Soaping in adjacent stalls, I found myself staring at Bill's body. He flicked water back at me, and said: 'Yes, boy. Black *all over*.'

HARRINGTON'S apartment was on the top floor of Robert Duncan's *hôtel*. He sat in his armchair, a big man with thick grey curls, on his easel a cartoon of Bootsie – his Schweik-like, know-all, black character – remarking of Burl Ives (the folk-singer, bullied by Senator McCarthy into ruinous admissions): 'There – he's completely thrown away his chance of a trial on coast-to-coast television, and a twenty-year sentence.'

Bill trusted Harrington's judgement. Shy of discussing his work, Bill had a plan for a novel whose protagonist was to be a black American draftee with absolutely no interest in anything except sex, drugs and money, a man prepared to do, or say, anything to satisfy his immediate wants, successful at it, too, until he is shot dead by accident, caught in a fire-fight between black and white American soldiers, in England, a few days before D-Day.

I could hardly believe my ears. Fire-fights between American soldiers in my country, in wartime? The patriotism roused in me by Austryn's casual rejection of the Peasants' Revolt as a serious political event – 'They were winning. They went home, and got massacred, when their lords told them to' – resurfaced. Yet Bill was no exaggerator.

'Are you sure such things occurred? Are you absolutely sure?'

Friendly-like, they laughed at me

'Oh, Chrissy boy, you are in for some turns, some nasty turns.'

I was in Paris because I felt there was no place for me in London in 1950; because Paris was beautiful; because I hoped to find people like me there. Alex was there, because he was naturally adventurous, and had fallen in love. Austryn and Dick, from a love of France, of French culture. George, from a wish to create something as interesting as had the big names of the Lost Generation. Austryn – speaking for us all – said: 'In France, a writer is esteemed. Feels necessary to the intellectual life of his country.'

'It was the same for Dick Wright,' Bill said, 'and for the rest of us black boys – Chester Himes, James Baldwin, me – with this extra: Paris was a refuge. There was no "Negro neighbourhood", no "Negro cafés", none of that. Being black didn't mean too much.'

After listening to Bill I found myself saying of so-and-so: 'He's a racist. The French are racist.' Bill was angry to hear it. 'Don't you mention racism. Oh, man, you are so stupid. It just kills me to hear you talk racism. You know *nothing*. I am happy in France. Happier than since I was small. When I see Algerians selling carpets and I know the holes they go home to, why not call me a racist? And those Algerians are *French*, man. They are *citizens*. This is their *own country*.'

JOSHUA Leslie, darker than Bill or Richard Wright, came from a middle-class, well-educated Jamaican family, and had about him that air of self-confidence common among English public schoolboys. He was, too, a graduate in mathematics, studying for a doctorate at the Sorbonne. 'Wright is right,' Joshua said. 'Because of my family background I have never faced active prejudice. Do I need to go to Hell to know it is hot? This much is sure: unless you defend yourself against such force, you are lost. The only way to deal with it is to gain political power.'

Bill was disturbed by Joshua. Ollie ignored him. Not so, Wright.

'Don't you give me that "power" talk, Joshua Leslie. Or you, boy' (me). 'None of your so-called *en-ga-jay*. You' (me) 'got nothing to fight for, boy. You are dying for a fight. You want some cause. Some police boy – as silly as you, with more excuse than you – to knock your head in on some demonstration.

'You both are so cheeky, if you were black, and American, you would be dead. Dead as the dead are dead. Just you mind that. Just you mind what I say.'

We did mind. Not as much as we should. Not as much as he did. Then he pulled his beret on to his greying head, put his smart leather paper case under his arm and trudged off down rue Tournon.

An important writer, Richard Wright taught me not to make light of what I know to be wrong. Also, faced with a seemingly overwhelming, amorphous danger, see where it comes from, see what it thinks. This helped me to think about Mengele, and later, Stalin. Once you saw that things like anti-Semitism are ideologies that must be taken seriously, they lose their air of evil triumphant.

Harrington knew more about active politics than any of us. In the 1930s he had been the first United States press spokesman for the now seldom mentioned, but then important, US National Association for the Advancement of Coloured People (NAACP). He was well informed. When alone with him, I returned to the subject of interracial fire-fights between black and white American soldiers in my country, in England.

'There were many such stories,' Harrington said. 'I tried, but I could not get close enough to get facts. You know what armies are like. They produce loyalty – even when the loyalty you feel is against your own interests. It was too shaming to admit. It will come out in time. Nowadays you would have to dig hard and long. I don't want to give offence. Leaving aside the fire-fights, you need look no further than the law your Parliament passed in 1942 accepting the US Visiting American Forces Act that said black GIs could not while in uniform marry white British women. Then there were the black GIs who were charged, and hanged, for rape in your prisons. Rape or no rape – you'll find, if you find out anything, that the evidence was mostly hearsay. The NAACP were approached by the families of those GIs. Some of your newspapers, the *Daily Mirror*, the *Daily Telegraph*, reported the cases.'

Harrington advised Bill against writing a novel with the fire-fights as part of its background.

'You know what people are, Bill. There's some things they

cannot bring themselves to think. Put it in a story – that's it. It's made up. Do it as journalism. As history. It's like Dick Wright says. People like our Christopher here and that Joshua Leslie think us black Americans are just waiting for a chance to rise up and fight for their freedom. The truth is they want to live out their time in peace, plenty and pleasure, man. That is freedom. They're nice people. Easy people. Americans. Easier going than most other Americans.'

On the table next to his easel Harrington kept the lid of a tobacco tin into which he put, or rather laid, the matches he used to keep his pipe going, building them into a two-inch-high stack. Then, still talking, laughing as he went, he carried them over to the waste bucket, carefully, before tipping them in.

'I'll tell you one of my mother's Polish stories,' Ollie said. 'A man is walking along the side of a field when he hears cheep-cheep from a young bird fallen out of its nest. As it's winter he pops the little bird into the side of a new-laid cowpat for warmth, and walks on. "Cheep-cheep-cheep-cheep," goes the little bird. Hearing this, a stoat comes out of its hole and bites the little bird's head off. The moral is: it's not always your enemies who drop you in the shit, and it's not always your friends who get you out. But when you're in it – keep your trap shut.'

PAUL Johnson was a regular at the Tournon. He was the only Englishman I knew at all well in Paris. On leaving the army Paul saw an advertisement: 'Assistant Executive Editor required for International Magazine.' This was *Réalités*, an up-market publication covering business, fashion, travel. Paul got the job. He would come to the Tournon with his flame-haired girlfriend, Jackie, the wife of a Breton count. They gave splendid parties and used to fight in public – Paul often getting the worst of it.

This was before he met his wife-to-be, Marigold. Paul introduced me to Marigold on the boulevard Montparnasse. They were walking hand in hand. It was spring. Paul said: 'This is Marigold. We are to be married. I am incredibly happy.' Then they wandered on.

On the left in those days, he and I got along fine, as we still do. He loved English poetry. He liked to take the opposite side. To make you defend your opinion.

He was the *New Statesman*'s Paris correspondent. Very sturdy stuff. I used to use it in arguments. When he became the *Stateman*'s assistant editor he introduced me there. It was he who – certainly with his editor's, the celebrated Kingsley Martin, approval – four years later published my poem 'To My Fellow Artists', and among the political, rather than the literary pages of the magazine.

'What was his name, that tall American, rather stout, worked as a clerk at US Army Headquarters at Fontainebleau?' Paul asked me twenty years later.

'Bob Silvers.'

'Right.'

'Now editor of the *New York Review of Books*.'

'A very influential publication.'

'Very good, too. Decent politics,' I said. 'Who would have thought big Bob would have become so powerful?'

'That's where you go wrong,' Paul said. 'You are quite inexperienced at judging character. No good at it at all. When Bob Silvers finished work for the day – which was pretty early, you know how things are in the army – he would be on the train and at his table in the Deux Magots by 6 p.m. In one way you are right about him. He was interested in literature. I would say he loved literature. He was equally interested in infrastructure, the politics of literary coteries, about which you knew absolutely nothing at all. Very silly of you. Pretending to yourself that they don't count. I told you to read Johnson. Not Boswell – I know you read him. Read *The Rambler*. Johnson explains how literary society works. As then, as now. Mark my words, Bob Silvers understood literary politics by touch. Naturally. Not in a nasty way, mind you. He was fascinated by such things. Partly, that made him a fine editor.

'The thing about you and your set, Trocchi, Seaver and Co. – the same was true of Plimpton and his set – was your indifference to French society. You knew very few French people. You never learned to read or speak French properly, did you?'

'No.'

'I found that most odd. A mistake.'

'True.'

'You people had an international community. Then there was

Jean, Jean Crouch. Such a kind, clever, young woman. A perfect girlfriend for a poet. Interested in scientists though.'

AT around this time – the end of 1954 – another matter came to a head. Although Senator McCarthy's reign was over, the widespread fear in America that America was still threatened from within by subversives had not died down.

The energy liberated by this fear affected the Paris expatriate community, particularly Richard Wright, Bill and Ollie. Not between themselves. There were unpleasant figures hanging around the Quarter. It is easy for a small group to be infected with suspicions, to become the prey of malicious gossip. This person accused that of betraying a third to the CIA, the FBI, the French security police.

It was difficult for me, an outsider, to see what measurable difference the accusations made. Clearly, though, the atmosphere was spoiled. It was just another burden to which the blacks were subject. Wright had been a thorn in the side of the American government, defending his fellow blacks in the face of prejudice, criticizing white America outside America – rightly so, in my view. Austryn, closer to Bill than anyone, felt it most strongly, could hardly speak of this hostile undercurrent without growling.

I raised the matter with George. For the only time in his life – we are close to this day – he got cross with me, saying I sounded like any other anti-American bore. Usually too quick to rise to a charge I find unjust, I found myself relaxed, saying that I had grown up on American films, songs, singers – black and white. That modern American poetry – Eliot, Pound – meant more to me than modern English poetry. That I did not associate him, or the American people, with the actions of their State Department and the Senate Committees. And regarding my own country's governments, I hoped he would draw the same distinction. I was sure he knew, better than I would ever know, that to be born an American black is to be born subject to very powerful, not wholly conscious, cruel forces.

DIARY SCRAPS:
Lowering and overcast. A day of indecision and doubt. Took refuge by discussing motorbikes with Patrick who is to

leave for Vienna. During the day slept a heavy sweat-soaked
sleep. Woke choking on an imaginary string of plastic objects.

Idled until 7. Went out. Idled in Tournon. Am disgusted by
my 'satire' which has been published in *Nimbus*, a London
literary magazine started by a young man called Tristram
Hull.

What on earth am I so ill-tempered about? England? No
one has harmed me. John Coleman came into the Tournon about
9 p.m. He has applied to become the *New Statesman*'s film critic.
In the meantime, new out of Cambridge, he is writing a book for
Maurice and has been appointed business manager of *Merlin* by
Alex. He said: 'You'll get no criticism here, Logue. You're scared
of London. It's cosy sitting here thinking you are better than
everybody else.' I took this very badly. I began to shout at him.
The Tournon was almost empty.

Then Simon Vinkenoog arrived with a young Roman senator
lookalike arming a blonde-goddess style woman dressed in a
black raincoat, six-inch white heels and a white Homburg.
Simon ordered *fines*. 'This is Hugo and Elly Claus,' he said. 'Just
arrived from Rome.

'No,' Elly said, 'we have just been thrown out of the Ritz.'

'No, no, no, asked to leave,' Hugo said. 'I will tell you
everything. I had a big cheque from my book *The Duck Hunt*.
We decided to go from the train for a drink at the Ritz. Who is in
the foyer – very nicely dressed? – Hans Oosterman, a son of my
father's best friend, Eric – owner of the best hotel in Ostend. Very
rich. Hans is learning the business

'"Oh, it's Hugo Claus, our biggest young author," Hans says.
"I have read *The Duck Hunt*. Exemplary. Have you come to stay
at the Ritz?"

'His words carried me away. I heard myself saying: "Yes. But
I must have a white piano in my room." In a moment it was
done. We were on the first floor drinking champagne. A white
piano is brought in. I played and Elly sang: "These Foolish
Things". Beautiful.

'After we had made love I telephoned for a pedicure and Elly
had her hair done. Then we had spring lamb with redcurrant jelly
and Jersey Royals in the hotel restaurant.

'As we were returning to our room, Hans re-approached us.

He had been asked to establish how we, as new guests without luggage, were going to settle our bill. I showed my cheque. He said it had to be money or travellers. I told him it was all his fault. He had disgraced the Belgian flag. A fine young author and his beautiful wife had been humiliated. There were tears in his eyes. Nevertheless we had to leave.'

The Clauses were companionable. More of them anon. Another scrap:

Met Jane in place Saint-Sulpice. She will move upstairs into the little flat Dick and Jeanette have left. Jane said she wanted to be more private, to live her own life. She was tired of living in a storeroom that was also *Merlin*'s office with people calling at all hours, never leaving, expecting to be given coffee. As well, Alex has relinquished editorial control. Austryn was his co-editor. There was an editorial committee – Patrick, Dick, and the poet Robert Creely. Maurice had become the magazine's legal owner. He asked Jane to pay for the next issue, Spring '55. This will mean her going home to get the money. I said he was making a fortune. 'He never liked me,' Jane said. She asked me if I was going back to London. I said soon.

PATRICK introduced me to Beckett in 1954. In cold weather Beckett wore a windproof half-length overcoat, its fur collar making him appear like a seventeenth-century North European aristocrat/scholar. In summer he wore grey: a grey sports jacket, grey trousers, a grey roll-neck sweater. Tall, gaunt, ascetic, full of energy, he walked fast, his eyes about him, moving gracefully through crowds. His days of poverty were over. His luxury was to travel first class on the métro. As you descended beside him – you had to look slippy, he went down the stairs at speed – he would remove two tickets from his *carnet* giving you yours with a nod. He treated you like an equal, though you knew you were not. He was friendly, generous, always asking after others, particularly Patrick. 'How is he? Is he working at his own work? I don't want to take him away from his own work. We worked at writing my book again. This time in English. I could not have done it alone. I needed someone who knew English as I once did.'

Beckett loved Samuel Johnson. He was always referring to Johnson. 'Rasselas is a grand book. He could be rude – but he had a kind heart. Towards the end of his life he suffered from dropsy. Water was blowing him up. When the doctors would not drain more of it off, he asked his servant, Barber – a negro, they were together for years – for a knife and stabbed and stabbed his own legs.'

I was surprised that he thought little of Eliot's poetry. 'He is hiding. You never feel there is a man there. He keeps on telling you what you already know.'

'That's not true of Prufrock.'

'I'll look at it again.'

Beckett could be sharp, impatient. He was very interested in a dream Descartes was said to have had in which the philosopher saw himself floating above the world. As well as the incident, I liked the idea of Descartes hovering about, taking notes – as I supposed him to be doing. Then I forgot about it until I met Beckett again. 'What was that story you told me about Descartes' dream?' I asked, keeping up with him as he strode along. He repeated the story at length, then said: 'Don't ask me again.' A few steps later, he said: 'You can ask me again if you wish. I'd rather you didn't.'

Beckett rated Balzac.

'You know his house in the rue Visconti?'

'Yes.'

'He worked on the first floor. On either side of his table there was a hole in the floor. On the floor below, his printers.

'When he finished a page he dropped it through the hole on his right and began the next. Later, his pages came up through the hole on his left as proofs to be corrected, dropped back down, then printed and published.'

'Gosh . . .'

Then Beckett would look straight at you for an instant, saying nothing. Then: 'Balzac died at fifty-one. Alone. His wife left him to die. His friend Victor Hugo went round and felt under the blankets for Balzac's hand, and pressed it, but there was no answering pressure. He had begun to decompose before he died. Think of that.

'When they went next morning to take his death mask, his nose fell off while they were applying the plaster. So no death mask. He was too far gone.'

'Do you believe that?' Patrick asked me.

'Yes. Don't you?'

'I don't know.'

'We could check it.'

'Yes.'

We never did.

The interested world knows the power of Beckett's work. What struck me was his character. He was, if one can have such a word, anegoistic.

Anthony Cronin, Beckett's eminent critical biographer, cites Jérôme Lindon:

> I do not dare to express the enormous admiration and affection that I have for him. He would be embarrassed and on that account I should be so too. But I would like this to be known, and only this: that in all my life I have never met a man in whom co-exist together in such high degree, nobility and modesty, lucidity and goodness. I would never have believed that anyone could exist who is at the same time so real, so truly great, and so good.

OUR little group was breaking up. Alex had had enough of editing. He was to leave for Greece. 'It's over between us,' Jane said in a sad, casual way. 'Austryn and Dick will get *Merlin* 7 out,' which they did. Austryn then buying a plot of land in the hills above Nice and building a house on it, Dick returning to New York – whither George planned to take the *Paris Review* – and where he ran the Grove Press.

Before any talk of such things, George resolved that Jane, Alex, he and I would attend the Bal des Quatz' Arts, an annual rag ending at the Salle Wagram, where, following a parade through the streets, behind locked doors, the art students of Paris elected a beauty queen and danced, etc., until dawn. This year's theme was 'Ancient Egypt'.

At 10 p.m, painted gold, with blue mascara around our eyes, Jane bikinied, Alex, George and me in baby-boxers, we arrived at the Salle Wagram. The noise was overwhelming. The Salle had a balcony divided into straw-strewn stalls, on three sides. Along the fourth side was a temporary stage, from which the Paris Pompiers' brass band – dressed as characters from *Ubu Roi* – were playing the Triumphal March from *Aïda*, while the judges of the tableau, and the beauty-queen competitions, sprayed bottles of sparkling cider over the dancers, beating off with mops those of the 1,500 present who tried to clamber up among them.

Tubs of wine were emptied and replaced. The judging began at midnight. Spotlights travelled along the balcony stalls, pausing at those occupied by tableauists. Each tableau featured young women, naked but for feathers and body paint. All received tremendous applause except from Alex, who began to boo and shout: 'Action! Give me some action!' Booed back, he took Jane aside and they decided that when the spotlights returned for the winning round they would make love, naked, on a trestle table pulled forward from the back of the stall, thereby winning first prize – a massive papier-mâché phallus festooned with pigs' bladders.

I covered the table with straw. Jane slipped off her bikini and reclined. Then, while George fanned her, as the lights swept round, Alex, naked and erect, leapt on to the table, fists clenched ready to beat his chest before the action proper.

Alas, as he leapt, he forgot that the stall's plank roof was only seven feet above its floor, and, BAM! his head hit it, and he collapsed on to Jane, stunned, while George and I fanned like mad and the crowd booed with happiness.

At 4 a.m. we got a lift to place de la Concorde. There was no one about, so we climbed into a fountain and washed the gold off, scrubbing each other down with our shorts. I thought we would have to walk to the Quarter. But Alex had a F.5,000 note in his sock and we found a taxi.

IN Autumn 1955, soon after Maurice published *Molloy*, Beckett arrived unannounced at the storeroom. Alex and Jane were packing things up while Patrick and I hung about. Having asked if we would care to accept them, Beckett unwrapped a brown-paper parcel and distributed copies of his two books of poems, *Whoroscope*, from 1930, and, from five years later,

Echo's Bones. 'I was having a clear-out and found them in a box. There was no great demand for them,' he said, sounding pleased.

I had £30 for my move to London. If Maurice gave me half my advance on the *Ballads*, that would make £100.

'I have to have tests,' Maurice told me. 'A doctor has arrived from Washington. He has invented a urinometer. He has ana-lysed President Eisenhower's water. I dread to think of his bill. You want money, of course. Where would any of you be without Olympia?'

1956 – 1966

ON MY RETURN HOME

JEAN Crouch invited me to stay until I found somewhere of my own. She was editing *Girl* magazine – the female equivalent of *Eagle* – and living with James Hayes, a psychoanalyst, in Park Square East, Regent's Park – white-painted, stucco, wide windowed, heavy-fronted houses occupied by accountants, gynaecologists, and company lawyers.

James resembled a heron in a dark suit. Leaning forward, cigarette held at arm's length, the fingers of his other hand in his waistcoat pocket, he peered down at me in a patient, interested fashion. A good-tempered man, James regarded his fellow humans much as a vet his suffering animals, always ready to tie up a paw, administer a whiff of laughing gas, or, in my case, ask embarrassing questions like – us having settled at a restaurant table – 'What is making you so impatient? You can't be hungrier than you were a minute ago.'

My room at Park Square East was empty apart from a bed, a table, a chair and the books I had brought up from Bournemouth. I dressed out of army surplus shops: jerseys with shoulder slits for epaulettes, dark green denims. I favoured cookhouse jackets, their buttons attached by split pins (no sewing). James was not charging me for my room.

I had Maurice's advance. For Jean, I wrote strip-cartoon lives of exemplary British women: Florence Nightingale, Edith Cavell, Emmeline Pankhurst. I hoped to find material for Vicarion's *Ballads* in the British Library's Private Case – as its dirty-book section was called. To satisfy the Library's admissions department Alan Pryce-Jones gave me a letter on *Times Literary Supplement* paper saying that my subject, 'clandestine vernacular poetry', required my having a Reader's ticket. In I went.

And at once was devitalized by the firework-gasp factor of the famous – now abandoned – Reading Room. Warm, light, lofty, a cranium. The sight of the 28,000 books shelved below and above the catwalk circling the forty-feet-high drum wall that supported its dome, through whose lancets daylight tarried on the hundred-plus volumes of the catalogue, while, from the central desk, the superior gaze of the librarians commanded the readers, reminded me of my ignorance of everything, as well as of my disreputable cause.

I felt defeated, and left. Better beat a retreat to Bournemouth and work as a beach photographer.

Restored by a cup of tea, plus a buttered bun, I returned, ordered my titles, and whiled my wait away by browsing the catalogue.

LONDON had changed. It was still greyish by day, underlit at night. But there were signs of reinvigoration: black faces to be seen, tower cranes at work, new chrome-framed shop-windows. The static-water tanks, the stairways and bedrooms open to the sky, had vanished. Though not the dogshit.

Chiefly, it was the mood that differed. If London lacked the gaiety or the colour of Paris – a city that set about cleaning its public buildings the day the Germans fled – the marks of the war were fast fading.

From Paris, I had not observed the heroic and successful effort made by the British to release themselves from the material disadvantages of their past. My father's world was gone, and he, for one, would not have mourned its passing. There was a feeling of confidence in the air. What happened to Britain in the re-nowned 1960s – for me, the period between 1956 and 1970 – came from this act of national will: the creation of the welfare state.

I felt lonely, not afraid. London had no equivalent of the Latin Quarter. In Paris I had always known where friends were to be found, and while I lived there, I made, at most, ten telephone calls. In London people lived far apart. Charles Fox was here, working as a music critic for the BBC, writing the sleeve notes for LPs, reviewing. Still, one didn't pop over from Regent's Park to South Kensington on the chance of finding him in.

Although wary of drunks, I used to drop in to the French House in Soho – the haunt of artistic drinkers – when I ran out of Gauloises. Once there, you had nowhere to sit. Getting to the bar was hard work. When you reached it, it was awash with spillage. The customers shouted at, and occasionally punched, each other. There was no question of reading a book. As a

Parisian I was accustomed to having my own table and chair, a waiter, peace to read, write, study the passers-by, chat. London did have quiet pubs, though there the ethos was emphatically anti-book. You were supposed to be drinking, not reading. Certainly not writing.

In Paris you went out to get out of your hotel room. Here, people had their own flats, or shared them. I needed a place of my own. A house, preferably. And when I found it, I would not be sharing it. The thought never crossed my mind.

Strong, sexual urges never left me. I converted them to sex in the head; fantasies, dismissed – momentarily – by masturbation. I knew this for poor stuff. It meant my work was missing a certain kind of truth, a gravity. I was unwilling to commit myself to an adult relationship. The acceptance of another's demands and needs. The – in a way – death sentence it amounts to. You give your life. Not on a barricade, or in a cavalry charge, but humbly, as the world does. You have something more than your own life to lose.

Not that I had ever considered family life, marriage, children, regular employment, as a way for me. Rather, I told myself: to be able to stay in bed until midday, to spend all day in the library, or just mooching about the place, is worth £10,000 (now £100,000) a year. I seldom stayed that late in bed – though I did a lot of mooching about.

Intellectual quarrels I enjoyed – low-powered games that they were. Emotional confrontations I feared.

Seeing me downcast, unhappy, puzzled, James said in his amiable tenor: 'Love means quarrelling and fucking. You dislike the farmyard side of sex. The sloshing about. The smells. What you would like, if we could provide it and you were rich enough to pay for it, is geisha sex. Let us go to my bank and open an account in your name with that BBC cheque you got.'

ONE day on leaving the Reading Room I decided to visit the bookshop owned by Mr David Archer, a poetry specialist. I had brought a few copies of *Wand and Quadrant* from Paris. My next volume, *Devil, Maggot and Son*, was due later in the year. I needed a London distributor. Maurice had sent me a note to say that he was reprinting Vicarion's *Limericks*. If I went to Old

Compton Street his 'British Empire Distributor', Mr Cliff, would give me £50.

On the walk from Bloomsbury to Soho I saw KEEP THE ROPE painted on the wall of a school. The abolition of hanging was to be debated by the House of Commons. In the Lords, Dr Fisher, the Archbishop of Canterbury, had declared it was mistaken to regard the death penalty as un-Christian.

Dirty bookshops were much the same then as now. Smallish rooms, scrubbed floorboards, walls lined to the ceiling with same-height shelves, plus display space for the photographic material. At the far end, a bead curtain, through which, as it tickers, the proprietor's assistant soft-steps to make a sale. In my case, the assistant, after scanning Maurice's Olympia Press letterhead, directed me to the basement.

Mr Cliff had wiry, ginger-grey hair. He filled his blue suit. He was reading the *Marriage Gazette*, a newsletter for those seeking spouses. He was a specialist in works on bondage, spanking, torture. On the wall above his desk were photographs of Hitler surrounded by Nazi notables: 'The only honest politician,' Mr Cliff assured me, as he counted out my notes. For the first time I began to feel qualms at having written a dirty book.

It was Simon Vinkenoog who got *Devil, Maggot and Son* published. Simon was working in the stationery supplies office of UNESCO's Paris headquarters. He had invited me over – after working hours – to help myself to whatever writing materials I required. I took a lot. I used up the last of three large balls of parcel string in 1996.

Shortly before I left Paris Simon told me that the reputable Amsterdam publisher Alexandre Stols had been annoyed when the weekly *Elsevir* declared there was no poetry worth the name being written in Holland or Belgium. 'I met Stols when he was on his way to Ecuador or Guatemala, I'm not sure which, to organize a state publishing house with UNESCO's help,' Simon continued. 'He had read what Hans Andraeus, Rudy Kousbroek and Claus were writing and scattered contracts all around. Hugo stayed in his room and wrote a book in three days. I had a copy of your *Devil, Maggot and Son* manuscript, and Stols took it. Then he went to South America where he caught a bug and died.

'Most publishers would have been happy to dump the poets with the death of the proprietor – or perhaps it was his son. Not Stols Ltd. They fulfilled the terms of all our contracts to the letter. And very good-looking books they were.'

Emerging from Mr Cliff's basement I made my way through Soho to find David Archer's shop in Greek Street. His, and Mr Cliff's, were at opposite ends of bookselling.

Cliff's shop smelt of carbolic, the customers did not look at each other. David's was open, fresh, friendly, with people standing about, talking, trying to catch the eye of the black-haired, sumptuous beauty, whose name I soon learnt was Henrietta Bowler, working the coffee machine that stood on one end of the shop's counter, assessing new customers in a loud, always-on-the-verge-of-laughter voice: 'What's your name? Have you come to buy a book? Or borrow some money? That's David over there. The only gentleman you're likely to meet in this part of London.'

The ceiling of David's shop was covered with portraits of poets, historical and contemporary, chosen by David and the Italian graphic designer Germano Facetti, who had pinned and pasted them up, and so became the man who restyled Penguin Books – a change initiated by Penguin's Founder, Allen Lane, after he visited David's shop and admired Germano's ceiling.

A year before Italy made a separate peace with the Allies (1943), Germano, the seventeen-year-old son of a Naples furniture maker, together with a few friends, armed themselves with shotguns and 'arrested' the crew of a German anti-aircraft battery, making off with several boxes of their hand grenades. A week later they were rounded up. For which they were deported to Mauthausen-Gusen death camp, until it was liberated 1945.

David, now quite forgotten, was a man of importance where poetry was concerned. Nervous, with a mild stutter, never still, always anxious to help others, courtly in his ways, David, the homosexual son of a Wiltshire landowner who hated him, gave his life, together with the fortune he inherited, to poets and to their work, being the first to publish collections by Dylan Thomas, George Barker, David Gascoyne and W. S. Graham. Tristram Hull – he of *Nimbus* – was David's assistant, for Henrietta came and went as she pleased with this poet or that painter.

David was like my bookseller friend-to-be, Bernard Stone. Both preferred to give books away rather than sell them. If you asked to buy a particular volume, David would say: 'Oh, please, do you mind. I need that for the window. Try Better Books.' Then, fearing he had offended, he would rush to the nearest off-licence and buy you a bottle of wine. He was thin, grey haired, with large eyes set deep in a delicate face, smiling and blinking. He died alone, in poverty.

Tristram – lofty, well-built – had a casque of wavy brown hair, hands that fluttered, a big arched nose, and a falsetto giggle streaming out from behind gravestone teeth. He had that mysterious quality business people call 'confidence'. That is to say, when Tristram said a thing you were inclined to believe him. He was prudent. 'Oh, I shouldn't do that if I were you.' Or: 'Well, if you say that, he'll never speak to you again. He is vain to a degree. You know what writers are like.' Other people's problems did not frighten him. He liked to solve them.

A customer of David's who looked like a schoolboy wearing a three-piece suit was going through the shop's magazine rack. 'Let me introduce you,' Tristram said, his Adam's apple – it was prominent – bobbing up and down. 'I have just published his play *Don't Destroy Me* in *Nimbus*. Remarkable – for a sixteen-year-old. He's a tailor's apprentice. He made the suit he's wearing.'

This was the playwright, and future novelist, Michael Hastings. Michael's black hair bristled upwards. Now and then he ran a comb through it. His eyes darted about. A handsome lad. Henrietta came over for a close look.

'Watch this,' Tristram whispered.

But Henrietta's (to me) exciting *décolletage* made no impression on M. Hastings. Nor had Brecht's play *Mother Courage*. 'That's the one about an old bag who drags a barrow around Europe, isn't it?' he said. 'I didn't like it. No point to it. I want to write a play about a tennis champion' – saying these (to me) rather discreditable things in a light, friendly way, backed up by a grin. Then: 'Oh I've got to run.' And without more ado he hurried away out of the shop. Henrietta, neglected, sniffed, put her nose in the air and went back to her coffee machine. 'That'll be a girl,' Tristram predicted. 'They can't resist him.'

After closing the shop David took Tristram and me to the Colony Room, an artists' drinking club at the top of a flight of wooden stairs that made me think of the brothel in Rome. By the bar, a group stood around the painter Francis Bacon, then a rising star. Bacon's face was broad, moony, his voice, a whine. He was overpouring champagne into his admirers' glasses. He did not return David's deferential hello. One of his lot – you saw, instantly, they were a 'lot' – was remembering: '... then Lady Helen caught herself on the rope in front of Francis's pictures and Francis said: "Watch out, that's to keep the paint off the mink!"' And everyone laughed and laughed, except for Bacon, who continued to pour.

Outside in Dean Street, and scattered through Soho, there were art-school people about. Seventeen- to nineteen-year-olds. The boys wore donkey jackets. The girls black stockings, hoop earrings, black or mauve eye make-up, their hair in ponytails, or long and straight curtains – leaving no more to be seen than a tip of the nose or a flash of lipstick. And there were many less immediately placeable types, all young, people who came, so to speak, from nowhere – 'They just get an education grant and loaf about,' some said – standing outside jazz clubs, in the squares, laughing and whispering. Their self-confidence was manifest. For the first time in my life I felt: These are the young, and I'm not one of them.

ONCE a week I would take the 31 bus from Chalk Farm to Charles's room near South Kensington Underground Station. In different circumstances Charles would have become a scholar, or, perhaps, a spy of the listening-in kind. Poetry, jazz and murder were his subjects. Derek Drescher, among the BBC's principal music producers, said: 'When I needed to know the name of the saloon pianist substituting for Tom Turpin on the Rosebud Café's version of Scott Joplin's "Maple Leaf Rag" I discovered it was quicker to call Charles than go through the catalogues.'

It did not occur to Charles that he was eccentric. He had what might be called a mixed relationship to life. He kept a suspicious eye on it. He did not care for Abroad. Nothing personal. Even Scotland was dangerously foreign. Mind you, if it was necessary, one could reach Scotland by bus. Bus, after foot, being Charles's preferred mode of transport.

He loved newspapers. Always prompt for a train, he would take his seat, park his set of dailies beside him, cross his legs at the ankles, and beginning with *The Times*, start to read. When he reached the bottom of sheet 2 he tore sheet 1 off. Likewise with each page until he reached the end of the paper. Then he began on the next.

Charles had an instinct for discovering unusual poems. Peter Clarke said: 'I found a copy of *The British Prison Ship*, 1781, by Philip Freneau and took it round to Charles. After we examined it, he roamed his shelves and produced a copy of *The Convict's Appeal* by Bernard Barton, 1818. Several months passed before he showed me his rarest find, *The Washerwoman at Petersfield / Woman's Labour / a poem / 1736*.'

Charles and I passed our evenings in London as we had done in Bournemouth, reading poems, playing records – only now they were white-label acetates, his review copies. Then I would ride home on the 31, often the sole upper-deck passenger, through the unfashionable darkness of Notting Hill Gate.

I did not want to rely on Charles for company. In my mind, Charles meant Bournemouth. Until I had established myself in London, I was nervous about Bournemouth. In any case, I wanted to keep clear of my mother.

THERE was precious little for Vicarion's *Ballads* in the Private Case. I assumed that *Devil, Maggot and Son* had died with Stols. Then a parcel arrived from Amsterdam containing twenty copies of the published book. It was better looking than *Wand and Quadrant*. Creamy paper, the text set in elegant Romulus. As I read them my heart sank. They were so arty. Who on earth could be interested in such stuff? They raised a recurring wish: that my head might somehow be attached to my neck by a sort of bayonet fixture, easily removable for a thorough clean and a good polish before being locked back on.

I put ten copies in my shoulder bag and schlepped around to see if Better Books would stock a few. Likewise with David Archer. And who knows, David – that is to say, Tristram – might have sold a copy or two of the *Wand and Quadrant*s I left with him.

Better Books took three. Looking out of their window in the middle of negotiations I saw Michael Hastings signalling: 'Come out, come out.' He was dressed in a black suit, and spotted bow tie. Very smart. On the pavement, instead of suggesting we go somewhere for a coffee, he declared: 'I'm just off to the Royal Court Theatre. They're going to put on a play of mine. I thought you should be one of the first to know.'

Of my new book, David said: 'Oh, please leave them. Happy to have them. I really think we should pay you for them now, don't you, Tristram? See what's in the till.' Tristram looked up at the ceiling. Not a single copy of *Wand and Quadrant* had sold. One had been stolen. David remembered my talking about the *Ballads*.

'I say,' he said, 'that book of dirty rhymes you're doing for Olympia. A fellow was in the other day, a Captain Brown. Likes poetry. Has a very dirty mind – please don't repeat that. He has a copy of the *Royal Marines Song Book*. He left his number. Tristram?'

As well, Tristram had the number of a young man called Shakespeare who wanted me as one of several new poets he was interviewing. Shakespeare lived in Hampstead. I told him lies, claiming my prison sentence was given for gun-running, that in 1949 I became the only registered pauper in the parish of Poole, that I was versed in political thought, a student of Marxism. Looking along his shelves I spotted the first (and last) copy of *Lust* seen in other hands than my own. 'I wrote that,' I confessed. 'You mean that *you* are Count Palmiro Vicarion?' A truth he found difficult to believe, and omitted from the published interview.

Captain Brown lent me his copy of the *Royal Marines Song Book*. It contained the items the great library lacked.

A Third Programme producer, Mr Carne-Ross, accepted some poems of mine. The name was familiar. At Broadcasting House's reception desk an elegant middle-aged lady sent a uniformed attendant to lead me from one of its glass and marble hall's broad sofas, down long tan carpet-covered corridors to a studio. There, Carne-Ross, dark-haired, dark-eyed, with an inquisitive nose and a cautionary tone of voice, pipe in one hand, introduced himself.

When the recording was made, Donald, as I grew to know him, invited me for a drink. Not knowing why – unsociable fellow that I was – admiring and respecting the Third Programme as I did, I declined. In operation, I suppose, was the part of me that enjoys being an outsider of the kind who, not always, yet in any case far too often, is inclined to anticipate rejection from those he associates with insiderism, the conventional paths to success, but is, at the same time, ambitious to succeed in that very world.

Donald – with his invitation – was, of course, a living rebuke to this sort of prejudice. In fact, with one or two unimportant exceptions, those who have chosen a more conventional path than my own have always been ready to help me, often beyond what was called for.

Dimly, I remember making some kind of excuse to myself about needing to get home to talk to James. To tell the truth, I was worried lest I outstay my welcome at Park Square East. Since the J. Walter Thompson episode I had been avoiding Terence Conran. I knew he disliked failure. Then I called at a coffee bar he owned. He was working the machines.

'Well,' he allowed, 'if you really have nowhere to go you can have my groundfloor front room for three months at £3 per week, payable one week in advance. I'll supply the rent book.'

My stuff had been piling up. James drove it over.

For the first time in months I met Alex at a party in Kensington where we knew each other better than we did our fellow guests. We smoked his Gitanes.

'I'm going to live in New York, take heroin and write a textbook for dope fiends, old man. I want to cut off my retreat,' he said. I began to complain.

'Stop complaining. Not long ago you tried to take your own life. Perhaps you owe your life to me. I didn't say thank goodness Chris's misery will soon be over. While talking to me – though how much you talk to yourself about them, I wonder – you talk about Stalinism, Auschwitz, horrors with nothing to do with you except they stop you thinking about why you turned killer. For that is what suicides are – yes? And now I'm in your mill of complaints over a chemical you know nothing of.

'Rather than say we will lose contact, why not accept my

decision to take drugs as testimony to the courage and creativity of my spirit? As a friend? Someone who may need your help one day. Who is to say that my chemicals will not lead me to write a fine work?

'I propose to use heroin wisely. My consumption will be controlled. I shall be in a position to ask that my drug experiences become a part of public deliberations. It is indeed a horrible world where a Jew has to go to Auschwitz. And surely, Chris, me lying stupefied in a small room in an unfashionable part of New York is better than me asserting my rights over others in the House of Commons?'

'Compared to the vulture the crow is a pretty bird.'

'So I have heard you say, dear Chris. And what is your position? An anarchic leftist with an overdose of Catholic guilt? I was the first person to publish you, and probably the first to tell you what it is you *don't* like talking about: i.e., sex.

'I am looking for a vantage point. High art, low art – it doesn't matter. Falsifying is bad art. Don't fill up your verse with moral judgements from a cushion provided by the art lovers of an overdeveloped country. My chance is in drawing a contrast between one particular way of living and another general way. Myself as my subject. I, too, want to change the world.'

What he said to me then, regarding myself, was the truth. Few friends can do, let alone will do, as much.

Trocchi was charming in those days. Mostly, I avoid charming people. The kind whose faults bring their excuses with them. Who let you think you think alike, when you do not. Who, while talking to you of a subject, have another subject in mind.

Alex's charm was not like this. It lay in his critical acceptance of oneself. A willingness to help, to share his powers. He had a sensitivity towards others. What he liked, and what I disliked, was intimacy.

'You have never got your fucking right, have you, old man?' he said while we were having our supper on the train on our way back to Paris from Perpignan. 'You have to get over that.

'I'll tell you a secret. I'm having an affair with –' mentioning one of the *Paris Review*'s young American women helpers whom I knew, and had fancied. Miserable as I was at that moment, envy and jealousy flooded up.

'Now, don't go cold on me, Chris,' Alex said, laughing gently. 'Your tears bring me closer to you than your frowns.' Then: 'As a matter of fact, she' – the *Review* girl – 'is rather keen on you. She told me so when we were talking about the men she had had – and she's had quite a few. I'm not sure but I think there's a chance that, if I put it to her in the right way, she, you and me might make a threesome. You can watch her and me fucking, and then you can fuck her. She likes a lot of sex. If needs be I'll take your cock in my hand and ease it into her cunt. And a very sweet, tasty cunt it is. Then I'll leave you two to get on with it.'

But no, I wouldn't.

An hour after I arrived at the Kensington do we parted in bad spirits, me cross, Alex out of patience, not to see each other again for eight years, in a police court.

WHEN I told June Mary – whom you will meet – of Alex's offer, she said: 'When I was seven my middle-class parents let me play with the village boys. First it was "Mummies and Daddies" and then it was, well, we didn't have a name for it, but I was sucking the boys' cocks almost on a daily basis. I had very little idea what it really meant, just that I shouldn't mention it. Later, when I did know, I was jolly glad I had done it. It made things a lot easier for me at twenty.'

FEELING at home in London increased my restlessness. There was no question of my taking the underground to Chelsea and of walking up and down the King's Road hoping to meet people from the artistic world, as I had done in 1949.

Theoretically, my political/social ambitions were untrammelled. I was on home territory. Everything was possible. In Paris, the thought of writing a play, or printing a poster, or taking political actions – other than talking – was out of the question. I began to read and – like my father – clip newspapers. There were some champion stories: 'Astronomer Royal blacks his eye on telescope optic', 'Councillors cling to sewer'. And my top teeth started to ache again. It was February 1956.

At James's to collect my letters, I found one from Alfred

Chester to say that the Sullivans were moving and I should go and see them as soon as possible. The second was from Peter Russell, now 'Bookseller & Publisher' of Tunbridge Wells.

Hearing of *Devil, Maggot and Son*, Russell had asked Stols Ltd to print a small English edition for him. Did I mind coming down to sign them?

He was still stylish, now rather portly. What had been his enviable library was now his stock. I said my book no longer pleased me. In future my work would be politically committed. Those who did not work did not deserve to eat.

'What are you going to do with someone like my mother?' Peter wanted to know. 'She lives comfortably on her income at a small residential hotel in the New Forest. When her bills are paid she has little over. A new guest, Mrs Thompson, with more money than my mother, arrived and built a private lavatory next to her room. "How lucky you are being able to build a private lavatory for yourself," my mother said. "Ah, but *you* have two sons," Mrs Thompson replied.'

We looked at his stock. 'I was going to offer you an advance of £20 against sales,' Peter said. 'On the other hand, I've got a 1929 *Encyclopaedia Britannica* at £24. £1 per volume.'

'Will you post it to me?'

'What became of *Nine*?' I asked as he took me to the train.

'We have an issue out soon. Our last, maybe. Money . . .' he said. 'You remember my co-editors, Fletcher and Carne-Ross?' – *that* was where I heard the name – 'They have jobs. Rather like me.'

AT the station I bought an evening paper and read the arts pages and entertainment advertisements on the way back to London. Artistically speaking, the creation of the welfare state had, so far, changed nothing. The theatre, cinema, exhibitions of paintings by Laura Knight, Jack Yeats and Augustus John – there was no such thing as a 'poetry scene' – had a contented, self-satisfied air that reflected, perhaps inexactly, but closely enough, the taste and sensibility of middle-class England of 1939.

The beautiful young Queen rode by in her coach. The Guard changed at Buckingham Palace. Fashion was imposed from above. In any case, most people were hardly touched by fashion. The models were often aristocrats, young women earning a few extra pounds, while the photographers were gentlemen.

There were glamorous war films: *Ill Met by Moonlight* (agents and partisans), *In Which We Serve* (Noël Coward as Captain D: 'If they had to die, what a grand way to go!'), *The Wooden Horse* ('All the suspense I care to take' – *Sunday Chronicle*). Terence Rattigan wrote psychological comedy; Christopher Fry, poetic. John Masefield was poet laureate; J. B. Priestley was a sage. There was a comfortable, nothing-too-serious, mildly cultivated flow of amusements.

Perhaps my dissatisfaction was self-born. Or I could not face up to the demands of steady, regular work. My youth was gone. I had not shown the sustained concentration necessary to produce an extended poem.

I had sworn that, as soon as I had enough money, I would find a dentist who would take all my top teeth out – no inspections, probes or drillings, simply *out* – send me home with a mixture of decent, sore-soothing, pleasure-giving drugs.

James knew the right man. With dentures, £120. I had £80.

'Don't you own a wad of letters from Ezra Pound?' Tristram said. 'Your one-time god, so to speak? You didn't throw them away, did you?'

'No.'

'How many are there?'

'I'm not sure. Thirty?'

'I can get you a £ per Pound for them.'

'They're only typed – bar one. Which I'm not selling.'

'That doesn't matter.'

Tristram got Pound's letters. I got the money, my extraction and an upper set.

All the same, I felt helpless. Weeks slid by. I stayed in my room. People who went to the theatre, or to galleries, or who read, had what they wanted. I might as well return to France and help Austryn – he and Muffie had parted – to build his house in the hills above Nice.

Then, as they do, things started to change.

ONE morning as I was walking through Soho, Danny Halperin, a friend from the Tournon, called my name from somewhere above my head. Occupying the flat from whose window he had seen me was Annie Ross, then singing with the Count Basie band. Her other guest was a skinny, pale, long-legged, skull-faced man wearing a green suit, a pink bow tie, and a frilly purple shirt. I had scarcely heard of the *Observer*, let alone of its theatre critic, Kenneth Tynan, as Annie introduced him. Ken (the style he preferred) lay back in his chair, a cigarette between the third and fourth fingers of one hand, a stream of opinions, gossip and ambitious plans, broken by an occasional stutter, rushing from between his lips.

Unfazed by my ignorance of his position, he jumped from topic to topic. Did I think Arthur Miller's marrying Marilyn Monroe would improve them both? Perhaps we should give up art (Ken, rightly, thought of criticism as creative work; of himself as an important contributor to the art of theatre), and go to Alabama to support Martin Luther King's bus boycott?

I relished his confidence and, in an instant, he restored mine. How pleasant it was to meet someone who thought that to doubt the relationship between art and social responsibility was daft. Not only was it possible, it was essential to change the deadening effects of conventional cinema and theatre. 'If a thing is written about,' he said, 'it is exposed. Exposed, it can be analysed. If analysed, attacked, subverted, changed.'

We had power. By combining and working, we would increase our power. We had the strength to alter things. Never doubt it.

Before leaving he produced a slim diary, riffled through its pages, and picked an evening for me to go with him to see a play called *Look Back in Anger* at the Royal Court Theatre in Sloane Square. We were friends.

I felt good. There was a link between his brainy enthusiasm and the young – T-shirts, black stockings – people standing about, laughing, enjoying themselves. He and I had the urge to change the aesthetic output of the capital; they had the potential to bring the actual change. They, I felt sure, were as bored with, or as indifferent to, the prevailing art scene as I was.

I had seen a documentary film called *O Dreamland* directed by a Lindsay Anderson. It had transformed my idea of documentaries. Lyrical, barbed, it eschewed the usual, taken-for-granted, sentimental contract between audience and artist. It was not naturalistic.

Had Tynan seen it? Yes. Did he know Anderson? Yes. Would he introduce me? Yes. 'Don't wait, though. Just ring him up.'

'Thank you,' Anderson said, when I rang. 'I'm glad you liked the film. Not many people did.' We arranged to meet.

TRISTRAM lived in Notting Hill Gate. A place of bad reputation. Run down. Full of blacks. Designers like Terence visited its market occasionally. 'Look here,' he'd say, showing me a miniature chest of drawers. 'Note how the drawers slide. Perfect. An apprentice's masterpiece, I'd say. £1 on the Portobello Road street market' – off which ran Denbigh Close where Alfred Chester's friends the Sullivans lived.

I walked around. Chepstow Villas was a frontier. On its west side, the houses were large, reasonably well kept. On its east side – my side, as already I thought of it – the houses needed paint, their gateposts, plaster. Further east things got worse. Grass between the paving stones. The drains choked. Vast, five-floor houses, their window frames loose, their porticoes crumbling, their railings removed in the forties armament drive, overlooking shrubless squares filled with derelict cars. Each floor, a flat, holding a family.

Coming back up the Portobello Road I noticed a bakery and bought a roll filled with cheese and chives. There was a laundry, washing and ironing done on the premises, and dairy, 'Open from 5 a.m.', milk and cream served from china tubs decorated with pastoral scenes. There were three cinemas.

The Sullivans were out. I left a note to say that, as soon as they were ready to move, I would take No. 18 Denbigh Close.

In the same week I went with Tynan to see Osborne's *Look Back in Anger*. The Royal Court was packed. The audience buzzing with anticipation. Ken – in a wolf-skin overcoat – preened through the foyer. For several weeks running he had endorsed the play in his column.

'It proved just how little weight the *Observer*, the country's most intelligent, leftish newspaper, and I counted,' he said. 'I reckoned a rave review from me, plus good words from other critics, would fill a smallish theatre for a week. The Court has 400-odd seats. *Look Back* was in its fourth week. Audiences were falling off.'

Then the play was attacked in the wider press. The phrase Angry Young Man was coined. An excerpt showing Jimmy Porter – the play's self-pitying, lower-middle-class hero – railing against the state of England while his middle-class wife irons his shirts was broadcast on television, and immediately the nation was stirred in the way that, from time to time, it can be by works of art.

The material changes the country had established showed, naturally enough, in its most famous art: the theatre. It was extraordinary that in a theatrical world ruled by able conventionalists such as Coward and Rattigan, where teas were served during matinée intervals and the national anthem was played after the last curtain, a discourteous, loud-mouthed boor should be allowed to appear at all, let alone to rant about *class, money* and *sex*, while bursting with rage at the habits of the society that had borne him, and scorning – it seemed – the values of the men and women who had died in the Second World War. Nor was the play one of those gloomy, political tracts, dismissible as propaganda inspired by envy. It was funny, topical, quick, written in admirable, street-wise English. Worst of all, it was deeply patriotic. Osborne was emotional. He spoke directly. From love.

His play broke the mental spell cast by our role in the Allied victory over the Axis powers. To wit: that we were, at heart, still the same old lot with the same old ways. Bits of it embarrassed me: Porter's talk about love between men and women in terms of bears and squirrels. Nevertheless, *Look Back* said something previously unsaid, through the mouth of a character previously unknown, yet manifestly English. The acceptance of poverty, class obedience, unquestioning loyalty to Crown and Church, the power of blind, bad patriotism, things that had once bound us, had been changed, for ever.

Five years ago I saw a revival of *Look Back* which I loved – for sentimental reasons. In fact, the play is monotonous. Jimmy Porter goes on and on. It is a period piece. Its freshness cannot be recaptured. At the same time, I wish there was a playwright who could do for today what Osborne did for yesterday.

LINDSAY and I met in Soho. The son of a general and a wool merchant's daughter, he had – as David Storey has written – 'a high, broad, intelligent forehead, a prominent, inquisitive, inquisitorial nose, a broad, thin-lipped mouth, with a tendency to be drawn down at either corner in an expression of wry disbelief.' Short, sturdy, well balanced, he wore, as he entered the Dog and Duck, a cap and an anorak, and carried a slim document case under his arm.

Taking off the first, he put down the third, sat, leant back, crossed his legs at the ankles, put his hands behind his head, sighed and said:

'I don't think there's much hope for the English, do you?'

I said I would like to write a film script for him.

'Have you ever written a script?'

'No.'

'Have you ever read a script?'

'No . . .'

'Have you ever *seen* a script?'

'I'm afraid not.'

'Well, you'd better get started. What do you have in mind?'

'The mutinies in France at the end of the First World War. Half the British army demobilized itself rather than go to fight against the revolution in Russia.'

'How can you be so naïve?' Lindsay said. 'Can you imagine the people who made *The Dam Busters* putting up a penny for a film about mutineers? All your favourite films are American, Polish, French. Be honest: have you ever seen an English film that inspired you?'

'*Oh, Mr Porter!*'

'Then how about a comedy. Something for . . .' And he began to talk of actors.

I had never thought in terms of actors. That is to say, of their art. Lindsay (who was later to say: 'The only immoral thing about theatre is what it does to actors') talked about their art. He had critical, as well as inventive powers. 'Fortunately for people like you and me the general standard of acting in this country is at least eighty per cent higher than that of writing or directing.'

I began to choose my words with care. When you spoke, Lindsay listened. Hard.

'Have you seen *Look Back in Anger*?'

'I went with the Tynans.'

'You know Tynan?'

'Not well.'

'What did you think of him?'

'He's a fighter.'

'I mean – what do you think of what he *thinks*?'

'He's on the left,' I said, nervously.

'*That's* not very good,' Lindsay said. Meaning, as well as my lack of a proper opinion, my evasive tone. There was never a false note in Lindsay. I was pleased that Ken had taken me up, though I knew by now that he lacked, much as he desired and sought, firm intellectual opinions. In the middle of a conversation on matters on which you thought both of you agreed, Ken would suddenly bring in a reference to an intellectual system – Freudism, say – not only wide of the topic in hand, but subverting all the assumptions you – though now, it would seem, not he – had believed you shared from earlier occasions.

Pointing this out got one nowhere. If you said: 'That may be fine for' – naming the thinker – 'but what we were saying depends on a cloudy humanism matched to a leftist urge to share out the world's goodies', Ken would stare over the top of your head in complete, and to you, disconcerting, silence. It was as if he had been struck by a longing for universal coherence.

Unlike Ken – for whom he never cared – Lindsay had an analytical imagination. If you asked Lindsay for an analysis of a piece of writing, you got it – clear, direct, unflinching – provided he thought it was worth the effort.

'Tynan's a flash harry,' he said. 'You can't count on him.'

As we were walking towards Piccadilly Circus, from where he would catch a bus to the Royal Court, Lindsay began to sing in a wistful, melodious tenor:

> 'One night in gay Paree,
> I paid five francs to see
> A lady dressed in blue,
> Tattooed from head to knee.
> And up and down her spine,

Stood the Royal West Kent in line,
And on her back, was a Union Jack –
So I paid five francs more . . .'

as if it were the most natural thing in the world to do. The only other soul I had known who sang in the street was my dad. Whereas John Dominic's singing embarrassed me, so I would pretend to be elsewhere, I learnt the words Lindsay sang. Before parting, we agreed to see *Look Back* together – him for the third time.

I WAS in Bournemouth when the United States government exploded the world's first airborne hydrogen bomb over Bikini Atoll. Rumour had it that we were about to follow suit with a less expensive model from the same range.

Either on the day they did it (21 May 1956) or the day before, Peter Clarke and I had been to Salisbury, visiting Beech's Bookshop – then one of the finest in the West of England – and the cathedral. Peter's diary says:

> Christopher bought Trotsky's *Stalin* and I purchased a life of John Dee, a good indication of our contemporary tastes. The cathedral a structure of wonder and beauty, a great soaring pile of green-blue stone. Sombre and overwhelming.

For me, Peter's father embodied the idea of an Englishman. Six-two, with a long, horse-like face, and grey – formerly brown – curly hair, big-boned, comfortable on his feet, with a loping stride, not to be hurried, not given to conversation, the kind of man I – with an opinion about everything – fell silent before.

Usually, when he got home, Peter put his head around the kitchen door, said hello to his parents, then led me upstairs to his library.

On this occasion Mrs Clarke invited us to have a cup of tea. Mr Clarke had the *Daily Telegraph* spread out on the oilcloth covering the kitchen table. To my astonishment, without preamble, he began to read aloud from the paper:

> . . . the explosion this morning was the most stupendous ever released on earth. The fireball extended to a diameter of at least four miles and possibly larger, since part of it was hidden

by cloud. At a distance of 40 miles its luminosity exceeded 500 suns. After the fireball there came what was probably the most startling and incredible phenomenon of all – a vast, unearthly cloud that kept climbing upward and upward, and spreading outward and outward as though it would envelop the entire earth.

We drank our tea and Peter's mother said: 'That's something to write about.'

Peter walked me halfway home to my mother's flat. Except that BAN THE BOMB was no longer painted on the surface of the undercliff drive, we were back where we were in 1949.

'Worse off,' Peter insisted.

'They say they are meant for defence. They are useless for defence,' I said.

We agreed, appalling as the thought was, it was our duty to accept defeat at the hands of an enemy possessing such a weapon, rather than see the country destroyed.

'Every European country has been occupied at one time or another,' Peter said. 'We are as resilient as any of them.'

'The *New Statesman* has announced a rally against our manufacturing A-bombs,' I said.

Many people were out in the pleasant evening air.

'There is so much more money about since you went to Paris,' Peter said. 'Even I have more of it. Amazing. And now these bombs.'

Next morning I got my school atlas out of our attic, squared off a map of the British Isles, including Ireland, and calculated the total area to be 90,000-plus square miles. How many H-bombs would devastate that in perpetuity? The only people you can use them against with (relative) impunity are those who lack them.

Mother made coffee. We had never discussed big issues. We had never discussed anything. She had heard about the bomb on the radio.

'I was going to have my wedding ring made smaller. Perhaps it isn't worth it now.'

I remembered Chu Teh's words: 'Never mind the war. Study by moonlight! Study by the light of the falling snow!' and said: 'Of course it is worth it. Get your ring done. I'll give you the money.'

'Last night I felt so low I got my photos out,' she said. 'You and my mother. Your dear father teaching you how to hold a cricket bat. How nice you were in those forgotten days. If only you would make something of yourself. You are one of those people who has got to make his name. You won't stick at anything. You'll never be any good at anything if you don't stick at it. I'm sure I don't know where you get it from. And all that money we spent on your education.'

She gave me £30 to take back to London.

Then – that wonder, the bikini, was everywhere. Explosive swimwear. Aphrodité making trouble for the war bores. The papers were delighted to carry photographs of nearly naked young women showing off their bodies, and all sensible people were delighted to see them. The message was: screw your bomb. We redeem Bikini.

TERENCE's house had sanded, polished floors, with Moroccan rugs, chairs of his own design and manufacture, curtains with geometric, primary-coloured patterns. When my *Britannica* arrived he looked askance.

A letter came from John Sullivan inviting me to No. 18.

Denbigh Close was what my mother and aunt Gladys would have called a slum. Dead-ended, cobblestoned – mains water seeping over the cobbles in one place – two-floor cottages on either side, with washing on clotheslines strung between.

The ground floor of each cottage had once comprised a stable and a coach house, between which stairs led up to accommodation for the coachman, his family, and other servants from the houses of Chepstow Villas. A goat stood, and several chickens dodged about, on the cobbles. A donkey was tethered to a drainpipe. The stables were now garages, workshops or storerooms.

The Sullivans were having a second child. A Mr Warren rented the garages underneath. John Sullivan said he and his family would leave as soon as they found the house that suited them.

'There's a market on Saturday mornings. It doesn't come down the mews but the traders store stuff in the garages. Minky – that's Mr Warren – owns the shop on the corner there.' We were looking to the right out of the windows on the first floor. 'Minky is king of the mews. There's usually someone in the

Scrubs' – HMP Wormwood Scrubs – 'but you can get everything done. Drains, roof, decorating, electrics.'

For me, a dream come true. My little house. 'The hider of my failings', as the proverb says.

The rent was £5 a week. I would see to the legal expenses, lease transfer and so on, and the last three months' rent. Mum's £30 would nearly cover that. Charles would lend me the balance. In any case, a Xanthe Wakefield of the BBC's World Service, having heard me read my sonnets on the Third Programme, had written offering me a fee as reader – Blake, Clare, Wordsworth, all the great stars – on a set of educational broadcasts she was planning, so I had money to come.

'I'll introduce you to Minky,' John said. 'It's well to be on good terms with him. On warm evenings you can hear some interesting conversations through the window.'

J UNE 24, 1956
 Dear Mr Logue
If you are in town about six o'clock Friday 29th we could meet for a drink in the Salisbury pub St Martin's Lane next to New Theatre. I will be in the large bar, have got a dark beard and will wear a green tie.
Yours sincerely,
J. P. Donleavy

Muffie Wainhouse had given him my address at the same time as she sent me a copy of *The Ginger Man*. I rated the book highly. Tristram had invited me to edit *Nimbus*: 'Do what you like, I'll do the rest.' I wanted something by Donleavy.

JP was at the beginning of his twenty-year battle with Maurice Girodias over Maurice's having mispublished *The Ginger Man*. He, elegantly dressed as always, in a fine white, cufflinked shirt, tweed suit (with turnups), button-on braces and well-polished brogues. We liked one another. I was invited to supper next week.

The Donleavys lived in a terrace house under the shadow of Fulham gas works There were three substantial hardbacks on a shelf over his chair. As he stood at the window polishing a wine glass, slowly, carefully, holding its bowl to the light from time to time, I looked at the books. They were law books. On copyright. There were no other books in the house. For light reading, there was the local newspaper. Supper was delicious. On the mantelpiece was a cardboard sign that read: THE VOLUNTEERS ARE FIRING.

'I picked it up in Phoenix Park,' JP said. Then – stroking his beard – 'I hate Girodias. I hate him. My book, my fine book, deserved to be published as he published Beckett. Which is to say, as part of the Olympia Press/Collection Merlin series. Unless I can get it away from him, it will remain part of the Traveller's Companion Library. A dirty book. Unreviewed. Ignored by serious readers. A book that should bring me fame. The foundation of my fortune.'

How different JP's conception of himself from mine of me. I assumed I would go from one book of poems to the next, earning enough in other ways to continue what I wanted to do. I had a giant stapler and a store of pliable card. These and my typewriter would allow me to publish a small edition of a small book if nobody else cared for my work. I denied the existence of an influential world of poetry reviewers and literary sets. I asked JP for something for *Nimbus*.

It was late when we walked to my bus. He moved slowly. With deliberation. His feet pointing outwards at an angle of thirty-five degrees. His fingers in his waistcoat pockets.

'I am thinking of a play,' he said. 'It will be called *Wealth*. I see the main billing outside the theatre as follows: *Wealth*, new line, *by J. P. Donleavy*, new line, *Author of* The Ginger Man. I shall insist that these words are visible to the naked eye at a distance of seventy-five paces.'

He waited until the bus arrived, then gave me a chapter of his next book for *Nimbus*. 'We will be in contact,' he said, waving me goodbye, standing beneath a street light, one hand behind his back, smiling his circumspect smile.

IT was a brutal autumn.
    Moscow crushed Hungary's attempt to escape from its clutches at the same time as, provoked by Egypt's nationalization of the Suez canal, London and Paris – helped by Israel – invaded Egypt.

Moscow smothered Hungary while supporting Cairo. We – led by Sir Anthony Eden – bombed Egypt while supporting Hungary. Both invasions were accompanied by storms of self-righteous propaganda and shrieks of mutual recrimination.

Inflamed with rancorous nostalgia, our popular press roared: EDEN GETS TOUGH, SAYS 'HANDS OFF OUR CANAL'. IT'S *GREAT* BRITAIN AGAIN!

Sir Anthony was not alone. The majority of his cabinet, his party, and the Labour opposition were in thrall to a sentimental vision of their brave past. For all that, almost everyone I knew was filled with anger that a bunch of Anglo-French geriatric piss-artists should betray us into a war in support of a transport company that for eighty-seven years had taken quite a lot, in return for rather a little, from a country much poorer than our countries, while justifying our invasion with cries of 'India!' 'Empire!' 'the Gateway to the East!' long after our principal interests in these regions had gone.

Moscow got its way, Washington blocked London and Paris, Israel withdrew from most of the territory it had occupied.

THE Sullivans found the house they wanted. I could not spare the rent I now owed Terence. Instead of explaining the position with a view to an extension of credit – which I am sure he would have granted – I decided on a midday flit. Charles came over to Regent's Park Terrace. We loaded my cartons on to a barrow hired from a stallholder in the Inverness Street fruit and vegetable market, topped them with the mattress Jean had allowed me to take from Park Square East, and, leaving Terence a note of apologetic thanks began to push my all the three miles to Notting Hill Gate.

The main hazard was Bishop's Bridge, spanning the railway lines to the west. We decided to gather our strength by having a drink in the Duke of Albemarle below the bridge. Learning that most of the cartons held books, the two railwaymen who shared our table reckoned we would never reach the top without a rest. Which meant bother when the traffic piled up behind us.

There was only one thing for it – help.

'Right?'

'Right.'

Each railwayman took a handle of the barrow, Charles positioned himself between them, I pulled at the barrow's kerbside rail, and we attacked the bridge at a run, us shouting 'Thanks!' then 'There-you-go . . .' as the barrow cruised down the far side of the bridge, Charles now brakeman, me acting the part of a rope to keep everything on.

WEARING a green trilby tipped slightly forward, a white silk scarf, going up on the toes of his shoes after taking a long drag on a fresh cigarette, Mr Minky Warren was standing in the door of his shop as we trundled into the Mews.

Fifth-generation north-west London prosperous working-class, Minky dealt in scrap metal, rags, old bottles, second-hand clothes, bits of furniture, and lead – which he weighed on the shop's giant scales, the kind with a graduated boom and sliding gauge. He had a scar over one eye. During the Second World War he served with the Chindits – meaning he had experienced barbaric warfare.

'Right,' he said, hitching his shoulders, giving the brim of his trilby a twitch. 'You're Chris, taking over No.18 from John. He's gone, as you know. Here's the keys.'

Just at this moment, a totter (an itinerant, down-market street dealer – anything that would fit on a cart) arrived with some lead under a horse blanket.

'Right,' Minky ordered. 'Get your fucking lead on the scales and stop looking about. These two gentlemen' – Charles and me – 'don't want anything to do with your kind. And hurry fucking up. And next time let me fucking well know before you show your face.'

They went into the shop. Money changed hands. The totter released his donkey from the shafts of the cart – which belonged to Minky and, as I soon learnt, was garaged inside the ground floor of No.18. 'Two shillings a week. If that's agreeable, Chris.'

'Oh, yes, Minky. That's fine.'

Then Mrs Warren appeared holding a ewer with a cloth over it.

'Right. This is Mrs Warren with my tea. Have you got anything to make your tea with?'

We hadn't.

'Leave this lot' – my possessions. 'Go down to Jimmy James' –

a primitive supermarket in Westbourne Grove, open from 8 a.m. until midnight – 'get what you need. The gas is on in 18.'

Charles was my first guest.

LINDSAY invited me to lunch. The path leading to his Maida Vale door was surfaced with black and white tiles. I rang, and moments later heard him singing a hymn as he came down a passage towards the door, which he opened with a formal swing. There was an oven cloth over one of his shoulders. 'Oh,' he said, 'so you found it, did you?'

'Of course I found it,' I said. 'I can follow the *A to Z*.'

'Now, Christopher,' he said, 'do not be irritable with a friend who is cooking your lunch.'

He had just published his essay *Stand Up! Stand Up!*, with this (by the music critic, Ernest Newman) as an epigraph:

> It is beginning to dawn upon us all that what is needed most today is a criticism of criticism . . . For it is the critic, rather than the work of art, who should be put for a while upon the dissecting table.

His text – a discussion of how cinema was viewed and reviewed by the national press – revealed his critical intelligence, a faculty he assumed to be active in any artist of any worth, or in any spectator worth having, morally attuned creativity being impossible without it. He insisted on the link between imagination and social circumstance. The critic or the artist who claimed to provide non-partisan aesthetic judgements, or 'pure' artworks, was a fraud. Critic and artist have the same responsibilities as everybody else. Humanism was not exhausted.

He was frying bacon, eggs, sausages and tomatoes.

'How is the mutiny script going?'

'I have been checking things.'

'You mean you have been reading. Not writing.'

'I've made some notes.'

'Notes? That's not much good. You're supposed to be a writer, aren't you?'

'Yes.'

'Well, write then. Let me have an outline by the next time we meet.'

'It's not that easy.'

'You want something easy?'

Then softening: 'Just get something down. We'll go through it together.'

I had in fact made a start on the script. The problem was how to reveal action, plus character, without letting the mechanics show. How the words looked on the page was irrelevant. This was like writing a kind of poetry that had to vanish in order to be understood. And the main question was: how did you get poetry into celluloid? For Lindsay was a poet.

One wall of his kitchen was covered with stills: Ford, Vigo, Pudovkin, Renoir, Jennings, Grierson, Balcon.

'If Pudovkin and Ford are poets, if they can do it, other people can do it,' Lindsay said, talking of himself.

There was another problem. Writing is an abstract effort. Making commonly intelligible marks. I found no pleasure in making them. I like making the marks akin to those of painting or drawing. I have spent months decorating typewriter paper and note-cum-scrapbooks.

M Y possessions seemed meagre as soon as they were into No. 18's two rooms, with kitchen and bathroom, twenty-five by twenty-five feet overall

Dusting off one of the two built-in shelves, parking his trilby on it, Minky inspected the premises and said: 'Right. You need springs, curtain, curtain pole, table, chair, cup, saucer, plate, knife and fork. There's a sale on at Whiteleys.'

I had £15 in hand.

Minky opened the window and shouted: 'Harry!'

A small, thick-set man with watery eyes and a drinker's nose came up the stairs.

'This is Harry Dust, No. 9.'

'I do the drains,' Harry confided.

'Harry,' Mr Warren said in a patient, threatening tone, 'I am doing the introes. I will tell Chris who you fucking are and what you fucking do.'

'Yes, Minky.'

'Right. Chris needs . . .' He ran through the list. 'And he can't pay above £3.'

'Including the springs?'

'And delivery.'

I looked out of the window.

'And Harry, there's another thing' – offering him a Senior Service, thumbing up the flame of his Ronson.

'What people like Chris like is polished floorboards, right?'

'Right, Minky,' I said. How Minky knew this was beyond me. Terence had polished floorboards. Polished floorboards were just coming in.

'So what would you and your brother charge to sand this lot down, Harry?'

'The first thing we'd have to ask,' Harry disclosed in a professional voice, 'is: are Chris's boards fit for sanding, and who's going to de-nail them?'

'Chris's boards are the same as everyone else's boards in this part of London, Harry,' said Minky in his you-have-a-good-deal-coming-up tone.

'Um . . . um . . .' Harry said, peering about. 'Let's say £20 – using the best polish. A double polish.'

'That's fair, Harry. You and Chris can work out the details.'

IT was as well that Xanthe's work for me came through. She influenced the course of my life. Brought me close to Carne-Ross, by whom she was loved, and whom she loved. Through him, because of her, I came to Homer, and so to *War Music*.

Xanthe Wakefield was a gawky young woman, a classical scholar with an enchanting, musical voice. Grey-eyed, witty, inventive, reserved, a person with deep enthusiasms, troubled and lonely. Her father was a Conservative Member of Parliament, high in the Tory ranks, the sort of man who treated doubt as a minor infection.

From Xanthe I gained a notion of other than modern (post-B C that is) literary standards. It was not that the Greeks were better, they differed.

'But, actually, Xanthe,' I said, 'you think the Greeks are better, don't you?'

'Very well, I do. That is mere taste. Unless you learn Greek – it is not *that* difficult – you must take me, or Donald, on trust. The difference is critical. The Greeks are not humanistic, not

Christian, not sentimental. Please try to understand that. They are musical. Such music. And Homer ... Homer is close to your ear, and at the same time – so distant. He has a passage' – giving me the book and line reference – 'where he describes the snow falling on to the sea at Zeus's will. You feel that Zeus is so far away, so far . . .' And she looked out of the window.

Donald was planning a version of the *Iliad* to be broadcast on the Third. 'Get Christopher to do a passage,' Xanthe said.

PATRICK visited from Paris. He told me Alex had a job on a scow transporting stone up the East River. He had decided to become a pariah, an apostle for heroin.

'Did Beckett ask after me?'

'Of course. I said you were doing well. Publishing. Broadcasting.'

'Do you think Beckett would join a protest against our manufacturing nuclear weapons?'

'The French are like us. They couldn't stand not having as big a bomb as anyone.'

'And Austryn is . . . ?'

'Building. Translating.'

'And you, Patrick?'

'I've been offered a job in Africa. With the World Health Organization.'

'What about your long poem?'

He took out a blue folder.

'I'm thinking of a quotation from Dante as an epigraph,' he said.

'Good,' I said, pouring the tea. 'Can I read it?'

'I'd rather wait. Austryn said you had a row with your publishers.'

'Leave the manuscript with me for the evening.'

'What happened?'

'They came up with a pansified design. A cover scattered with forget-me-nots. I said it didn't suit my stuff.'

'And?'

'The designer hated me. He kept saying, "Tell me what you want".'

'Poor chap,' Patrick said.

'Why take his side?'

'Go on.'

'Finally he opened his book of typefaces and said: "You choose." So I went through them, there and then, saying: this one, that one, until there was practically a different type for every poem. I got a shock when I saw the proofs. And do you know what that bastard did? He put "Typography by the Author" on the prelims page. What about your poem?'

'It has corrections all over.'

'I'm used to your writing. I want to see what you have done. We are friends. I feel I have the right to know what you are writing. It might help me with mine.'

Soon afterwards he went to Brazzaville for the publications department of the WHO. It was ten years before we met again.

I ENJOYED *Look Back* more the second time. Sitting in the King's Arms next to the Royal Court, Lindsay said: 'Those who hate John's play see nothing but a loud-mouthed malcontent who loathes them. Once you stand back, you see the evening as an expression of temperamental disgust at our hypocrisy, and an image of our own sense of confusion.

'When Alison's' – Alison is Porter's wife – 'fifty-year-old, upper-middle-class father appears, you feel for him. He too is confused. He fought the war. He – almost unwillingly – resents the freedom the young are taking. As you said about characters like Attlee and Priestley, they feel they don't know what people want any more.'

Lindsay Anderson, Kenneth Tynan, John Osborne – though I only met the third once – personified much of what London in the late fifties meant to me. Each assumed that theatre was as important as politics, not simply entertainment.

Stemming from frustrated affection, Osborne's attack had been *ad hoc, ad hominem*. His play offered no comprehensive vision of the world, formed outside art, though expressed through it.

Ken, though more analytical than Osborne, was a creature of moments. Passionate for the theatre, undaunted when he lost his ill-planned battles, relishing – to some extent – the hostility he aroused, he lacked a vantage point, a settled view, going from

Marx to Freud, from Freud to Zen, from Zen to (not for long)
Wilhelm Reich.

What was special about Lindsay was his humane, demo-
cratic, sympathetic/satirical, independent-spirited picture of our
society.

To me it seems that, for a short time, the Royal Court Theatre
became a source of energy for three different generations. First,
that of George Devine – a founder of the English Stage Society –
himself. Then that of Osborne and his fellow pioneers. And after
them, those who produced *Beyond the Fringe*, started *Private
Eye*, set up the Establishment nightclub, worked at the BBC
under Hugh Carleton-Greene, or painted, designed and drew
cartoons in the new styles.

The Royal Court did not agitate alone. I was introduced to
some of the painters and sculptors at the Royal College of Art
by Germano. Though I only heard about it in the days that
followed, in the spring of 1957 the RCA was the scene of an
auspicious dispute.

John Minton, the well-known landscape artist, a college tutor,
assembled and then denounced his students for betraying their
art. They had abandoned traditional materials, were inspired by
the New York abstractionists, could not draw properly, took film
stars, boxers, etc., as their heroes.

Wrongly – I thought – Minton associated their rejection of his
artistic preoccupations with a don't-care attitude to the invasions
of Suez and Hungary, and to the proliferation by Britain and
France of nuclear weapons. Whereas the indifference lay with
his own generation.

From the point of view of artists like Robyn Denny and Richard Smith, which was shared by playwrights and film-makers,
the art produced by minds imbued with pre-war values, for all its
amiable qualities – tolerance, benignity (Bacon excepted), a sense
of fair play – could not represent the position in which they, the
younger generation, found themselves, and for which, as artists,
they were determined to assume responsibility.

The impulse was a questioning one, backed up by a strong
desire to help establish a fair, free, classless society. If you did not
have such a purpose, then your art was simply another form of
entertainment. The kind of art that confirms its audience in their

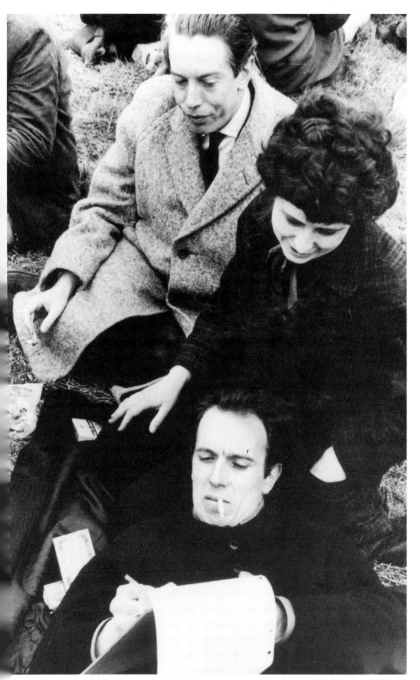

3 Ken Tynan meditates while Doris Lessing oversees my signing of a petition during the midday rest on the third day of the first Aldermaston March, 1958.

14 'Minky' Warren outside what was then his shop on the corner of Denbigh Close and the Portobello Road, *c*. 1950.

15 Denbigh Close, on the verge of respectability, in 1958.

16 With Peter Clarke marching between us, George Devine, artistic director of the English Stage Company, and I carry the Royal Court Theatre's banner as the second Aldermaston March reaches Kensington High Street in 1959.

17 Lindsay Anderson, a poet by nature, film director, stage director and critic by profession.

18 Nell Dunn, *c.* 1960, with whom I was much in love.

9 Douglas Cleverdon of the BBC (radio), Vanessa Redgrave and myself
rehearsing the text of 'Patrocleia' (part of my Homer poem, *War Music*) for *The
Death of Patroclus* ('77' Records, 1963), in the painter Elizabeth Moore's
London studio. Her self-portrait (she also took this photograph) is above and to
the right of Cleverdon.

6459

UNCONVICTED PRISONER			
Reg. No. ~~50062~~	Age 34	Location	F 95
COMMITTAL Date of 12·9 19 61		Place	Bow St M/c.
Remanded till 1 Month.			
To be tried at			
Labour for which fit with restriction (if any)			
1 RIV			

CIVIL PRISONER

AGNOST C

No. 49   (21816—14-8-44)

10 I took this card off the door of my cell in HM Prison, Brixton, where, as one
of Bertrand Russell's Committee of 100, I, among others, was taken after being
detained as a 'Civil' or 'unconvicted' (political?) prisoner by the Conservative
Cabinet in 1961.

21 Richard Ingrams, my editor at *Private Eye* and my friend since 1961.

22 Bernard Stone, author, poetry bookseller, publisher, always a genial companion, endlessly kind to me, *c.* 1965.

23 Reading my work at the International Poetry Incarnation, the Albert Hall, London, 11 June 1965.

4 Pauline Boty, painter, c. 1965.

25 Mr Carter's (once 'Minky' Warren's) shop with a display of the painted furniture he sold in substantial quantities. My house, No. 18, is just visible in the top right-hand corner.

26 Mrs Alice Carter, Mr Carter's widow, photographed at Rosemary's and my wedding lunch.
27 Mr Kenny Carter, 'the elder brother I never had', as best man on my wedding day, 1984.

prejudices, amuses them with displays of meaningless violence, corrupts their patriotism with nationalistic waffle, and deepens their self-deception.

I do not think it untrue to say that the writers associated with the Royal Court in its heyday echoed the ideas expressed by English poets such as Langland, Milton and Blake. In modern terms, the assumptions were that competitive individualism came second to public interest, low taxation was incompatible with general education and good health.

In the arts, no one I knew at all well identified with money-making and moneymakers. Their affinity was with those who gave service, not with those who sought wealth.

My father would have ignored the art, but not the thought. It was as if there was a wish in the air to revive the spirit of 1945, to effect a second national transformation no less thorough than the first. I wanted to do something on stage at the Royal Court. I was not sure what.

WHAT Patrick had said of me to Beckett was true. My poems were appearing in the *Times Literary Supplement* and *New Statesman*, and were being broadcast by the Third.

I had learnt that nothing was left to chance where the careers of promising young British poets were concerned. If your poems were liked by your fellow poets, you published a book. Its reviews (usually by your fellow poets) called it to the attention of the educated public. If favourable, these comments resulted in your being interviewed by the press and included in anthologies. Then a second collection, a visiting (literary) professorship, a prize or two, a *Selected Poems* (plus TV programme) and, finally, the incorporation of your work into the educational syllabus. A process taking twenty years or more. How horrible, I thought. I wanted poetry to be part of the wave that had broken at the Royal Court.

There was a second approach, with room for improvisation and collaboration – poets, composers, painters, singers and actors working together. What Jacques Prévert wrote, Yves Montand sang. This was the way.

At the same time, I was introduced to editorial discipline. That remarkable woman, Janet Adam Smith – then running the arts features of the *New Statesman* – had asked me to review Bertram Mills' Circus. After the show, I saw a sign inviting ticket holders to see the animals in their cages. They looked droopy, half-asleep. 'As if they were doped,' I wrote in my review, and thought no more of it.

A fortnight later, when I popped into W. H. Smith's at Notting Hill Gate to buy the latest *Statesman*, the headline 'Bertram Mills' Circus, an Apology' caught my eye. There it was, signed 'Christopher Logue', a grovelling retraction wherein I declared myself to be a complete fool who knew nothing about live-animal entertainment, indeed – aside from one or two dogs I might have passed in the street – had never seen an animal in my life before I mistakenly implied that this nationally recognized, regularly inspected, RSPCA-approved circus ever gave their non-speaking performers as much as an aspirin without a doctor's prescription.

My call was put straight through to the *Statesman*'s editor, Kingsley Martin, who boomed: 'So glad you called. It's about your apology, yes? I thought I made a fine job of it. Just the right note. A word from the lawyers to say all's well. Guessed you'd be pleased . . . Bye.' And he was gone.

Then something else came up. The *Times Literary Supplement* published a review that, in passing, mentioned T. S. Eliot's anti-Semitism. I paid little attention to the imputation, even though, having read all Eliot's poems, I knew it was justified. I was too much in love with the beauty of his verse to admit to myself that good poets can express bad thoughts.

The next issue of the *Times Literary Supplement* carried a letter from Eliot saying that he would like to know on what grounds he had been charged with anti-Semitism. In the following issue no one replied to him. I looked the poems up. There was no doubt. They expressed anti-Semitic thoughts. The edition I consulted was dated 1951. I telephoned Alan Pryce-Jones and asked him if a letter from me citing the passages would be welcome. He said it would – and to be careful I got them right. Four issues later, still no one else had written in, so I did.

My motives were mixed. Self-righteousness, giving daddy a kick, puffing myself up, all played their parts. As well as my letter, the thing to have done would have been to write a poem, the Fifth Quartet, among whose themes the power of art to serve poor aims, and of high literary standards to protect bad thoughts would have been evident. I do not say that Eliot's anti-Semitic sentences actually caused a Jew to suffer, or an anti-Semite to inflict a blow. But everybody knows how easy it is to turn humans against one another.

Eliot concluded the correspondence by saying that the passages I quoted were what those who shared my frame of mind usually produced against him.

My frame of mind? Presumably I had such. Certainly Eliot did: a mind to restore the unity of thought and feeling through the reintroduction of religious concepts to art.

I felt let down. I told myself that, overtaken by events, Eliot could not handle his fame. He had increased the misery in the world. He lacked the strength to apologize. I decided to discuss the matter with Beckett when he came over for the first British production of *Endgame*. I never had the chance. The Lord Chamberlain refused the Royal Court a licence to present the play.

As I came out of Notting Hill Gate underground I met Michael Hastings, now a Royal Court playwright, with a very nice-looking dog on a clothesline lead. It was a London dog – half lurcher, not large, dark brown, one ear cocked, fairly intelligent, very friendly, genetic engineering at its most traditional.

'This is my dog Russells,' he said proudly. 'I'm giving him a run in Holland Park. Want to join us?'

Russells's peculiarity soon became known to me. Amiable dog though he was, he could not stop farting. More: Russells's farts – about one every five minutes – had an invasive, melting pong that you could have bottled.

Once in the park, Michael untied Russells who shot off while we meandered towards the refreshment pavilion. Five minutes later, Michael said: 'Russells is lost.' So he was. We called, we walked, we listened, we asked. People were concerned. We retraced our steps, calling again. There was no sign of him.

After an hour, I – impatiently caught up in another's anxiety – persuaded Michael to come to Denbigh Close and use Minky's telephone to inform the police. 'That's not much good. He doesn't have his name on his collar,' Michael mumbled, very upset, his head hanging down, his hands in his pockets, as we walked along.

Then, just like that, there ahead of us at the corner of Chepstow Villas and Portobello Road, wagging his tail into a blur, was Russells, bounding up, emitting, like a kettle on a casual boil, a sequence of happy, overpowering farts.

MAD John, the brother of Mrs Goodie Sheepgrove, of No. 12 Denbigh Close, was fiftyish. He wore big black boots, a full-length overcoat (in all weathers) and a black broad-brimmed hat of the kind associated with artistic people of the twenties. John looked through you, smiling his wide, lunar smile, or said 'Hello, hello' as he passed, carrying, as always, his always empty, patched leather shopping bag. Goodie gave John his meals. He slept on a paliasse on the stone floor of No. 14.

Mrs Sheepgrove had confided in Harry Dust, who had confided in me, that nobody was sure who Mad John's dad was.

'My mother, Joy,' Goodie told Harry, 'was very easy-going. One summer around 1910 she went to Herne Bay for a week taking our youngest, Mary, then two, with her. And when she came home she had John with her, but not Mary. Our dad – he was a rat-catcher, he had the rat-catching rights for the new villas on what was the old Chepstow estate – was very upset and went down to Herne Bay to speak to Peggy, Joy's sister. All Peggy could tell him was that Joy had come in after a walk on the seafront, saying that a young woman holidaymaker she had met confessed she had always wanted a girl, and John was her third boy. As Joy already had two girls – me and Mary – the mothers decided there and then to make a swap. And that was that. There was no point in getting upset.'

ONE day, Minky announced: 'Right. Lead's out. Pine's in. Decent stuff. None of your fucking rubbish here.'

He meant stripped pine furniture. Dressers, corner cupboards, kitchen tables. 'People who talk like Chris are coming down here on Saturdays. They want fucking pine.'

On Saturdays a young man called Kenny – at first I took him to be Minky's son, it being 'our Ken' this and 'our Ken' that – ran the only used-goods market stall at our end of the Portobello Road. Kenny was married to Alice. A looker, pink-complexioned, blonde, hazel-eyed, talkative, with no doubts of her opinions. Alice was, compared to her Kenny, highly conventional.

Once we had become friends, Alice said: 'I have never voted Labour, Mr Logue' – which was how Kenny and she addressed me – 'and I never shall. When I earn a pound it is my pound.

'When I had my Douglas' – their first son – 'I said: Ken push a pram? Never. I don't agree with men doing housework. Sit there and read the paper, Mr Carter' – meaning Ken – 'or talk to your friend Mr Logue. You two are never short of something to say to each other. Though Ken insists on doing his share of the housework. But the pram? Never. I wouldn't have it.'

'You' – Kenny interrupting her after five minutes – 'are so Conservative, Al. So Conservative.'

And Alice: 'He's off.' Though on this occasion he said no more.

Sometimes Alice brought Minky his tea. Then it was: 'Thank you, Alice' – with a small smile. No bad language.

It was Kenny, not Minky, who spotted pine. Kenny's stall was always busy, half-empty by 8.30 a.m., the dealers crowding round while Alice managed the shop and Minky – loosening his shoulders, up and down on his toe – fixed prices by the customer's appearance.

Before we grew close, Kenny – fair-haired, handsome, twelve years younger than myself, broad-shouldered, steady, with an inquisitive, disbelieving grin – brought me a note.

Denbigh Terrace
8.9.1957

Dear Mr Logue,
   Seeing as your kitchen window overlooks my back garden may I thank you not to throw the matches you light your oven with out of it onto my ferns. I hope I have spelt your name correctly.
   Yours truly,
   Brigit Vaughan

Kenny said: 'That's Brigit all over. Better do what she says.'

MY mother was seventy. Not that she thought of herself as old. Peter Clarke said: 'I met your mother in the street. "I'm throwing a lot of stuff away," she said. "I wrote to John Christopher saying, if he wants the papers he left in the loft to take them now or never set eyes on them again. Not a word of reply."

' "I'll have them, Mrs Logue."

' "You had the last lot, didn't you?"

' "I did, Mrs Logue. When shall I collect them?"

' "I'll drop you a line. I'm off to Felixstowe with my nephew, Lionel."'

After Dad's death, my mother started to see a lot of Lionel and Gladys, spending Christmas with them when she moved back to London, helping them househunt when they went to live in Felixstowe.

I shall not say that Lionel was, politically speaking, on the extreme right. He was a Superconservative. When I remarked on Lionel's views, my mother said: 'Lionel is not so much of a stick-in-the-mud as you suggest. Take his marrying. He was driving his motorbike along Maida Vale when he noticed a young woman – who turned out to be Gladys Parker – looking out of an upstairs window. He stopped his bike and shouted up: "Will you marry me?" and Gladys – she was working as a saleslady in Liberty's needlework department – said yes. There's action for you.'

Hilda was soon to upset Molly and the Bridges.

You will recall that my uncle George's marriage to Edie Langford was a failure. Edie sank into depression, George, philosophical-mystical, a member of Whiteway, the utopian-socialist Gloucestershire community – fell in love with Hilda and she with him.

My mother condemned the relationship. Hilda was little better than a fallen woman. Her brother George was as wicked – worse.

'That girl has abandoned her God for his silly ideals. It is hard to say which one of them has sunk lowest. It must be him. She never had a brain in her head. Never. And she could never speak the truth.'

There was no question of George and Hilda living together. He was sixty-seven, she, fifty-three; they were children of their time. Then Edie died. A month later, Hilda and George married. More:

they sold their houses, pooled their money, and bought a house in Felixstowe.

'In Felixstowe! Would you believe it?' my mother said. 'There are a hundred places those two might have gone. A hundred. Now poor Lionel may have to bump into them at the shops, and, wearing her "butter-wouldn't-melt-in-my-mouth" look, Hilda will enquire after Gladys's bowels.'

'How are they by the way?'

'That's enough from you, my son. They needn't think that I shall be paying them a holiday call. The next thing we shall hear of is their putting up a VOTE LABOUR poster in their front window.'

'I thought you were apolitical.'

'Non-political. Non-political is non-political. That means no politics.'

'Because of Hilda I have my pension. Because of George I saw I could make things. They are in love. That's enough for me.'

'It is high time you were married. That's my last word.'

CHARLES, a member, had introduced me to the London Library. Bargain though it was, I could not afford the ten-guinea annual membership fee. I would say: 'Charles, see what they've got on Mad Songs' – I was very keen on mad songs, a variety of eighteenth-century ballad-sheet verse – 'or riddles. Oh, yes, and Charles, would you mind getting me vols. two and six of Dryden's *Collected*?'

We met at the working men's café in Duke Street at the back of the Library for Charles to hand over a big load of books to see me through Christmas.

Christmas was a difficult time. The art world closed down. People went home to their families. If I went to Bournemouth, I must stay with my mother. The picture of the pair of us sitting for two days in a quarrelsome silence was not inviting. From time to time we exchanged letters.

The Brangwyns were living in the respectable part of Notting Hill. Pat was working on the *Daily Mirror*. Our positions were reversed. Outside work, he had stopped writing. I, after a fashion, was a writer. A published poet. Patrick and I spent

Christmas sketching out a musical set in the world of motor racing: *Sweet Chariot*.

'How are you going to get a car race on to a stage?' Audrey enquired.

'We'll use film,' I said.

'Mixed media,' Pat said, introducing me to the phrase. 'The coming thing.'

Then the season was over. People returned to life – slightly stunned.

Women pointed me towards the *Iliad*. Xanthe first. Then Doris Lessing. Doris and I met at one of the Tynans' Sunday afternoons – them inviting various friends over to their flat in Mount Street for tea, then drinks, then (sometimes) out to supper.

Doris – her namesake Achilles' half-sister – had the most beautiful eyes, straight from a Persian miniature. There was something heroic about her openheartedness, her willingness to trust you. Equally, she was acute, direct.

'Are you happy?' she'd say. Or: 'No. That is quite wrong. How ignorant you are, Christopher. I know you like women. Simply like them, sex aside. But you are complacent about women's position in the world. We are as good as you are. It is very difficult for men to understand. Keep trying.'

Doris and I sat beside each other under Ken's room-wide, wallpaper reproduction of Hieronymus Bosch's painting *The Garden of Earthly Delights*. We were – as was Ken – interested by J. B. Priestley's demand for a movement to be started against Britain's becoming a proliferator of nuclear weapons. In a statement to the Commons, the then Minister of Defence, Mr Duncan Sandys, had admitted: 'It must be frankly recognized that there is at present no means of providing adequate protection for the people of this country against the consequences of an attack with nuclear weapons. Though, in the event of war, the fighter aircraft of the RAF would unquestionably take a heavy toll of enemy bombers, a proportion would inevitably get through. Even if it were only a dozen, they could with megaton bombs inflict widespread devastation.'

A week or two later Doris called at Denbigh Close to say that Bertrand Russell, A. J. P. Taylor and others were on the point of founding a campaign against our spreading these immoral armaments and to plan what we, as writers, might do to act against their apologists. Then the conversation turned to Homer, the *Iliad*, which Doris had been reading. 'It would suit you,' she said.

'I find it boring.'

'I'm not thinking of you as a reader, but as a poet.'

'What does that mean?'

'I'm not sure. Something to do with heroism, tragedy, that sort of thing.'

'You mean like *Godot*?'

'*Godot* is comic.'

'Yes, but . . .'

'I know what you mean. *Godot* is what we who don't know any Greek think of as Greek. Ancient Greek, that is.'

'You mean translating Homer would suit me?'

'Obviously not. But I'm telling you, the *Iliad* suits you.'

A few days later Donald gave me lunch at Broadcasting House and, at Xanthe's bidding, proposed I translate a sequence from Book XXI of the *Iliad*. To the question of my knowing no Greek, Donald answered: 'Read translations by those who did. Follow the story. A translator must know one language well. Preferably his own.'

We called the passage he chose for me 'Achilles and the River'. This is the moment when a swathe of Trojan soldiers hide among the River Scamander's marshes. It does them no good. Achilles slaughters them. Whereupon, outraged by the pollution of his waters, the River Scamander inundates the hero.

My copy of the *Iliad* was in a box marked 'Sell'. The translation – in prose – was by the poet E. V. Rieu. It was grangerized with maps of the ancient Aegean engraved in the eighteenth century. Looking at the maps, I recalled that in Bournemouth I had discovered a waste yard through whose gates I saw a council-house-high mound of sopping paper, not only of newsprint and magazines but from ruined books, their signatures thrown here and there prior to pulping.

'Take what you want and don't come back,' said the foreman.

I hesitated between a work on heraldry, on vellum, with

hand-coloured illustrations of escutcheons and crests, and two small octavos of a four-volume Pope *Iliad*, 1763, with engraved illustrations. These included the maps I stuck into my copy of Rieu's *Iliad*.

Thinking of it as a job to be done as well as possible and then forgotten, I did not mention Donald's commission to Charles or to Peter. I read various translations, making an abstract of the sequence as I went, listing this or that turn of phrase, dropping or conflating this or that speech, these or those actions, until I had a clear storyline.

As time went by, when I walked up to the Gate for a newspaper, or as far as Kensington Gardens for a stroll, I found myself thinking of Achilles and Scamander, running through the events listed as easily as I might the alphabet. More, I could reverse the sequence to test its strength overall, as painters hold a canvas to a mirror to inspect its composition afresh. And when this – my inspection, so to speak – provoked ideas of what might be added to it from a different part of the *Iliad*, or for that matter, from the day's newspaper, I would realize I had come without means to write, and, repeating the possibilities in my head, I hurried to the nearest newsagent's for a jotter and pencil.

I have discovered that, sometimes, while working on a poem, or on a passage from an extended poem, you reach a point some two-thirds of the way through when, pronto, you see how it should end. Then – this being the oddity – you rough out the end and work back up to the point of departure, writing the text backwards, or rather, back upwards – if you see what I mean.

Although still at the bed-springs-on-the-(sanded)-floor, one-big-table-chair stage, I had begun to alter No.18 by removing an interior wall to make a bigger room. A reason for this change came with Harry Dust's finding a fourteen-foot long tailor's bench on a skip. Teak. A lovely thing. A true working bench pitted with tiny needle marks. £2. For another pound Ken got me a pair of trestles. The table would just fit into my biggest room. It looked wrong. So Kenny, Harry and I took the wall out. Harry's brother, Foxy, plastered over the brickwork. No mention was made of landlords. Anyway, they lived in Wales.

I am one of those people who miss what is right under their

noses. Day after day, I sat at my bench working on 'Achilles and the River'. The sweat ran out of me. I forgot myself entirely for hours on end. The moment I stopped I disregarded the work and its principal source – the various translations I was studying. Perhaps I was afraid of it. In any case, I was drawn into the *Iliad* and towards Carne-Ross. At times I could make nothing of what the translators had written. I wanted to know *exactly* what it was Homer said in the first instance.

'There is no exactly, no first instance,' Donald said. 'The poem comes from a world that did not have art over here, and "real" life over there. We have developed the notion of "originality" and "originals" as a natural part of modern – I mean post-ancient – thinking.

'Our *Iliad* may or may not be the work of a late – at present 700 BC is the favoured date – master poet who inherited centuries of material. The Greek-speaking people of the Aegean invented Achilles. Homer – we reckon – gave him literary perfection. I will make you a crib.'

'Will you make it *à la* Greek? Greek word order, no English articles, etcetera.'

'I'll put it in the post.'

Then I would go to his flat for Homer tutorials.

I had decided that Achilles was some kind of a Nazi.

'Nonsense,' Donald said. 'Think Greek. Achilles is not "bad". Hector is not "good". Homer is not sentimental. He is sympathetic to everyone. Inescapably ironic. Frankly, I am surprised that someone with your obvious disadvantages can do anything. I begin to like your other stuff. I'll back you at the BBC.'

When Donald read the *Iliad* aloud in Greek a hush born of respect came into his voice. When he put the text down, he, whose concentration could be ferocious, was abstracted. Looking neither at Xanthe nor at me, nor at his pet white rat, he would say: 'This is miraculous. There is time for the size of the boat, for the struggle at its prow, and the noise of the flames *all in one line.*'

As well, the thing under my nose that I missed then, and for a long time afterwards, was that I am happiest when I have a guide. A text, a painting or a photograph, to work from. I like recomposing. An existing text makes starting easier. And starting is always difficult. At least for me.

When 'Achilles and the River' was transmitted in June 1959 it interested a number of literary grandees. The broadcast was repeated; parts of it were televised; then it was published by *Encounter*, a serious, non-specialist magazine. Finally, backed by the grandees, I was given a grant by an American foundation to produce more of the same.

Gratetul as I was for the praise and for the promise of support – for the grant materialized later – I told myself 'Achilles' was irrelevant. Important to me was the publication of my anti-nuclear-lobby poem – partly based on a poem of Brecht's – 'To My Fellow Artists', in the *Statesman*. My mind, ever ready to suggest causes for dissatisfaction, ignored the possibility that those who gave my Homer poem critical support knew better than I what was best for me. Not that 'To My Fellow Artists' is a bad poem. It is a good one, and unusual for its time.

S HORTLY after 'To My Fellow Artists' was published the second Free Cinema Festival was held at the National Film Theatre. 'Free Cinema' meant films made by young directors minus the constraints of conventional entertainment.

As at the Royal Court, the mood at the Festival was exhilarating. Typical of him, and of the time, Lindsay said: 'Why not read your poem to the house? We'll put you on between films' – as if it was commonplace, poetry reading in cinemas.

I had not faced an audience since my recitation of 'Christopher Robin Is Saying His Prayers' twenty years ago. The auditorium was packed. Several hundred people. 'There is nothing to fear. The poem is a good poem. The audience are young, intelligent. On we go,' Lindsay said. On we went. My knees shaking.

Lindsay introduced me. I gave the title, and began. To my amazement the words held me up. Reading verse aloud is a quite separate art from writing it. I hoped to get the business over quickly. Then my fear quelled and I slowed down.

At the bar Lindsay introduced me to Karel Reisz – calm, quiet, perceptive, like Lindsay, someone who listened carefully to what you said, and then, in a flash, developed your notion, taking it forward.

What was imminent became evident. It was a year since the Prime Minister, Harold Macmillan, had made his 'the people of this country have never had it so good' speech. Far as Macmillan's assertion was from the things that I, and many I knew, wanted, his words were true. Men could have cars. Boys, bikes. Women, good kitchens. Girls, fun – which, for them, meant the start of unprecedented freedoms, of liberty. The last, though I did not know it, being the most important change of all those that occurred.

'Charles,' I said. 'I think I'll put "To My Fellow Artists" on a poster and sell copies, stick them up.'

'What about length?'

Then I remembered Germano and his ceiling for David Archer's bookshop. I rang him.

'Facetti. Yes. I know it. I like it. From the *Statesman*. A poster? Of course. Come round.'

In his workroom, one of its eighteen-foot-long walls covered with books on typography and graphic design ranged along three-inch thick shelves – 'They are hollow, made of varnished cardboard. From an abandoned window display at Harrods' – Germano spelt out his ideas while he selected paper and type, while for me, watching him, the excitement of my visit with Alex and Jane to the Imprimerie Mazarine was recaptured.

'No long blocks of print' – standing back from his drafting board. 'When you stand back, the sheet has its own interest' – suggesting the lines of verse with zigzag pencil strokes.

Others, too, gave time, their services, their skills, for nothing. Tom Maschler – managing director of Jonathan Cape – found the money to produce an LP of the second section of my Homer poem – as I had begun to think of my work on the *Iliad* – *Patrocleia*. Douglas Cleverdon – among the Third Programme's most experienced directors, *Under Milk Wood* being his show – produced it. Vanessa Redgrave – met on an anti-nuclear-lobby demonstration – and Alan Dobie – met in the bar of the Royal Court – read and refused to be paid. Roger Mayne, the photographer, gave prints, proud of his work. Karel Reisz and Ken Russell gave me ideas for poems, for plays. Jimmy Logue gave me the money to pay John Sankey, the printer/editor/critic, to produce – at cost – the 'To My Fellow Artists' poster that Lindsay and I pinned up in bookshops, cafés and the new-style,

Terence-led, espresso and cappuccino coffee bars. Germano, as well as the poster, designed *Patrocleia* when it was published as a book. Carne-Ross and Peter Levi provided the cribs. Mirella Ricciardi, her photograph of a young Masai warrior, used on its jacket, and now on the front of *War Music*.

ONE evening I was taken to a house on Chelsea Embankment for drinks. About fifty people. Posh. Among the crowd was a young woman with fine blonde hair done in a ponytail, and, as I learnt from her words to the young man whose interest in her was diminishing with every syllable she spoke, a serious, innocent nature.

'Why say that,' she said, 'when a moment ago you said the opposite?'

'A joke, I suppose . . .'

'Well, if you don't mind my saying so, I didn't find it at all funny.'

He did mind. He was keen to escape. She wouldn't let him.

'You think it all right to make a joke about someone whose heart has been broken by what her love said to her?' This put gently.

'Oh, Nell . . .' the young man said. 'Look, there's . . .' mentioning a name. 'I must have a word with him . . .' leaving Nell, if that was her name, gazing down at her black button-over shoes and white stockings.

'Would you like a drink?' I said.

'No thank you. I don't drink very much. Do you?' she said, looking up, looking straight into mine with her own wide blue-grey eyes. And I fell in love.

'Only when I eat,' I heard myself saying, thinking: What a stupid answer.

'I'm Nell,' she said. And when I gave my name: 'Oh, I hoped you would come. I have been reading your poems. I liked some of them a lot.'

This was too much for me. I had to sit down.

'Let's sit over there,' I said.

'I can't sit,' she said. 'I'm the hostess. You sit. I write stories. if you like I'll get my stories for you to read.'

She came back through her guests holding a green ring-binder.

'This is your house?' I said, not wanting to lose her.

'Mm. I don't like it. You never see your neighbours. I'm going to give it back to my father.'

In a large, flowing, well-proportioned hand, the title page read: *Stories / by / Nell Dunn.*

The spelling was bad. The grammar anarchic. Tenses changed mid-sentence. Sometimes in mid-clause. As soon as characters appeared, the irregularities ceased to matter. The dialogue was keen, plausible, clear. One scene between two middle-aged working-class women went:

'When Mandie died I bought a budgerigar.'

'What did you call it?'

'Tiddles.'

'That's a cat's name.'

'It was all I could think of at the time. A few days after I bought him I came down in the morning and he was lying on the floor of his cage. Dead.'

'No. . .'

'Yes. Completely dead.'

'What happened then?'

'I put him in the dustbin on my way to work.'

'Poor thing.'

'His cage cost three shillings.'

I – who had read the letters pages in women's magazines to discover what women really thought – found myself in the presence of women talking openly to each other. I entered a world where men were treated as instruments of fate, trouble you put up with, obstacles or problems to be worked around, not too bad – if you picked carefully.

Nell and I began to see a lot of each other. Part of my delight in her came from wanting to know how she was going to approach this or that subject. I relished her formally uneducated, feminine intelligence.

She and Lindsay had something in common. His educated intelligence was masculine, acute, critical, but both were inspired by a lyrical sympathy. They shared a respect for ordinariness, insight into the transient beauty of the commonplace, appreciation of what was glimpsed for a moment, then gone for ever unless caught as it flew.

From Nell's silences I learnt that matters of considerable interest to me, to those like me, had little significance elsewhere.
When I made, as I was apt to do, too much of a fuss over her, she
would insist: 'The world sees me as an ordinary person, pretty
enough, friendly enough, nothing special.' If I became cross at
hearing this, upsetting us both, she would say, moving the fall of
her hair to one side with the brush she took from her bag: 'Let us
just sit quietly together reading our books, saying nothing for an
hour.'

Nell regarded my work more seriously than I did. She had
commitment. Part of my mind was always looking out of the
window.

Writing what one hopes will be valued and preserved requires
faith. Mentions in a one-volume history of literature, items in
popular anthologies, books by others on your books, prizes –
these are worth having.

As it is to write something that will help others to hoe their
row, or be comforting to read when they are ill in bed in a foreign
country.

Money is a decent, low reason for writing. Self-expression is
not. Well, I suppose it can be – provided that it is no more than
a motive to drive an accomplished writer. To write well today
requires ardour, concentration, method, pride in your art. Even
the blessed – Picasso, Shakespeare – needed these.

Away back in Bournemouth I had decided that to write for
money was disgusting – whatever Samuel Johnson said. You
wrote for the art of writing, for literature. Now I see that that
view disregarded many forms of literary art. But in my heart I
still hold it to be true.

I lacked a firm routine. I worked in the late morning, early
afternoon. For how long? Seldom very long. An hour or two.
Three at most. One of my few memories of me writing is of the
surprise I felt at my exhaustion while at work on what became
War Music. Another, of my pernicketiness, obsessive tidiness,
making sure everything is in exactly the right place before I can
start.

Hugo said: 'Few writers work long hours. If you wrote 250
words – a page – each day, every day, from your twenty-first to

your seventy-first birthday you'd leave fifty books. Dickens worked like that. Shakespeare even harder, plus acting, and helping to run the business. Norman Mailer works hard. I admire Norman Mailer.'

I had no subject matter of my own. I wanted to write an extended poem just because I wanted to. I had no theme. Homer gave me something to do, though I was slow to see it.

I would leave my work mid-sentence, especially if it was going well. I do not mean that ideal break point where you have roughed out the next paragraph or unit of verse. I mean leave it flat, like that. Just walk away.

'You did that with people, too,' Isobel said. 'You did it with me.'

As Doris had predicted, the Campaign for Nuclear Disarmament, CND, was founded in February 1958 by well-known figures such as A. J. P. Taylor, J. B. Priestley, Kingsley Martin and Bertrand Russell. Three months after its inauguration the Campaign had attracted support enough to become a mass movement of a kind rare in British history, involving, as it did, mainly the young and middle-class.

Without the lead given by these reputable souls, and by certain distinguished Christian ministers, it is unlikely that the Campaign's attempt to rid the country of a misguided defence policy based on the possession of nuclear weapons would have been taken out of the hands of a number of small, albeit honourable, groups.

Contemporary British intellectuals outside journalism are inclined to dismiss any suggestion that they constitute a significant minority – what is elsewhere called the intelligentsia – and that this minority, blessed with the power of detached, informed, analysis fails in its duty if it fails, when necessary, to criticize, as well as to support, the institutions that sustain it.

The dissident voices I have mentioned, plus those listed in my notes, challenged this complacency. Far from being estranged from their fellow countrymen, the founders of CND demonstrated a belief in the nation's sensible conduct regarding its defence, at the heart of which lay the conviction that idealism and self-sacrifice were essential features of a successful country.

SHORTLY before Easter 1958 the Campaign announced its sponsorship of a public march starting at Trafalgar Square on Good Friday, and finishing on Easter Monday fifty miles away in Falcon Field opposite the Atomic Weapons Research Establishment, a government factory dominating the Berkshire village of Aldermaston, where our weapons of mass destruction originated.

This event, known in the years that followed as the Aldermaston March, caught the imagination of many thousands of people. Accommodation for the marchers, who came from all over Britain, was provided *en route* by schools, churches, village halls, institutes, libraries and private dwellings.

The Film and Television Committee for Nuclear Disarmament decided to make a documentary of the march.

In the weeks before the march, the Committee, composed of film technicians (plus Karel and Lindsay) borrowed the equipment and begged 18,000 feet of 35mm film stock from around the cinema industry. Then, from Good Friday, from the plinth of Nelson's column onwards, they photographed the four-day march, interviewing marchers, covering the bands and the speeches of CND's leaders until the Research Establishment had been passed.

Lindsay, Karel and Mary Beales assembled the material. 'And a tricky business it was,' Lindsay said. 'Few of the sequences had numberboards. When the work was done I asked Richard Burton to read the narrative passages linking the interviews – which he did.'

The film, *March to Aldermaston*, opened, and ran for six weeks, alongside Jean Renoir's *La Grande Illusion* at the Academy cinema in February 1959. A video of it was issued this year (1998).

I enjoy the moment in the film when the march is seen entering Reading and we marchers respond with a cheer as the bells of a church we are passing begin to peal. However, as the church's vicar emerged to explain, he had had his bells rung to drown out the sound of the marchers singing, not to ring them into town.

As a political act the march was scorned by the majority of Britain's professional politicians. Confident that the electorate would believe them, not the Committee for Nuclear Disarmament, the apologists for nuclear weapons excited natural fears with stories about Moscow's plans to drive Austria, Germany, France, the Netherlands, Sweden, Norway, Italy, Spain, Portugal, Ireland and Britain into the Atlantic, *en bloc*, making their predictions plausible by detailing the foul behaviour of Stalin and his followers, while – as an aside – they characterized the Committee's efforts as feeble-minded ('loony').

The government's confidence was unshakeable. Was there any reason to be disturbed by this new movement? None whatsoever, London assured Washington.

The *Daily Mail* said:

The marchers were mainly middle-class and professional people. They were the sort of people who would normally spend Easter listening to a Beethoven concert on the Home Service, pouring dry sherry from a decanter for the neighbours, painting Picasso designs on hard-boiled eggs, attempting the literary competitions in the weekly papers, or going to church with the children. Instead they were walking through the streets in their old clothes. They were behaving entirely against the normal tradition of their class, their neighbourhood, and their upbringing.

Among other things, we sang:

> Men and women stand together,
> Do not heed the men of war.
> Make your mind up, now or never,
> Ban the bomb forever more!

Nell and I marched together. The weather was dreadful. Good Friday the coldest since 1917, the wettest since 1900. Roger Mayne's photograph taken on the morning of the second day shows a drenched, bedraggled line vanishing into a rainy mist. The organizers had expected 300 marchers. Nine thousand filed in to Falcon Field.

Among the enjoyable consequences of the march was the huffing and puffing of its opponents. 'Jivers . . . babies in prams . . . Communist dupes . . . moral fantasists . . . irresponsible . . . traitors to the Queen . . . emotional fools . . . amazing to find pretty young girls among the great unwashed . . .'

'Everything they call the marchers describes themselves,' I argued as we walked along. 'It is they who are hysterical, irresponsible, unpatriotic, militarily stupid, wasting the defence budget on pride-pleasing bombs. It is a compliment to say a non-conformist movement has attracted pretty girls.'

Nell was silent. We walked on surrounded by people who were talking and smiling. Out of the corner of my eye I saw Nell had tears in hers.

'I'm sorry. I said the wrong thing about pretty young women.'

' "Wrong thing" makes it sound like a *faux pas*. And it's not that you *said* it. It's that you *think* it. It came out pat,' Nell said, brushing her hair back. 'As if there never had been any fighters for what is right who were also what you would call "pretty".'

We decided to march apart. As usual after such words I walked along feeling like death. Then I saw a black cab cruising down the side of the march with Ken looking out of the window. A moment later he fell in beside me – dressed in a fawn ankle-length overcoat and blue kid gloves. He produced a clipping.

'L-l-listen to this from the *Daily Express*:

In a statement issued yesterday the Archbishop of Canterbury, the Most Reverend Geoffrey Fisher, said: *The very worst the Bomb can do is to sweep a vast number of people from this world into the next into which they must all go anyway.*

'And on the same page:

How to make a Million. 1. Be tough. If your best friend stands in your way, sweep him aside. 2. Be ambitious. Smash your way forward, trample others down, and wear hobnailed boots for the job. 3. Apply your Mind. Think money day and night. Live with it, dream about it, talk about nothing else, and above all – get in with those who have made it.'

Towards evening we arrived at Reading. A letter appeared shortly afterwards in the *Daily Telegraph*:

Sir – The people of Reading, together with hundreds of thousands of others on the route have had to suffer the attentions of an unruly mob. The majority of this rabble seem, from their appearance and behaviour, to have gained their experience and training for this performance in students' 'rags'.

I see that a senior Berkshire police officer is reported as saying: 'I have never in 22 years' experience in the police seen such a large body of people so well organized. '

What he meant by this I do not know. If however, it was by means of good organization that the noise caused by thousands of people marching, singing, chanting and enjoying the music of such people as George Lynch and his Hi Fi Steel Percussion Orchestra at 7 o'clock in the evening, I feel that the police should be prosecuting the organizers.

On the last day of the march the sun came out. I met the painter Richard Hamilton carrying a life-size cut-out of Marilyn Monroe – who was thus present in spirit. With him was a young student, just entered at the Royal College of Art. Her name was Pauline Boty. She was handing out pamphlets for an Anti-Ugly meeting to protest against the boring, inefficient designs of the office and tower blocks rising by the dozen over central London.

Miss Boty was resolute. Above her smile, her gold-brown eyes challenged us, as we sprawled on coats spread over the damp grass, to do something to improve the urban landscape. 'Our leaflet states', she said in a serious voice, 'that architects never criticize architects. We will protest outside the horrible Agriculture House in Knightsbridge at the stated time. I expect to see you all there.' Then she waded away through the crowd.

When we had eaten our sandwiches everybody went home. I had that pointless feeling.

EARLY in 1958 the Tynans took me to see a play called *The Tenth Chance*, one of the Royal Court's Sunday-night productions – that is to say, single performances, without décor, of new plays by young writers.

As neither Elaine – Ken's first wife – nor I had heard of the author, Ken read out the press release. Stuart Holroyd, it said, was a young thinker who believed that only the lives of heroic or inspired individuals, outsiders of genius, could show the world how to act under stress.

The play concerned a man finding God under torture by the Nazis. The theatre was full, the audience excited. I sat between Elaine and Michael White.

By the interval the mood had changed. *The Tenth Chance* was oracular, with long philosophical speeches. Towards the end of the second half the torture scene began. The hero, tied to a chair, was beaten by officials of the Gestapo, while other members of the cast paced the stage, intoning: 'Receive him into the kingdom of light! Receive him into the kingdom of light!' At which point, rather to my own surprise, I shouted out: 'Rubbish!'

The cast froze. The chanting died away. Then, in the silence, the voice of Anne, the author's wife, rang out with: 'Christopher Logue, get out of this theatre,' which got the only laugh of the evening, and whose command Elaine and I obeyed.

Nervous, we went into the King's Arms for a drink and to wait for Ken. Five minutes later, when the curtain had come down, the door burst open and, bent on squaring accounts, in came the author, plus several supporters, led by Mrs Holroyd – a most attractive young woman – who ran through the tables and jumped on to me saying: 'I'll crush you with my Daimler!', overturning my chair and bringing us both to the floor. As Michael called out: 'Don't worry – she can't drive,' I got up, expecting a fight. Elaine, flourishing one of her heels by the toecap, said: 'Forget the women, Christopher.' Then, two handy-looking barmen appeared, and that was the end of it. Or almost.

It being a Sunday, not much else was going on, and several newspapers reported the incident on the following day. Their reports were accurate, except for that in the *Daily Mail* which described me as 'a Communist' poet. I was not a Communist. When some I knew repeated the description, or asked me if it was true, I disliked having to deny it. I wrote to the *Mail* pointing out the mistake, but they did not print my letter. Eventually – wherein I was helped by Alan Pryce-Jones, and David Jacobs, a rather grand solicitor – the *Mail* printed an apology.

I still feel uneasy about it. Richard Wright, who had changed long since, and Ken Sprague, a friend from my Bournemouth days, were the only Communists I had known. Both of them praiseworthy men. Albeit a mistake, this has been my only brush with false representation. I found it alarming.

IN Paris I had become a friend of the Yankee wit and political analyst, John Phillips Marquand. We had kept in contact by letter. Now married, he and his wife, Sue, were renting a house at Palamós, a village on the Costa Brava. Would I care to visit?

I went via Paris.

Maurice was buoyant, no mention of his health. Was I owed any money? He was going to expand. A nightclub. A restaurant. The books were doing better than ever. Did I know that Alex was married? A beautiful American girl? Take this (£50).

Beckett had aged. 'Are you all right for money? Give my best to anyone who remembers me.'

I arrived at Barcelona Central Station in the early evening. The local train, drawn by a steam engine with a tall brass-collared funnel, had open carriages. Soon we were running through orange and lemon groves, their leaves scenting the air. I began to worry that John might have forgotten I was arriving.

It was dark when the train reached Palamós. There was no sign of John. The only person waiting was a short, dark-haired man, his hands in the pockets of his car coat. He came over and said: 'Hi, you're Christopher. John asked me to pick you up. I'm Artie Shaw.'

And it was! It actually was *the* Artie Shaw, king of swing, the big-band maestro, world-famous for his recordings of 'Begin the Beguine' and 'Frenesi', putting my rucksack into the boot of his Mercedes coupé.

I expected us to purr away at once. Not at all. The maestro switched on the car's internal lights, slid back the driver's seat, took out his penis, and said, in a formal voice: 'Christopher, to let you know that you are now in the big time, take a look at a prick that has fucked Lana Turner and Ava Gardner.'

A uniformed maid opened the door of the villa where we drew up. Artie briefed her, in Spanish: 'This gentleman needs a bath.' And to me: 'See you tomorrow.'

While showering in the circular, tiled bathroom, I asked myself: had Artie 'gone down' on either, or on both, of these world-famous beauties? How did they taste? Delicious? Were their clitorises large? Like acorns? Did Artie tickle these highly responsive organs by brushing the tip of his tongue across their heads? All this was too much. Remixing the sequence with myself in the great virtuoso's rôle, I took a satisifying wank on the bathroom's sofa, wiped myself off – the towels were monogrammed RR – dressed, and made my way along a corridor towards the voice of a squeaky, almost-recognizable singer. At the head of a staircase leading down into a large studio room, I saw John and Sue side by side on a sofa.

By them was a grey-haired man of about sixty who came forward and put a glass holding half a pint of Bloody Mary into my hand, saying: 'My name is Robert Ruark, and you are Chrissy Logue, the little pinko-Brit who aims to beat my Rolls-Royce into a ploughshare.' He pronounced my name correctly.

Nodding towards the LPs stacked on the player, Sue said, 'Why don't you try 33, Bob?' The squeakiness came from Ruark's playing a Sinatra disk at the wrong speed.

'I hate that cock-sucking son of a spick bitch,' Ruark said. 'One time I went on my knees outside his hotel room door and shouted through the keyhole: "Come out you commie spick. Come out and fight." He didn't. He couldn't buy heavies then.'

Mrs Ruark lifted her glass to her lips at regular intervals while staring straight ahead.

Next day John took me for a drive along the coast. 'You reckon to get what you call politics in your new poems?' he said. 'As the one with the good luck to be driving you around Europe I note that what you say in your published poems has nothing to do with what you say when lecturing me on the art of government.'

'They are the work of my ignorance.'

'You think so? You really mean that?'

'Yes.'

'That still leaves how you're going to get this new vision in.'

'By an act of will. I'll force it in. I'll just copy Brecht.'

'You mean plagiarism?'

'Yes.'

'As a duty?'

'Yes.'

'Even a form of patriotism?'

'If it's any good, my work will be a patriotism in itself.'

We waited on the terrace of a bar while the owner sent his son down to the rocks for a netful of baby squid. These were served to us sliced and (barely) fried with hard bread. Even after living in France, after M. and Mme de Ruyter's cuisine, I had never eaten anything so delicious that was at the same time so ordinary, so inexpensive.

Outside Port Bou we saw a Franco road sign: *No Hay Libertad Sin Orden* – 'A sentiment you never appreciate, Christopher'. On the following day I showed the first signs of a condition known as EMOS (Enormous Marble Object Syndrome) from which I have suffered intermittently ever since

Artie had offered to drive us to Cadaqués. The outing included a plan to knock on Salvador Dalí's door and get him to sign several postcards of his better paintings. On the way, we stopped at Armentera. Opposite the bar was a yard full of what is now called 'architectural salvage', i.e., heavy junk. And there it was: a lion-mask fountainhead. White marble curls, blank eyes, a drip spout – and only £10.

John pointed out that I was letting down the International Left by coveting an object that should by rights be ground into cement to build holiday homes for elderly Pillars of Labour. Artie worried for his suspension. Sue was on my side. The trouble was weight. The head was carved from an eighteen-inch cube. No two of us could lift it.

I settled for a (large) mortar and pestle, also in white marble – £2 – which I dragged across Europe and which, ten years later, Kenny exchanged for the (composite) statue of Venus that came off a gatepost to the Venus Pencil Factory in West London and that Harry bolted on to the disused chimney stack of No.18.

HOME, I learnt there had been two days of race riots in Nottingham and parts of Notting Hill. The police had managed to control, and then disperse, crowds of up to three hundred young white men chanting 'Down with the dirty niggers', attacking local blacks, breaking their windows, trying to break their heads.

To my relief, the trouble did not spread. When Harry

complained that because of the recent immigration his way of life was in danger, Minky replied that his way of life was so disgusting – 'Day after day with your nose down a fucking drain' – he should be thankful. As for Harry's opinion that the blacks were turning the district into a slum, Minky reminded him that the district had been a slum for fifty years: 'And you, Harry, are a fucking slum dweller like the rest of us. And if this wasn't a slum, you wouldn't be living here. So fucking shut up in case when the property boys turf out the blacks they turf you out with 'em.' Which is what happened, though it took twenty years.

I asked Kenny what he thought.

'You're bothered, aren't you?' he said.

'And you're not?'

'Not specially. There's been plenty of anti-black anger about for years. A lot of bad lads came up from south London.'

'Do the police know that?'

'Of course'

'Well?'

'Well, what are they doing about it – is that it? Nothing. If the Mews was full of people playing Blue Beat all night, you'd be the first to shout.

'Minky has just bought a bungalow in Essex – and that's what he says. And, Mr Logue, for your information, Minky Warren is not my father. My father was killed fighting in Italy. Mum had two boys to raise. She walked from door to door for sewing. Then Minky proposed. She took him. You like him. He likes you. You're a curiosity. But he's not a nice man. Take it from me.'

People blamed the riots on the Fascist politician Oswald Mosley. Wrong. His people were not active in Notting Hill until after the riots. Mosley stood for North Kensington in next year's (1959) election.

'And lost his deposit,' Alice said.

STREET stalls – once restricted to the fruit and vegetable sellers – were spreading. Kenny had two outside the shop. Typically, he had the up-coming goods: leather cases from the twenties and thirties, embroidered pictures, tin toys.

When I wanted to buy a friend a present I asked Kenny what

he had in the garages – the garages under No.18 that is – his and Minky's storage.

'How much for that embroidered angel with silky wings with "I'll Walk Beside You" stitched underneath her?'

'Gone. I told you to have it. You turned your nose up. "I don't like folk art," you said.'

'The reason so many people like your friend Kenny,' Isobel remarked, 'is that he has time for everybody. He never turns you off with a word. It's "Try so-and-so. He knows. Come back if you don't have any luck." And that's even when he's unloading at the end of a day on the road.'

I KNEW a little about jazz. In Paris, Danny Halperin had taken me to hear Kenny Clarke and Art Simmons. One evening Charles played a record called Jazz Canto, poems read to jazz. The balance was wrong. The music too loud for the words, the words unrelated to the music. One track was exhilarating. Lawrence Ferlinghetti's poem *Dog* read by Bob Dorough, an American french-horn virtuoso, to music composed by him, played by his Quintet.

Next day I called Carne-Ross at the Third. Would he back a poetry and jazz programme?

'Send me a proposal.'

'I'll bring *Dog* in.'

Donald was a scholar in the world: Greek, Latin, French, Italian, Spanish, Portuguese – knowing the poetry in these languages as well as that composed in English. Equally, he was to be found in theatres, cinemas, bars, parties, or breezing across Hyde Park on his scooter on the way to Broadcasting House with his rat looking out of his overcoat pocket. 'He gets stares at the lights.'

Dog was enough for Carne-Ross to see the possibilities. He commissioned a thirty-minute programme.

Charles introduced me to the drummer/composer Tony Kinsey, who, with the pianist/composer Bill le Sage, ran the Tony Kinsey Quintet.

Best suited for music plus speech were the poems Patrick Bowles and I had made out of Neruda's love poems – impressionistic, lyrical things without argument or narrative. I hoped

Kinsey and le Sage would like them for their mood, imagery, strength of feeling. 'They are the ones to do it,' Charles said.

Tony lived in Maida Vale. 'I took you into our sitting room where my wife was reading in an armchair,' he said. 'You darted towards her, knelt at the side of the chair and introduced yourself by saying: "Hello! My name is Christopher Logue. I am a socialist and a poet." '

Fair, curly-haired, with an engaging countenance, Tony took the poems over to the window of his music room, holding them up to the light as if they were slides, murmuring: 'Ah . . . ' and 'Um . . . ' for several minutes. Charles smiled occasionally. I felt anxious. Then Tony said: 'I can't say anything now. I'll see what Bill says. You had better come down to the Flamingo on Saturday night to hear us.'

'In fact,' Tony said later, 'I was very excited. Bill and I divided the poems between us and set to work.'

The Flamingo Club was in a Wardour Street cellar. It was packed. Hushed. The Quintet were on. Tony behind his drums, Bill centre-right at the piano, angled, a glance over his shoulder taking in Kenny Napper (bass), Les Condon (trumpet) and Ken Wray (trombone).

Tony's eyes were closed. There was a smile on his face – whereas Bill was right *there*, on the moment – both attitudes characteristic of the 'cool' New York style music of the late forties.

We decided to call the programme *Red Bird Dancing on Ivory* (from a Caribbean riddle – answer: a tongue). The balance of the words and the music was hard to get. The BBC's sound engineers put me in a box in the middle of the band. Then I couldn't see the Quintet. I was relying on Tony to cue me.

'It's no good,' he sighed. 'We have passed eight takes and you are *still* off the beat. I want to concentrate on the music. You're part of a band. Do you know the meaning of the word? A band. Other people. Music means talking/listening to one another.'

Still no good.

'I'm amazed,' I overheard Tony say to Bill. 'He's supposed to be fairly intelligent.'

'He'll have to learn how to count bars,' Bill said.

They sat me at the drum kit. One stick only.

'Now. A-one, a-two, a-three . . .'

Bill began the piano part, while Tony, his hand on mine, marked the beat.

Still no good. I could not connect score to sound.

Charles solved the problem. He would do the counting for me.

The engineers put a light in my box. I could manage the first bars, then, as my rests ended, Charles pumped the button.

Carne-Ross was pleased. Broadcast, the programme was well covered by the press.

DIARY SCRAPS, April 1959:
A telephone call from someone called George Martin who works at EMI records. Tony has told him about *Red Bird*. He is interested in words spoken to music. His office is next door to the Wallace Collection so I can combine my seeing him with a view of Miss O'Murphy's bum.

George Martin is a tall, thin, softly spoken, silvery looking headmaster-type of chap. His office overlooks Manchester Square.

When I told Tony that Martin had asked me in, he looked serious and said: 'He runs the Parlophone label.'

Consequently I had expected a bigger office, not a slot-in-the-wall affair hardly bigger than my room at the Poitou – which is what Mr Martin has. But I felt quite at home as the office resembles Charles' room in Bournemouth. Cram full of papers, record sleeves, white-label disks, press-releases, publicity photographs of his label's artistes. George's – so I am to call him – chair in among them. Unlike Charles' place, George's is orderly. The 'phone goes. Something is required. He stands up, reaches up, and, lo and behold, there is the document: moments later, a hand with red-painted fingernails comes around the edge of the door and, leaning back – but not looking round – George hands it over.

It is agreed that he will record and release seven items from the *Red Bird* broadcast on a 45 r.p.m. EP Parlophone disk. Tony and Bill will title them. I learn the term 'A and R' man.

The O'Murphy bum is one of the finest painted. It turns out that there were two O'Murphy girls, Victoire and Louise, both painted by Boucher. Lucky man. But whose bum is it?

DIARY, 29 May 1959:
At EMI's Abbey Road studios to record *Red Bird*. George is a treat to work with. No nerves. No fuss. Always quietly spoken:

'Yes. Quite good. But still a little hissy. Watch those "esses". We'll do it again. Tony? . . . '

We visited the control-room to hear the playbacks, George at this huge 'desk' – its surface is nothing but dozens of small levers set in long slots by means of which George 'plays' and 'mixes' what he has recorded. Definitely part of the inventive effort. Leading from behind. I went back down into the studio much encouraged.

The recording took two days. We were rehearsed meticulously and knew the material backwards. Without the BBC and Carne-Ross there would have been no record.

SINCE abandoning my hopes of going to Oxford I had not thought that much about the city. When a letter came inviting me to read from my work at New College, my heart lifted. I *would* be going to Oxford, after all, and for professional reasons. I would see Uccello's *Hunt*. Then I realized my invitation had nothing to do with literary Oxford. It came from the University Labour Club and was signed by one Dennis Potter.

Even now, I suppose, my use of the word 'professional' vis-à-vis a poetry reading may raise an eyebrow. Before my appearance at the National Film Theatre there were not many readings. I remember one in 1957 in Greenwich – the result of my broadcasting. After the NFT I received a number of invitations to read my verse. The inviters (schools, literary societies) paid between £3 and £5, plus travel expenses, per reading.

Literary people of those days could be hostile to the public reading of poetry. Some said that the invention of writing had made it redundant. Or that the reader's interpretation, however skilled or sensitive, deprived the text of its autonomy, imposing on the poem's purely intellectual voice.

Not so. The literary voice is a fabrication. In verse, sound and sense are inextricable. Read silently, or aloud, poems perform.

They do so whether the interpretation is your own, or another's. A poem's life is as much a history of performances as a history of reprints. The invariant, replicable text is a myth, too.

I once made a list of historically recorded poetry readings, chiefly British, though I could not resist that given in AD 540 by Arator of Liguria of his epic based on the Acts of the Apostles, which 'was interrupted so many times by applause that it lasted for four days'. That's one I'm glad I missed.

Some 425 years ago, our very own George Gascoigne was booked to read his *Princely Pleasures* to Elizabeth I at Kenilworth Castle: ' . . . but did not perform owing to unfavourable weather – it being June'. Worse, having presented the Queen with his *Tale of Hermetes the Hermit*, Gascoigne was vexed when a Mr Abraham Flemings was appointed to read it to her, then outraged when Flemings claimed to be the *Tale*'s author. Gascoigne protested, only to be led away by the royal security.

Suffice it to say that poetry readings, mostly in private, were common in Britain from Langland and Chaucer onwards. By the 1960s, a fashion had developed for paid, publicly advertised readings by poets of their own work.

The New College porters directed me to the room of an undergraduate called John McGrath. It was, he was, as I had imagined: a well-proportioned space with white-painted window seats, a bottle of sherry standing by three glasses on its mantelpiece, and a tall, thin young man with stand-up curls, who, after admitting me, stood by the fireplace with one foot on its fender looking shy. Scarcely had we introduced ourselves when, knocking and entering at the same time, D. Potter appeared, red-haired, heavily freckled, eyes alight, his hand out, shaking mine. And with him, quieter, smiling, shifting his weight from one foot to the other – as (though now somewhat stout) he still does – my friend-to-be, Roger Smith.

Dennis took charge. Down we went, through several courtyards (it was dark by then), out of a back door, along a twisty lane, up a garden path into what looked like a small eighteenth-century provincial town house (what facilities these children had!) into a crowded room.

To some present on that evening I was *the* politically committed poet, the only one in the country writing about things that mattered. I probably looked the part, too, in my blue-cotton Chinese worker's jacket. ('Just the thing,' Roger certified.) At any rate, Dennis was keen on my stuff. The other stuff coming out was boring. One or two had heard I had written a dirty book in Paris. Dennis – he took a strict line about such things – brought the subject up. I said it was a bad book not because it was porno-graphic but because it was badly written. That a good writer should make use of the power of words to stir people physically as well as intellectually. None of the women there took me to task.

I was impressed – as I was later, when I read in Cambridge – by the intellectual pressure these young people generated. They were clever and grave. Their questions were sharp. Some were witty. They had been well taught. Method. How to question.

In the morning Roger took me on a tour of the colleges and the Ashmolean Museum. I saw the *Hunt*.

Going home on the train, I felt pleased. It seemed as if I had been of some use, even in Oxford. A kind of graduation. Though I was not, of course, a regular heterodidact, I won-dered if I might return some day and be allowed to use the Bodleian Library, which was – to speak only of things – with the buildings, the pictures and the Botanical Garden, what the city had to offer. Yet I was glad to be on the train returning to London.

Walking home from Paddington I noticed that Olivier's *Richard III* was showing at the Westbourne Grove Odeon. The cinema was full of schoolchildren, a mix of black and white. The silence, intense at first, gradually gave way to flagrant, unrestrained cheering for Richard. The stealthier his lope, the deeper the wickedness beaming from his eye, the more he was loved. Finally, when he met his fate, the audience booed – me included.

I HAD more money. I acquired a telephone.

Nell visited No.18 fairly often. 'Things cost so little,' she reminded me when we were discussing the first version of this book. 'If I was coming to see you I bought some tomatoes, bread, butter, cheese – there was never anything to eat in Denbigh Close except chocolate biscuits and jam – they cost 50p. You got enough notebooks for a novel for £3. And when we stayed in Dusty Wesker's brother's cottage our supplies for the week, good stuff, came to £8. Arnold said we must not pee near the house or the nettles would flourish.'

A CALL came from Ken inviting me to meet Marilyn Monroe and Arthur Miller at his flat.

Then a call from Lindsay. I am to meet him on the steps of the Royal Court at 10 a.m. sharp. George Devine has a proposal for me.

From John Marquand, now in New York, I heard that Alex's earnings as scowman did not cover the cost of his heroin. As Maurice had said, he had married a young American woman. She too was taking heroin, prostituting herself to buy supplies; Alex sometimes reselling the heroin he had bought with the advances for unwritten books; or borrowing money from John, George and Dick. John said Alex was sure to be caught. If prosecuted and found guilty, he faced years of imprisonment.

THE Tynans' flat in Mount Street was worth a visit on its own. Circular – the building centred on a lift shaft and a spiral staircase – its two spacious living rooms were connected by Ken's study. One of these rooms contained Ken's library and record collection – both shelved on glass – and had black walls. Its lights, operated by the new-style dimmer-switches, were concealed by Mexican masks, as were the loudspeakers. You sat on tubular steel chairs. The other room had sofas and the Bosch wallpaper. There were no fireplaces. There was a hanging wicker chair in the bathroom.

Each of these broad rooms had a broad drinks tray, ice cubes, boxes of cigarettes, lighters, nibbles. There was a selection of magazines on low, glass-topped tables. Ken loved musicals. As soon as a new show opened in London or New York he had the LP of its score. When the record of *West Side Story* arrived I wanted to learn the words of Stephen Sondheim's lyrics. So did he. We must have played the disc thirty times, correcting each other's mistakes as we sang them back. The flat's kitchen was empty. Milk, a tea bag or two. The Tynans ate out.

As far as dress went, I was still in my roundhead days, varying my white shirt, black pullover with the Chinese worker look. For my audience with Monroe I had bought a new shirt, had my trousers cleaned and pressed, polished my shoes, washed my hair, brushed my teeth. What would she be wearing? How would her hair be done? If she smoked, would I be able to light her next cigarette? I made sure my fingernails were clean.

Ken let me in. He was wearing his powder-blue suit, yellow shirt, a green and white dancing-dolphins tie, and python-skin boots. He looked worried.

'We have a problem,' he said. 'Marilyn is crying.'

'How about Arthur Miller?'

'He's fine.'

'Well, I can talk to him.'

'Not really. He's on the phone to Marilyn.'

'How – '

'The house phone. She's in the bedroom, he's in the Bosch room.'

'When he comes off, then.'

'He's been talking to her for an hour. It doesn't sound as if he's going to be off for a while.'

'Oh.'

'Elaine is in the kitchen. Have a cup of tea with her.'

While I did, Ken wandered in and out, cigarette on the go, saying: 'He says she's soon going to feel better ... He needs another cup of coffee ... He's still on the phone ... '

I left an hour later without even seeing her handbag.

AUSTRYN called to say that Maurice was about to open his restaurant/night club, La Grande Séverine. A performance of Austryn's translation of *The Bedroom Philosophers* was to feature at the opening.

This was bad news for those of us owed money by Maurice. If the abrogation of British publishing censorship threatened by our parliamentarians did not ruin him, running La Séverine would. (It did.)

Buying No.18 had been on my mind. Once the thought of owning a house had seemed far-fetched. Then it started to crop up first thing in the morning. If I owned it, I would never have to pay rent again.

A man called Garrow, living at No.2, knocked on my door.

'Do you want to buy the Mews?' he said.

'You mean the whole Mews, 1 to 18?'

'3 and 8 have gone,' he said. 'Yours and No.17 belong to an old lady in Wales. You can have the other fourteen for £2,000. I've got to have the money by five p.m.'

He took a bundle of papers out of a carrier bag. 'Here are the deeds.'

'Why ask me?' I said.

'You're the only one in the Mews who is likely. I'm screwed. Finished. Don't ask why. If you can't get it, tell me.'

Kenny said: 'You missed your chance. Garrow owns them.'

'I've never seen £200 let alone £2,000.'

'Buy your own then.'

'With what?'

'Never mind the with what. Al and I are buying Minky's shop from him. Borrow. You've got possession. OK?'

'No one's going to lend someone like me money.'

'You haven't got debts. You're on the BBC. What about your car dealer cousin?'

I – EARLY as usual – was cold on the steps of the Royal Court at 9.30 a.m. Lindsay was late – as usual.

In his upstairs office overlooking the square I met George Devine, a friendly genius more concerned for others than for himself. He was dressed in a tweed jacket with leather elbow patches and a woolly cardigan. *Songs*, my newly published book of poems, was on his desk. Devine eyed me over his spectacles while lighting his pipe, then said: 'I have been asked to find a new Shakespeare with more sex. Do you think you fit the bill?' I said I'd do my best, though my mind wasn't as dirty as his (Shakespeare's).

George – as I thought of him after this meeting – had a peculiar gesture. He would shake his pipe by his ear, slowly, as you shake a light bulb to find out if it is gone.

Then the telephone rang. George: 'Mmm ... Mmm ... Yes. Oh. He did? Yes, a fool. A complete fool. I'll deal with it. Make a note. Yes. Tonight.' By which time his pipe had gone out. Picking it up. 'Money.' Shaking it. 'Now, this is' – lighting it – 'what I'd like you two to consider . . . '

Which was for Lindsay to direct, after I had rewritten, a play by one Harry Cookson, called *The Lily White Boys*, that Ken had spotted at a festival. Plot: three juvenile delinquents and their three girlfriends opt for legitimate success, fail and return to a life of petty crime. We decided to turn the boys into winners. The enterprising boy becomes wealthy; the time server, a powerful trades unionist; the rough, a policeman. Most of the text was to be replaced with songs – for the Girls, the 'Song of Natural Capital', for the Boys, the 'Song of the English Salesman', and so forth.

When I brought this plan in to George, who was wise in writers' ways, he said: 'What else are you doing?' I replied ambiguously. In fact, the Bollingen Foundation had awarded me a fellowship of £50 a month for twelve months to get on with my Homer poem. I decided to run the two projects concurrently. Donald had left the BBC to teach Greek in America. My letter to him said: What shall I do?

'*Iliad* 16. *The Patrocleia*. It is the *Iliad* in miniature,' he wrote. 'It begins with a quarrel, continues with a making-up, then a human cheeking a god, and, as a result of that human's punishment (death), an irreversible change that brings destruction to Troy. Good luck. Donald.'

I set about it as before. The list of events being longer, I carried a set of index cards with me. On a bus, wherever, I would try to run through the sequence quickly, then work back up through the separate events consulting the cards for detail. I abandoned the translations I had depended on. When I had some lines written, I memorized them, added them to those done, then went through the lot 'from the top', as singers say – a phrase I learnt during rehearsals for *The Lily White Boys*.

I missed Carne-Ross. But he was faithful to me, and to *Patrocleia*, as I began to call the text, sending long, detailed letters. 'Bear this in mind.' 'Forget that.' 'Remember: no hanging about. If there is imagery, it must be part of the movement. Keep your distance.'

Different as they were in tone (sometimes in content), the

translations I had read were easy to understand. Which meant they were clear. The clarity created the impression of speed.

I'm sure I looked odd – upstairs on the bus on my way to Sloane Square, carrying the lyrics for *The Lily White Boys* in my shoulder bag, muttering to myself about Troy. When stared at, I thought of Wordsworth's dog. Wordsworth composed aloud while walking. To avoid accusations of madness, he had taught his dog to trot before him and bark when another human appeared, whereon he fell silent.

IT was at about this time that I fell in with June Mary. I had been invited to read to the students at Brighton's College of Art. She was somewhat older – in her thirties – than the rest of the audience. We got chatting and went for a drink afterwards. Auburn-haired, with a passion for listing her day's agenda and then of crossing the items off 'on location' with a gold propelling pencil, June Mary, a devout Catholic, owned a chain of shops supplying accessories for pets. She was mad about driving and personal hygiene, and knew nothing whatsoever about poetry.

'I was at a loose end. I went into your reading by chance.'

She drove a Healey two-seater. She would put the passenger seat far back for me, fold down the canvas roof, and drive us across the downs by night with Sinatra records on the player, me lying back looking up at the stars. Writing? Fuck it, I thought. I can't be fished.

Then she vanished for ten days. Then she telephoned. From Lourdes.

'I'm upset.'

She was. I could hear it.

'I'm coming home. Will you come to the airport?'

'Of course. What's up? Some man bothering you?'

'I'll tell you when I see you.'

She took her time. Finally: 'I visited the Grotto. I know you think nothing of it, but I wanted – only as a precaution – to put a foot into the sacred spring. You have to queue up. When I got to it, the top of the water was covered with greyish crud and I couldn't bring myself to put even a toe in.'

With June Mary, instead of learning how to enjoy sex, I decided to force myself to fuck. Likewise, furious with my inability to produce rhymed verses for *The Lily White Boys* on tap, I made dummy lines from dummy words and tried to force the ideas for songs into the shapes they made.

Think of a set of short films called, *Scenes from the Life of an Impatient Man*: (i) C. Logue, stabbing, then ripping apart an envelope of vacuum-packed smoked salmon; (ii) C.L. smashing his palm on to the keys of his typewriter when for the fourth time he has failed to thread a new ribbon; (iii) the same chap, slashing, scraping the point of a carefully sharpened pencil across the surface of a drawing that has proved beyond him; or (iv) sighing to the ceiling as the person at the head of the queue gets out his cheque book. As a child, I was so quick to speak, I bit my tongue; so eager to drink, I cracked a tooth on the rim of a drinking fountain.

There is not a lot to be said for impatience. Perhaps, when the time comes for me to die, unable to stand the waiting, I'll just go for it.

B ECAUSE she suffered from wringing migraines, Xanthe visited a healer, a titled woman living in Dorset, who banished them for a year. Pretending to share Xanthe's complaint I, too, visited the healer. I explained that, when the moment arrived, not only did I not want to fuck, I would lose any existing erection no matter how patiently invited to continue. Lady Smythe asked me for a sample of my head hair and said that she would do the rest. One other thing. In humans – her practice covered several species reminding me of James Hayes, Jean Crouch's psychoanalyst companion – lovemaking involved want. Was I sure I had the right sex? Had I never desired a man? No. Very well. Let me know how you get on.

June Mary knew of my visit to Lady Smythe. When I got back to the Mews we took off our clothes. To my astonishment I produced a substantial erection, by which she led me across the room. And, would you believe it, no sooner were we on the bed than I shrank. June Mary moved on.

I was content when alone. I needed company – but on my terms. When I wanted to leave, wherever I was, I left. Why wait until someone else was ready? It must be now. At once. I had no wish to be with the sort of woman I could not leave alone at a party. At home I had things just so. On a visit to No. 18, the poet Brian Patten said: 'It's nice to see a girl's shoe or a hairbrush lying around forgotten, don't you think?' 'Sure,' I said, meaning 'No', and changed the subject.

My dilemma kept me in a state of ungratified yearning. Afraid I would not be able to please the woman in question, and taking measures to avoid the rejection that this might entail, equally I feared the hold another's complaisance might bring. Now and again I saw my married friends quarrel. Unsympathetic, I wanted no part of it. I was an only child and disliked sharing. Often irritable, disconsolate, vexed with myself, with the world, I found it better, on balance, to be alone. Before answering machines came in I kept my telephone-that-always-rang wrapped in a blanket in a cupboard and the extension (that could be switched off) to hand. After four days without a call – panic. Had I done something to put everyone off for ever? No, merely forgotten to switch the extension back on.

It was a relief to close my front door behind me. That was the world dealt with. Now I could do as I liked. I decided against having a bed, just a mattress on the floor. Harry's son, Jeff, painted No. 18 white throughout. Somewhat like a cell. The books, spines out, stacked against the walls. The kitchen empty as the Tynans'.

THE market was expanding. Pine was still big. Unloaded on Friday afternoon, overnight the pieces were dipped, stripped, waxed, had new brass knobs screwed on, and now, ready for the Saturday market, stood (unpriced) from the corner of the Mews down to my door – all of ten yards. But stalls were getting bigger.

'Chris?'

'Yes, Minky.'

'A word in your ear' – voice lowered. 'I'm not saying this for laughs. Understand?'

'Yes, Minky.'

'Your garages join up at the back.'

'Yes.'

'Right. Open both garage doors. Whitewash the garages inside. Run the electric down from upstairs. Buy twenty stalls. What have you got?'

A pause. A look around.

'A fucking antiques arcade is what you've got. The crowds go in one side, and out the other. Our Ken will run it.'

'He'll need planning permission,' said Alice.

'I'm sure Alice is right,' I said.

Minky put his china mug down on a newly stripped dresser.

'Planning permission? I'm English. I know the law. Harry' – Harry was just passing – 'have a fag.'

'Right, Minky.'

Minky hitched his shoulders. Harry took a drag.

'Harry – these garages of Chris's. Have they ever been used as garages?'

'Never, Minky. My gran used to keep her donkey and cart on one side and Mad John lived on the other. Before we moved him down to No.14 that is.'

'No, Harry, my friend. Think again. Your gran kept her donkey in Harry Major's garages at the bottom of the Mews. Right?'

'Now I remember it, Minky, that's just what she did.'

'And these so-called garages were used by my gran, Vesta Warren, for storing and *selling* furniture, doors open, all day, every fucking day. Right?'

'Right, Minky.'

'Then Tom Arthur got them. And he sold furniture from them. Then he got killed at Dunkirk. Then his wife married a Yankee. Then the anti-black-market police closed the road down until VE Day. Then it was back to lead and rags. Now we're on to furniture and stalls again. Right?'

'You bring it all back, Minky.'

'I remember the Sullivans mentioning furniture,' I said.

'Well, there we are then,' Minky said, picking up his mug, giving Alice a 'that-proves-it' nod. 'Chris's premises have been used for selling furniture and allied articles since 1944. That means Established Use. Chris doesn't need planning permission for Established Use, does he, Harry?'

'He does not, Minky,' said Harry, dropping his lighted butt on to the cobbles.

'Just because you've finished your fag, Harry, doesn't mean you can slip away. As a matter of fact, you, Harry, may turn out to be Chris's key witness in case of Public Inquiry.'

'What Public Inquiry?' Harry said, nervous.

'I didn't say there *was* going to be an Inquiry, Harry,' Minky said. 'I said in *case* there is a Public Inquiry – into the Established Use, that is. Harry was born in the Mews. Therefore he's your key witness, Chris. How old are you, Harry?'

'Forty-four, Minky.'

'You look sixty-four. Forty-four means born in '14–'15. Right?'

'1915, Minky.'

'We'll hear about that another fucking time. Meantime, Chris's drains will need a full inspection. £10.'

'Yes, a full inspection,' I said.

'£20 gets you twenty stalls. £1.10.0 per stall per Saturday. You and Kenny decide the split.'

'Won't the Council want to see the books?'

'Alice, the books are in here,' Minky said, tapping his brow. 'And I can't read or write. The Sullivans have reached an unknown destination in Australia' – Kingston-upon-Thames, actually – 'Chris found some old books when you moved in, didn't you, Chris?'

'Yes, Minky.'

'Right. We'll start this Saturday. Goldie Wills wants a stall.'

KENNY and Alice and I became extremely close. As often as I had been round at the Kerswells' in Southsea, now I was over at Kenny and Alice's place in Chepstow Road on Sunday mornings, Alice doing the books – 'We can never have enough of those engraved mirrors, Ken. Those you got when they knocked down the Shepherds Bush Albion fetched £150 – in notes.'

Kenny had no schooling worth the name. Loyal to a fault outwardly, cleverly judicial indoors, inventive, quick, obstinate, kind, suited for marriage, for fatherhood, a lover of jazz, of singers, of walking the Fells, with natural authority – Minky gave orders, Kenny you wished to please – Kenny Carter, when first I knew him, could barely read or write. Alice – as proud as they come – mentioned the fact discreetly, and asked me what to do.

I told her that reading and writing were mechanical skills, on the same level as driving – and look at the number of fools who had mastered all three. 'You teach him, Alice,' I said. 'It should take a month, half an hour a day.' That was it. The first books Kenny bought were on furniture.

Then he collected over five hundred china faces – small wall plaques of, mostly female, profiles, the oldest examples dating from about 1890 in Vienna – which he sold to an American dealer. Then, on the pattern of nineteenth-century engraved mirrors, he produced inexpensive, framed mirrors with a variety of popular designs offset on to the mirror's surface – and made a lot of money from this for about ten years.

There was another quality of Mr Carter's that impressed me. Far apart as they were class-wise, Kenny shared with Nell, and with Richard Ingrams when I got to know him, the gift of viewing common affairs from an unusual angle.

To illustrate my meaning: the only other soul I knew who possessed this gift was Auberon Waugh. I have forgotten whether it was on a television or radio show that he came out with it, but I shall not forget the silence that followed, when, in response to a question about the possible reintroduction of judicial hanging in Britain, Auberon said: 'There is only one good argument in favour of capital punishment: it gives so much pleasure to so many people.'

Kenny had noted my involvement with CND. When it came up one Sunday morning he stated: 'The anti-bomb lot get it wrong, Mr Logue. It's like that shop girl in Bournemouth you mentioned ages ago, the one who reads trash but knows what people like you find in OK books – everybody already knows everything they need to know about the bomb, and about those people who are in favour of it.

'You can't argue with the-bomb-stopped-the-bomb, or the-bomb-saved-us-from-the-Russians gang. Number one is their philosophy, and far as number two goes, everybody knows it was the Russians who saved *us* from the Nazis. And don't tell me we did our bit, or how the Yanks sent a lot of help. I know we did our bit. My dad died doing it. But if Russia had lost, sooner or later we would have made a deal with Hitler and most people would have settled down under British Nazi rule with the Duke of Windsor as our Nazi king.'

'Oh, Ken,' Alice burst out, 'don't say such terrible things. That could never have happened.'

'Yes it could, and yes it *would* have happened, Al. You and Mr Logue are together on this one. You're a Catholic. He was one. You two can't stand Nazi thinking. Most Brits don't care that much what happened to the Jews and the gypsies and the homos. Get it into your head. Chris can march till he drops. And perhaps he'd like to carry a banner saying the government should issue family-sized doses of morphine so that mothers can finish off their children who are already half-dead from burns, and then themselves.

'What's the name of that good-looking friend of yours – the one with the hair – does conjuring tricks?'

'Heathcote. Heathcote Williams.'

'Whatever. I heard him tell you he was an anarchist. I looked it up – or Al did. What did it say, Al?'

'It said it meant "no rulers", "rulerless", something like that.'

'I wrote it out. What's happened to my exercise book?'

'Chris is sitting on it.'

'Gosh, Ken, I'm so sorry . . . '

'Forget it.

'Here it is. "An" means "no", and "arch" means leader, ruler, that type. There was a lot of other stuff about chaos and so on, but that's where the word began. OK?'

'Yep.'

'Well, that's what we've got.'

'We've got the opposite. More rules and more rulers, every day.'

'Not as far as the bomb goes. Every country for itself. Mr Macmillan has his lot – us – and we've got our bomb. The Yanks have got theirs. And the Russians. And the French. And those that haven't got it today will do their best to get it tomorrow. They all distrust each other. If that isn't anarchy, what is?'

'You can't win a war with nuclear weapons.'

'America did. One bomb to finish the war. One to make up for Pearl Harbor. Serve the bastards right. Hitler would have used it on us if he'd had to. Not London. That would have spoiled his victory parade. Birmingham. Hull.

'Now I'll walk you back round the Mews. Al, I'm going to load the van.'

'Will you get me ten ciggies?'

On the way I asked him what he thought about Minky's arcade of stalls idea.

'It'll work. The trouble will come from the Council and the new neighbours.' Whoever had bought Garrow's fourteen cottages had soon found two middle-class buyers.

Sure enough, they complained. It took four years and two inquiries to get the stalls legalized. Kensington, the local Council, didn't believe a word of Minky's pre-and-post-war shop-not-garage use.

I appealed to the London County Council – its decisions over-rode Kensington's. An LCC inspector was sent. I was still in bed on the morning of his knock. Putting my head out of the window, I yelled at whoever it was to piss off. He did. His – official – note informed me that his office, room 537, County Hall, would give a decision by such-and-such a date. That afternoon I rang to apologize for my rudeness. He laughed and suggested I visit his office to explain matters. When I did, he said: 'The LCC is becoming the Greater London Council and I am retiring in ten days' time. Your papers, along with many others, are being returned to Kensington. I shall file them under Examined and Returned. Without further complaints, you are unlikely to hear more. Good-day, Mr Logue.'

Kenny ran the arcade. Once a week he put £20 into my hand. With my pension – now £3 a week – I had a decent private income. Talk about luck.

JIMMY LOGUE was at his garage studying a collection of log books, a mug of tea in his hand.

'You want money,' he confirmed, without looking up.

'I want to buy my house.'

'How much?'

'£1,750.'

'Who's the seller?'

'An estate agent.'

'Pity. Local?'

'Islington.'

Jimmy bought No.18 and sold it to me for £2,000, payable over five years. Each week I used the money from the stalls to pay him. Kenny said: 'We'll increase the rent next summer.' When I made the final payment Jimmy gave me lunch. 'No need for thanks, boy. I bought Nos. 17, 16 and 15 at the same time and cleared £3,000 on them in a week. Have another slice of apple tart.'

An item on the television news caught my eye. The Anti-Uglies had demonstrated outside the new Kensington Central Library, with Pauline Boty, dressed as an eighteenth-century shepherdess, pushing a blindfolded, silvery-wigged man labelled 'ARCHITECT' in a bath chair. The demonstrators had called out: 'Pull it down, pull it down', and Miss Boty was questioned. She dismissed 'What's a pretty girl like you doing at this sort of an event?' with a friendly grin, and went on to say that the building was an expensive disgrace. When the interviewer reported that many people thought it was 'very efficient inside', Boty replied: 'We are outside.' Then the architect, Mr E. Vincent Harris, appeared. Having called the demonstrators 'stupid, duffel-coated, long-haired students' he described his library as 'a well-mannered building in the best contemporary-traditional style'. Finally, the poet John Betjeman was interviewed. He backed Boty & Co. 'The art of architecture is at last getting the attention it deserved,' he said, smiling at Boty.

Hugo Claus wrote to say a novel of his had made a lot of money. Why didn't I join Elly and him on a trip to Greece?

Agreed.

O NCE a week during the summer of 1959 I met Lindsay in the transport café by the stage door of the Royal Court to show him what I had done on the songs for *The Lily White Boys*. As George and Lindsay liked *Red Bird*, Tony Kinsey and Bill le Sage were invited to compose the music. Showing my lines to Lindsay made me nervous. I handed over a lyric to be sung by the Girls.

Lindsay: 'It's not very good, is it?'

Me: 'Oh, I rather liked' – pointing to a stanza I'd spent hours on.

Lindsay: 'Yes – that's OK. But what is the song saying?'

Me: 'That the girls face a different set of hurdles to the boys. The Girls are supposed to help the Boys. The Boys don't help the Girls.'

Lindsay: 'It doesn't say that, does it?'

Me: 'I suppose not. At least, not in so many words.'

Lindsay: 'Then this isn't the finished thing, is it? This isn't what Georgia, Shirley Anne and Anne' – Georgia Brown, Shirley Anne Field and Anne Lynn were playing the Girls, while Albert Finney, in his first London show, was the leader of the three Boys – 'are going to have to sing?'

Me: 'Well . . . '

Lindsay: 'Either it is, or it isn't. If it isn't, why are we discussing it? If it is, it's no good. There is no more to say.'

Me: 'I'll have another go at it.'

'One of the irritating things about you,' Lindsay continued, 'is the air of clarity you impart to the things you say. It's the same with your handwriting. At first glance it looks clear, elegant. When you come to read it, it isn't that clear – and neither is the thought it expresses. I have to go back over it several times to dig the sense out. When you talk about something – politics, say – people who don't know you think you have everything worked out, you are ready to start running the world tomorrow, when in fact you are as confused, more confused, I would say, than most of us.

'Your friend Michael White calls you "Crystal". Don't be fooled. Michael White is a one-man-band. He has not achieved what he has achieved without flattering many mediocrities.'

Then, seeing me worried: 'Some of this stuff is good. With this song – the Girls' – why not say that the Girls are not as free as the Boys? That's the point, isn't it? If I were you I'd ask our Girls before you start rewriting.'

Anne, butter-blonde, cautious, a reader, said: 'I think you'll find that us Girls are being paid less for doing the show than the Boys.'

Not since getting the proofs of my first poems for *Merlin* was a moment so enlivening, as when, on the stage of the Royal Court, Lindsay handed out copies of the script of *The Lily White Boys*, and then, after Tony had spread the music of the opening song along the front of the piano for Bill to play, we stood shoulder to shoulder – Lindsay having ruled that each rehearsal was to start with the principals singing together – we sang the words straight off the sheets:

'It says in the Bible, it's better to be idle,
   For the good neither toil nor spin;
But the glory of our nation is its lads' determination
   To do whatever must be done to win.'

It was a treat to follow Lindsay in rehearsal. To watch him watching Albert, say, create his part, trimming a movement here, adding a touch there, leading by hints followed by queries – he used questions as others requirements – thereafter remembering the details of intonation, movement, the pauses, before blending the six parts.

Lindsay's art drew on the confidence he felt in others, and that in return he sought from them. It was his habit to say what he thought, rather than think of the effect of what he said. If this made him disliked – as it did – also it made him loved and trusted.

At rehearsals in Brighton, where the show was to open, I can hear Eleanor Fazan – Fiz – the dance director, saying to Anthony Page, Lindsay's assistant: 'There's something wrong. Look at Lindsay's mouth.'

'The corners of Lindsay's mouth were a reliable guide,' Anthony said. 'If they were down, the rehearsal was going to be stopped. If the eyebrows were up at the same time, it meant an analysis.' 'You want to be influenced by him,' Shirley Anne told me. 'He believes in you. He makes you do more than you thought you could.' How true.

Albert was a wizard at mental arithmetic. After rehearsals half a dozen of us might eat together at an inexpensive Italian restaurant. When the bill came, Albert, running his eye down the menu, checked and then divided, the total, plus tip, in his head.

'I get it from my dad,' he said. 'He was a bookmaker.'

A great actor, Finney. Full of courage. Turning on stage and telling an ignorant, self-satisfied audience at Keith Waterhouse and Willis Hall's *Billy Liar* that he would go home unless they came to their senses and stopped giggling at every word.

Walking along Brighton front in the December sunlight Lindsay said: 'When I retire I shall open a boarding house and give advice to my lodgers. Do a bit of cooking for them. Walk on the front. Especially in blowy weather. Blowy weather is my element.'

When his admiration was aroused, no one I have met was as good as Lindsay at presenting his thoughts with verve and fire.

'Poetry in film is not just feeling. It is in the film's style. Take Jennings' – Humphrey Jennings – 'his images are composed with great care. They reveal his vision. Not much camera movement. Almost no rhetoric. Natural sound, selectively used. Dialogue expressing character, not fact. The context is the fact. Music often ironic. The world he shows is moral, humane, innocent. You can only analyse art so far. Then you must experience it.'

The newspapers gave us 'mixed notices' (reviews) – meaning, not so good. Still, the public came. Jimmy came and said: 'I don't know how you people can get away with that subsidized cheek.' I could see he was pleased.

One day, six weeks after the first night, I met a gloomy-looking Anne on the Royal Court's steps.

'We're closing next Saturday after the evening performance.'

'But we're doing well. Albert says it's over sixty per cent for each performance. I'm earning £80 a week.'

'A new show opens on Monday. The management kept it back for a fortnight. There's no transfer for us.'

On the last night Lindsay and I joined the cast on stage for the show's closing number:

> 'Time to go now, time to tell you,
> Life is short and men are fools.
> Fall in love, but ask no questions,
> Pay your taxes, keep the rules.
>
> When the future finds you wearing
> Plastic teeth while counting shares
> And you're begging God for mercy,
> Don't forget us in your prayers.'

IN September 1960 Bertrand Russell resigned as president of the Campaign for Nuclear Disarmament. With others, he thought that, having produced an educated minority opinion on the subject of nuclear weapons the Campaign had served its purpose for the time being. No one, as Kenny had guessed, had taken Duncan Sandys' warning as a basis for anti-government action beyond that of the march. This despite CND's estimate of the number of Britons who would be killed by a Russian nuclear attack – 23 million immediately, a further 15 million after eight weeks.

Thirty years later, when the Ministry of Defence's own estimates were declassified, CND's figures – persistently rubbished at the time by the government's supporters – were shown to have underestimated the number of deaths by a further 15 million. These losses – 80 per cent of the population – to result from warheads released by seven enemy submarines reaching fifty-six British cities. The Russians were estimated to have a fleet of over a hundred submarines armed with nuclear weapons.

There was no doubt that the governments of the day were prepared to sacrifice so many of their people. A British chain of Regional Seats of Government had been established in bunkers up and down the country, from which, if the warheads finally came, our representatives would reassert their authority over what remained of us. There was no estimate of the effect such a catastrophe might have on the survivors.

Still, astonishingly – to me – the public accepted Westminster's insistence on Britain's possession of nuclear weapons and readiness to engage in nuclear warfare.

This left those of us who were convinced that such weapons put the civilian population in unacceptable peril with an obligation to take things further. It was plain that, for us, such weapons served nothing aside from the urge to vengeance, and plainer still that, regardless of the 1952 Washington/Westminster agreement that the United States would come to Britain's 'aid against invasion by nuclear weapons', no American president would risk his own country's destruction for the sake of avenging another's. On top of it was our conviction that the conceivable good brought about by a nuclear war would never equal the harm.

I had begun to think of the bomb's apologists as more of a danger to us than the Russians. A quotation from one of Brecht's poems made the point:

The enemy marches at the head of the column.
The voice that gives orders, is the voice of the enemy.
And he who is forever speaking of enemies,
Is himself the enemy.

The pro-bombers were out in force. Witness Viscount (Field Marshal) Montgomery:

We are basing our plans upon the fact that if we are attacked we use nuclear weapons in our defence. The proviso is that the politicians have to be asked first. That might be a bit awkward, of course, and personally I would use nuclear weapons first and ask afterwards.

Challenged by such seditious nonsense Russell invited a number of people to form the Committee of 100. That is to say, a hundred conspicuous individuals (he hoped) prepared to break the law through acts of peaceful civil disobedience – trespass, obstruction, sit-ins, vigils, etc. – and by these acts increase the possibility of a rupture between Westminster and Washington which, if effective, might lead to the withdrawal of the latter's nuclear capability from Britain and its territories. Among the scientists and artists Russell approached, some of the latter were associated with the Royal Court Theatre.

The inaugural meeting of the Committee was held in October 1960. Lindsay, Doris, John Osborne, Arnold Wesker and I were present. John Berger, Robert Bolt, Augustus John and Sir Herbert Read were named as supporters. No scientist of importance attended. Disruption of Trooping the Colour, the establishment of a pirate radio station, the kidnapping of the Chancellor of the Exchequer were considered as appropriate crimes. After the meeting, Osborne – whom I met for the first time – Lindsay and I went for a drink. 'Would you go to jail for the old boy?' Osborne said. We agreed we would.

This was my only meeting with John. Lindsay and I were too old to count as Angry Young Men. Osborne, not concerned with theories unless they served his dramaturgical needs, was charming, determined. There was no question in my mind that if the politicians were going to get stroppy these two would stand firm. The press were hostile. Mad Monty denounced us. Austryn came to stay.

As predicted, the police had raided La Grande Séverine to stop the production of *The Bedroom Philosophers*. Maurice responded by reading the text of Austryn's translation aloud.

There was bad news of Alex. Marquand had telephoned to say that he was a fugitive from justice. Accused of selling drugs to a juvenile he had crossed into Canada where the songwriter Leonard Cohen found him a berth on a ship bound for Aberdeen. Alex's wife and child remained in America. *Cain's Book* had been selling in good numbers, but the Department of Justice had ordered his royalties to be impounded.

I did not know what to do. I half-feared, half-hoped that Alex would ask for my help. I had some savings.

I spoke to Marquand and Plimpton. John said: 'He's changed. He's become very hard. Importunate. He insists on being given money. Sue gives it. When I said "no more", he got angry and called us names. "Rich shits," etc. I sat there wishing he was right.'

George said: 'When he was on his way to Cohen he put on my three best suits. I was sorry to see him go like that. He has no idea how unforgiving our Federal law-enforcement agencies are.'

'Do you mean they would come after him?'

'No. They'll tell their opposites on your side. Make sure you tell Alex that.'

I had no address for him. He didn't telephone.

In June, forgetting about Alex and the Committee of 100 I left for Greece with Hugo and Elly.

We had decided to drive.

'Shall I help you load up?' Kenny said.

'I can do it.'

There was a lot of stuff. Books, maps, compass, drawing materials, medicinal tablets, my water bottle – not that for 'crossing the desert by night' but one of a superior, light-weight, US-army issue – clothes, washing and foot powder, a rope. Minky and Harry Dust watched. Minky insisted on the foot powder. He was haunted by feet. 'If your feet went in Burma, you fucking died. I look after my feet. You look after yours. Right?'

'Yes, Minky.'

When everything was on the rack, I shook hands and said goodbye all round, reversed out of the Mews on to Portobello Road, gave a wave and put my foot down. Whereupon the roof-rack shot forward, tipping everything over the windscreen and on to the street.

Kenny reloaded the car.

A month later, the three of us were the only people sitting in the sunshine on the terrace of a quayside restaurant overlooking the bay of Navplion. Far out in the bay is a rock topped by a fort, once – according to Hugo's guidebook – reserved for the country's public executioners; men so detested they had to be sequestered; now a luxury hotel. We had asked the price of its rooms. There were no vacancies. King Constantine of Greece had taken the entire hotel for himself and his guests. He was due ashore at any moment.

Four large men wearing dark glasses settled on the terrace.

Then some high-ranking naval officers. Then a number of senior policemen, plus a group of suited men carrying brief-cases.

Soon the terrace was full. The waiters were in heaven, the proprietor beside himself with pleasure, cigarettes were handed round, everyone was laughing over their brandy, their coffee.

Then a hush. From the fort a launch began to speed shore-wards. Cigarettes were extinguished. One of the men in dark glasses stood up and blew a long note on a whistle, at which six lorries drove on to the quay. From them jumped what at first sight appeared to be an entire operatic company's worth of schoolgirls, priests, local farmworkers, grannies, common citizens – even a man on crutches. Four assistants unrolled a length of broad red carpet, and, as a limousine with police outriders replaced the lorries, these welcomers lined either side of it.

The launch reached the quay. The King stepped ashore. The Mayor of Navplion kissed his hands, and as he walked to-wards the limousine those flanking the carpet waved Greek flags, cheering, cheering, until he was driven away. Two minutes later, except for us, the terrace was empty again.

W HEN I arrived home at the beginning of September, Alice, who had been taking care of my mail, handed me this:

Christopher Logue

Complaint has this day been made before me, the undersigned, by William Gilbert, Superintendent, 'A' Divn. for that you in the County and District aforesaid are a disturber of the peace in that you have incited members of the public to commit breaches of the peace and breaches of the law and in particular have incited diverse persons unknown unlawfully to obstruct the highway at or in the vicinity of Parliament Square, Westminster s.w.1 on 17th September 1961, and that you are likely to persevere in such unlawful conduct.

You are therefore hereby summoned to appear before the Bow Street Magistrates' Court on Tuesday the 12th day of September 1961, at the hour of 10.30 in the forenoon to answer to the said complaint and to show cause why you should not be ordered to enter into recognizances with sureties for your future good behaviour. Dated the 31st day of August 1961.

'Inciter of the public' must refer to my membership of the Committee of 100, I thought. It did.

On 6 August, Hiroshima Day, the Committee had laid a wreath on the Cenotaph in Whitehall. A statement attached to the wreath linked Japanese civilians who died at Hiroshima with the Allied soldiers killed while fighting the Japanese army. On the 31st, responding to Moscow's resumption of missile tests, members of the Committee had obstructed the road outside the Soviet Embassy in London. As well as this – hence my summons – Russell had called for simultaneous, Committee-led demonstrations against Westminster's defence policy at Holy Loch, the nuclear submarine base, and at Trafalgar Square. The date set was 17 September, Battle of Britain Sunday.

Among the rest of my mail was a copy of Thoreau's essay *On the Duty of Civil Disobedience*, a gift from Marquand.

I 'LL drive you to court,' Kenny said.
    'Thanks. I'll take the tube back.'
  'You're not coming back. You're going to prison.'

'Oh come on, I've not been charged with doing anything. I'm entitled to a fair trial.'

'You don't have to have done anything. *They're* in charge. You're going to prison. Ask Alice.'

Alice came out of the shop.

'Al, read Chris that bit about the recognizances.'

Alice: 'Blah-blah-blah – "to show cause why you should not enter into recognizances with sureties for your future good behaviour".'

'Recognizances mean promises,' Kenny maintained. 'Sureties means money. Good behaviour means not doing anything they don't want you to do – in your case, demonstrate. If you refuse the recognizances they'll lock you up.'

At the time there was talk of our being prosecuted under a law from 1381 passed against freebooters returning from a phase of the Hundred Years War. I never understood this part of the business. Roughly speaking, Mr Carter was correct. The belief that a fair trial – namely, a trial where you are presumed to be innocent until found guilty in a court of law – is the right of British citizens, is false. Means exist whereby British governments may imprison any of their citizens without trial. This is done by a government (the Cabinet) allying itself with the executive (in our case, the police) to manipulate the judiciary.

For instance: having taken the decision to hinder the demonstration the Committee had called for the 17th, Harold Macmillan's Cabinet asked the police to summons over a third of the Committee, including Russell, under the Public Order Act. This act gives magistrates the right to bind over (oblige under sanction), for unspecified periods, all and sundry to keep the peace ('the peace', in our case, meaning 'you will not demonstrate', as Kenny had guessed), though those to be bound over have not themselves broken any law. True, members of Russell's Committee were bound to demonstrate, and if at that time they broke the law, very well, let the law take its course.

The message from the Cabinet was: 'We cannot try you because you have not committed any illegal act, but we don't intend to put up with what you have said you are going to do in five days' time. So: be bound over – or be locked up.'

I went back into No. 18 for my washbag. It turned out that our magistrate, Mr Bertram Reece, had been on the bench for eighteen years. What lay behind our being summonsed may never be known. My guess is as follows:

Macmillan, not a panicky man, was pressurized by President Kennedy into challenging Russell. After consulting his Home Secretary, R. A. Butler, possibly Viscount Kilmuir, his Lord Chancellor, and a number of legal advisers, Macmillan decided to offer Russell a choice: binding over – that he knew, bearing Russell's record in mind, he was unlikely to accept – or imprisonment. The names of thirty-six other Committee members were added to that of Russell's, and the summonses were issued.

There was a crowd outside the court.

Kenny dropped me and drove off, saying: 'Don't worry about things at our end.'

I joined Arnold Wesker and Robert Bolt. John Papworth – one of the Committee – explained that if you agreed to be bound and then were involved in a breach of the peace – 'almost anything' – you would lose the sum given as surety, and, in addition, be fined for the offence.

I asked if the usual remission for good behaviour – one-third of the sentence – was given to people who chose to go to prison. It was. A police sergeant added: 'You can leave the prison at any hour if you sign the binding-over order.' Arnold asked if we were going to be bound over. Bob said he would refuse. Both the law and the weapon were bad.

Journalists were going through the crowd gathering particulars. Russell arrived. The photographers set to work. One getting a remarkable head-and-neck shot of the philosopher looking like an angry ostrich. In we went. Mr Reece took us political offenders last. The Cabinet's lawyer said we were people who might cause breaches of the peace.

When Russell's turn came, Mr Reece said, as he did to us all: 'I am about to order you to enter into a recognizance of £25 to keep the peace and be of good behaviour for twelve months. Are you content to be so bound?'

'I am not,' Russell said.

'Then you will go to prison for two months.'

This fetched cries of 'Shame!' and 'Poor old man!' from the public gallery as Russell's lawyer submitted medical evidence on his client's behalf.

Reducing the sentence to seven days, Mr Reece was tempted to say: 'It is a sad thing for a man of your age, my Lord,' – eighty-nine – 'to be taking part in these activities.'

'Your Worship,' Russell replied, 'I came here to save your life. But having heard what you have to say, I do not think that the end justifies the means.'

THE Court adjourned for lunch. Arnold, Bob and I went to a nearby steakhouse. Bob was worried. He was working on the screenplay of *Lawrence of Arabia*. The shooting of the film had begun. If Mr Reece sent him down, Sam Spiegel, the film's producer, would be furious. Millions of dollars were involved. We drank two bottles of wine between us and were late back to Court.

'We'll get six months,' Arnold said. I was frightened. I was not sure I could take six months. We were given a month apiece, political prisoners in all but name. Thirty-two out of the thirty-six summonsed chose the same course.

DIARY SCRAP:
HM Prison, Brixton.   12.9.61
We strip. Shower. Our arseholes are inspected. We are issued with grey trousers and blue and white shirts. Shouted at throughout. Then we are locked up for twelve hours. The prison smells of excrement and Dettol. Everyone is afraid. All the gossip is about violence. Very little about sex. We are in the Remand Wing. Rather than depend on their rations I have decided to stop smoking.

A visit from an Assistant Governor, wearing a trench-mac, smoking, accompanied by two large prison officers. We have decided not to call the prison officers 'Sir'. The other regulations we will keep. Who will have to be the first to refuse?

'Come here, Papworth,' said the Assistant Governor. 'What's your full name?'

'John Papworth.'

'Say *Sir* when you speak to the Assistant Governor!' shouted one of the prison officers.

'Occupation?'

'Sports outfitter.'

'Do you want me to wash your bloody ears out for you, Bomber?' said the prison officer.

'You must say Sir when you speak to me,' said the Assistant Governor.

'Well, Sir,' John said, 'if it's simply an exchange of courtesies, I have no objection.'

15.9.61

Mr Goods, PO, told us where the term 'Screws' used for prison officers came from.

'There was something called Unproductive Labour. You stayed in your cell all day long. Across the cell was an iron shaft with two handles fixed to it. When the bell rang you stood up and used the handles to turn the shaft for two hours. Whether or not the shaft turned easily was up to us because its tightness was controlled by a large screw in the outside of the cell.

'Don't believe a word you hear in here. On this floor we've got larceny, robbery, buggery, assault. You needn't think they care. Whistlin' and winkin' at each other. Braggin' how much they'll get or how easy they'll get off. When the wife comes to see them pre-trial it's: "Bring us 100 Seniors, a chicken and a bottle of beer." This with two kids, another coming, on National Assistance. Don't leave any letters lying around. They'll copy out the address then go round saying you told them to collect money.'

16.9.61

By bus to Her Majesty's Open Prison, Drake Hall, Staffordshire. I took the card on my cell marked UNCONVICTED PRISONER.

SURROUNDED by rolls of barbed wire, Drake Hall, north of Eccleshall, lay in open Staffordshire countryside. We were given a hut number and told to be on parade for tea at 4 p.m. Regarding 'Sir', we kept our rule. No other advantages were to be taken. We chose our beds. Arnold on my right, Bob on my left.

At 9 p.m. (lights out) prison officers came round to make sure we were in bed. Arnold asked the inspector if, as well as counting us, he would bid us goodnight. At first his request was refused. Then, when Arnold persuaded everyone in our hut to say together 'Goodnight, Mr Jones,' if that was his name, he gave in.

Next day the prison's governor, Mr Glynn Edward Griffiths, explained that our work would be helping to demolish the Royal Ordnance Factory at Swinnerton, where many of the bombs dropped during the Second World War had been made.

We went there by truck. The remains of the factory covered many acres. Its site abounded with wildlife. 'Built here,' Prison Officer George Graham informed us, 'because the valley is in the Mist Belt. Often invisible from the air.'

Narrow gauge railway lines ran into tunnels marked: DANGER. DO NOT ENTER UNDER ANY CIRCUMSTANCES. There were bunkers, their doors torn out, smothered with buttercups.

'Thieves haunted this place after they shut it,' PO Graham said. 'They were after what you have in your hands.' We were stripping four-inch copper cables. 'Some of them drowned in the holds.' Meaning the deep lockers where the explosives were stored. 'They flooded them in '48. 160 feet down. Alive with rats.'

In the sun, stripping a couple of inches of cable a day, or cleaning the odd brick or two, Bob and I roughed out a play featuring a new, internationally acclaimed star – Joan – playing the lead in an imaginary smash-hit musical: *Kisses*. We had Vanessa Redgrave in mind for Joan.

Our play opens with the closing number of *Kisses* after which the cast is called back onstage by the producer who explains that Joan has decided to demonstrate against the stationing of US H-bomb-loaded aircraft on British soil – and may well be arrested. Everything – the long run, the tour, the film, the record of the score, the TV interviews, the New York production – are in jeopardy. She will become 'controversial'. The show will not go on.

Some members of the cast complain that she is threatening their jobs, their mortgages, their children's schooling. She is a fool. She knows nothing about politics. She is a traitor to her country. A selfish bitch.

Joan goes to the bombers' base. The demonstrators break the perimeter fencing and attack the aircraft carrying the bombs. As is their duty, the soldiers guarding the planes shoot, and kill, several demonstrators, all of them young women. Joan is reported to be of their number.

Joan has been wounded, not killed. The country is in an uproar. It is revealed that the American sentries have shot twenty English girls.

Then Joan makes a statement.

The shots were fired by British, not American sentries. As she lay among the dead she could hear them talking. They all had English voices. Some were crying. Some threw down their weapons. She believes she can identify the senior officer who counted the dead.

Some demonstrators had chained themselves to the wheels of the aircraft.

Others had actually got their hands on armed bombs on the loading trolleys. She repeats these allegations to the Court of Inquiry, where, *in camera*, she identifies the senior officer correctly. She is given a suspended sentence.

Our play would be called *King Joan*.

SPIEGEL was angered by Bob's decision to choose imprisonment. That he had resigned from the Committee on signing his contract, and that his summons had been issued in error, made no difference. Spiegel bombarded Mr Griffiths's office with telegrams and telephone calls. Finally Spiegel arrived at the prison. 'From a yacht in the Middle East,' PO Graham – amazement in his voice – told us of the demolition party. 'His chauffeur was in livery. His blue Rolls-Royce was followed by an Austin Princess full of lawyers. Prisoner Bolt left with him.'

Later, Bob told me Spiegel had threatened to sack 200 extras if he did not sign himself out. I said he was right to sign. Arnold, who used to spend the hours before lights-out planning his Centre 42 art-in-the-workplace scheme, disagreed. I now think I was wrong. My impression is, leaving early remained on Bob's conscience until the day he died. Rot *Lawrence of Arabia*.

We were allowed one visit a week after the first of the three we had to serve. Nell came.

'We met in a sort of café-type room,' she reminded me. 'Tables with chairs. You looked terrible. Agitated. Upset. At first I thought it might have something to do with your seeing me. Then you started to talk. You talked about nothing except freedom. Your freedom. Not being free. Yes, you had chosen to go to prison. It was different from when you were a soldier in the Middle East. Freedom was everything. The thing. The only thing. If you had no money you could walk a hundred miles to see a friend. Begging – if it came to that. You were free to do it. Then the hour was over.'

Watching the television news on Sunday the 17th, we saw over 1,300 people – including Osborne, Redgrave and Shelagh Delaney – being arrested for taking part in the Trafalgar Square demonstration that Russell had called.

Louis came. In next to no time we were talking about the merits of Flemish as opposed to Florentine painting. One of the staff asked us to lower our voices. Then he was gone.

On our last full day, Mr Griffiths reminded us that he was entitled to read anything we had written while in his care. Arnold handed over a sheaf of poems he had composed. I produced a typescript of *Patrocleia*, with a month's revisions. Last year (1998) Arnold reminded me that Mr Griffiths, returning our material, had said 'Mr Wesker, I suggest you leave the poetry to Mr Low.'

Arnold's cousin Maurice drove us back to London. First, we stopped at a local newsagent's for a pound's worth of sweets to throw over Swinnerton's fencing at a prearranged spot – currency for the demolition gang. Once inside the shop I was dazzled by the slope of glittering confectionery. I had to let the shopkeeper choose.

That evening, George Devine gave a party for us on the stage of the Royal Court. A woman friend invited me to stay the night. Next day I walked home from Highgate. London looked so comely. So large that no one could know it all. And so varied, so diffuse, you could hope to know no more than a small proportion of those who were interested in what interested you. That was what I liked about London.

Lovely as Staffordshire was, I could never live in the countryside.

KENNY was away on a buying trip when I got back to Denbigh Close. Alice gave me my stalls money and my mail: 'There's something wrong with your drains, Mr Logue. Harry's been on the job.'

'You had a bung-up,' Harry said, drawing on a Senior. 'Two hours with the worm, then nine rods. Can you believe it? What's Chris been doing up there? Some of his French friends?'

'It's nothing to do with Mr Logue,' Alice said. 'He's been away for a month.'

'Greece again?' Harry said.

'No. Prison,' I said.

'You in prison?' Harry said. 'Never.'

'I have been in prison for a month,' I said, hurt.

'That's right,' Alice said. 'Mr Logue's been in prison. His friend Nell went to visit him. In the north of England.'

'In the north of England?' Harry said, as if it was Peru. 'And your friend Nell had to go all that way for a visit?'

'Yes,' I said, feeling better.

'You should have gone to the Scrubs, then, shouldn't you? That's where everyone from around here goes.'

'It was a short sentence in an open prison,' Alice said, stressing 'open'.

'Oh,' said Harry. 'Hardly worth going all that way for. Your drains hadn't been touched since the war, Chris. Klonk-klonk-klonk, then – unng-unng-gol-gur-schloop . . . a . . . PLOOSH! . . . PFWAAA! . . . Ten pounds.'

'That's five pounds too much,' Alice said. 'Mr Carter won't like it.'

I didn't care. Before I went to Drake Hall our side of Chepstow Villas had been smartened up. Artists on the verge of commercial success were moving into the Gate: David Hockney, Roger Mayne, Derek Boshier. Pauline Boty, too.

Reading by an open window after dark, I heard:

'Mr Churchill was the greatest man who ever lived. The Straits of Dover should be renamed the Straits of Churchill. When I was a lad he said he wouldn't rest until every striker was eating grass – I respect that.'

'He did nothing but talk. I lost my mates in the war. We should have gone in with Hitler. There's a lot of Churchills about. People longing for another war.'

'Not with Chris's bomb, they're not. That'll stop war, won't it, May?'

May: 'I had a wonderful war. Down in Shepton Mallet with the Yankees. Silk stockings. Southern Comfort. The blacks were so gentlemanly. Chris doesn't know a thing.'

'May's right. In any case, Chris has done himself a favour. Name in the papers. Man of principle. You coming for a drink?'

'Poor old Chris, he's a bit thick. It must be all that reading.'

It was true. I had risked little. I had no family apart from Molly. No job to protect. My friends wouldn't drop me.

I RESIGNED from the Committee of 100. Remaining a member meant further imprisonment. I could not face this. As well, it would demand my taking politics seriously. I had only the vaguest idea of how the country was defended, taxed, policed – in short, how it was run. Politics means meetings. Endless meetings.

Two incidents had made me doubt the sincerity of my interest in politics.

The first came at a party given by the film director and producer Tony Garnett. Along one wall of his sitting room several hundred books were shelved, almost all of them about politics. Fat biographies of Disraeli, Gladstone, Canning, Wilberforce, Paine, Robespierre, Lincoln, Trotsky, Kennedy, all, by the look of them – pages tagged, notes on the flyleaves – studied.

I owned no such books. Aside from John Buchan's *Oliver Cromwell*, I had never finished the life of a politician. As half my time was spent reading, this signified.

Orwell and Gladstone – my father's hero – were the only political theorists I had read, and in Gladstone's case the work in question had been his *Studies on Homer* where I had found: 'Decision by majorities is as much an expedient as lighting by gas.' And: 'If we cannot conceive of freedom without perpetual discord, the faithful performance of the duty of information and advice without coercion and oppression, it is either a sign of our narrow-mindedness, or of our political degeneracy.'

Paging through one of Garnett's Kennedy biographies, I came across a – to me – disturbing fact. By the end of his presidential campaign, the flesh of Kennedy's right wrist was scraped red raw by the fingernails of his supporters whose hands he had shaken. 'Stick that,' I thought.

The second incident involved Noël Picarda, a witty eccentric, an aspiring politician, a man who spent hours knocking on the doors of voters in his proposed Northamptonshire constituency, sitting in motorway cafés, convening small question-and-answer sessions to learn what people thought on this or that issue, wanting to be influenced by, and to influence, those thoughts.

Intemperate of speech, quick to judge, averse to dissimulation, useless at entering into others' lives, my idea was to get it all over in one quick push for paradise.

I had never known the pleasure of changing somebody's mind on a matter I thought was of social importance. Indeed, I had never been able to persuade anybody of anything. I was beginning to understand that the notion of so doing made no appeal to me. To persuade, you need to know what it is you want to happen. These are childish truths. Things, as Kenny would say, that everyone knows. Convinced that, only by empowering the United Nations will humans avoid self-destruction, I have not joined the United Nations Association. Invited by a short-range weapons specialist to visit him at NATO headquarters and be shown some of its armament, I never went.

'Tell you what,' Noël said. 'Let's you and I spend next weekend going to cafés and pubs in and around Northampton. We'll both learn a lot.' I didn't go.

The memory of these occasions has led me to regard my political thinking with embarrassment. Oh yes, I am on the left, and I will fight my corner as required. Yet as far as political theory or political facts go – and they go far – I am fit to carry no more than a musket.

KENNY had been in Wales and the Cotswolds. When he finished unloading – marble-topped road-house tables, the last of the pine – he came upstairs for tea and I told him about Drake Hall. It made him angry.

'You people are misfits. Yes you *are*. More people are having more of a good time than ever before They don't care about the bomb. What can they do about the bomb? Some of them have work because of the bomb. You've never gone looking for a job. I know you. If someone turned you down, you'd either burst into tears or start shooting. Learn to put up with things. It's not "giving in", it's "holding on".

'I'm not saying nobody cares about the starving masses or the bomb. They'll give some money if they've got some left over at the end of the week. What else can they do? Go to prison? "Why bring that up? It'll all be over quickly," is what they say. You don't understand a thing. People *know*. And at the same time they don't want to know. You think you are better than other people, that's your trouble.'

'I do not.'

'Not in your head, perhaps. But in your bones. It makes you feel good being "left-wing" – whatever that means. Most people think there's no difference between reading a poem and playing a game of darts. You think poetry should be on the National Health.'

'What is wrong with that?'

'The best thing to be said for it is that it will never happen. You don't like what most people like. You want everyone liking the stuff in museums – not the stuff on the Hyde Park railings. Remember the *Daily Mirror* poll that showed '*If* . . .' was the most popular poem? You almost threw up.'

'It's a whorish poem. Worse for being well written. An SS man defending a death camp can draw strength from it. And the stuff sold on the railings is crap.'

'Who says so?'

'I do.'

'That's what I said. You think you are better than other people because of what you like. You are one of the we-are-better-than-you gang.'

'I am not. Anyone can do what I have done – which isn't that much. You can still buy the best poetry in English from the last six hundred years for less than a fiver. You can read it while on the dole. The National Gallery is free. I'm not going to make Harry read Milton and he's not going to make me have a beach holiday. In art, some things are better than others. I want people to know what is best. Nobody *has* to like it. I just hope they will.'

Kenny started to laugh.

'And then you'll come home complaining you can't see anything for the crowds. And by "people" you mean working-class people. Right?'

'Stop "righting" me.'

'Well, I'm the only working-class man you know.'

'Ex-working-class. You and Alice have more money than me – or my parents.'

Kenny continued laughing.

'You have never had a working-class girlfriend except Pamela. And she was much too good for you. You never eat fish and chips at six, or Indian at eleven-fifteen.'

'I thought we were talking about nuclear weapons.'

'I've got a shock for you. I'm voting Conservative at the next election.'

'You're *not* . . .'

'Alice has convinced me.'

'Ken . . .'

'You going to prison helped me make my mind up. "If Chris can go to prison, I can vote Conservative," I said.'

TODAY, my views have changed. But not that much. The virtues of nation states are obvious, fundamental, though belonging to such a state does not excuse avoidance of choice. Nuclear weapons, by removing individual responsibility in warfare, have weakened the traditional claims of duty and loyalty, replacing them with feelings of irrelevance and disgust, while empowering, above all other professions – vocations, if you will – that of politicians. Codes, engineering skills, secrecy and buttons grant this minority sway. You may find my interest in this dated. I hope you are right. I don't think you are.

Soldiers know that nuclear weapons are insusceptible to 'command and control' – as the saying goes. Several poor, presently non-nuclear states are hard at so arming themselves. National armies must use every weapon they possess to avoid defeat. The strong like to have their own way. Defied, they wax temerarious: 'How dare they?' 'Something must be done . . .'

Some say that warfare between humans is unavoidable, and that, in so far as is possible, nuclear weapons have kept peace among us. Really? – Vietnam, Afghanistan, Rwanda, Biafra, Bosnia, Kosovo, Iran–Iraq, Israel–Egypt, Syria–Israel, Britain–Argentina, Algeria – add your own names to my list. I would like to test their first assertion by using the amount of money spent world-wide on war weapons, on anti-war weapons.

All wars are civil wars. Warfare is a criminal activity. With the above-mentioned budget to provide for the planetary establishment of the Declaration of Human Rights, supported by a United Nations inspectorate of those rights, itself supported by an international military police force … Don't tell me about the problems involved. They are our good luck. Worth solving.

To mark being home, I decided to have half-a-dozen people to supper. As we were about to start the meal, who should knock on the door but Michael Hastings. Meanly, I said that there was not enough food for an extra guest. If he liked to come back in an hour, he could have coffee. Off he went, returning, as suggested, then settling himself on the bed. Later, when I went to bed, I found that he had left a raw lamb chop between the sheets.

Among the mail Alice had saved for me was a letter signed 'Andrew Osmond', inviting me to contribute to *Private Eye*, a magazine I had not heard of. At its Soho office – one room of a run-down house in Neal Street, Covent Garden – Andrew introduced me to his friend Richard Ingrams, the magazine's editor. Ingrams gave me a set of back numbers. I read them on the tube home. They were funny, clever, rude. The magazine's appearance was unique. A paste-it-up-yourself job. Its cartoons and caricatures, all drawn by one Rushton, with a style of their own. Its jokes absurdist.

I was flattered to have been asked to join in. The *Eye* chaps – there were no women writers or illustrators – were ten to twelve years younger than me.

This was at the same time as I refused to share a volume in the Penguin Modern Poets series with two other poets, demanding one to myself. Brian Patten remarked: 'That was a bad mistake. Some people could not stand Christopher's arrogance. Others thought him a fool. It damaged the chances of his work being known. More people have heard of him than know what it is he does. When I was editing my magazine *Underdog* I wrote asking if he had a poem for me, starting my letter "Dear Chris". By return I got a note saying: "Dear Mr Patten, I use Christopher, not 'Chris'. Yours sincerely".'

TAKING a cue from my father's habit of clipping them, I suggested to Ingrams that I should produce a column of funny or bizarre newspaper items précised, and called *True Stories* after the romantic magazine.

As they could not be checked it was important that the stories rang true. And as the people involved were not fame seekers, if the stories were hurtful I would alter their names. Ingrams liked the idea. When my own collection of stories was exhausted, he invited the *Eye*'s readers to submit clippings for me to rewrite. If they were used, the senders were paid. One of the stories reminded me of my own efforts to explain to sceptical poetry lovers what I was doing with the *Iliad*.

A production of *Hamlet* by the Keswick Polytechnic included many changes. The text was cut to 15 minutes, 'because there are several other things on the bill', and retitled *Hamlette*, 'because we could only get two male actors,' said Miss Joanna Ripe, the director/adaptor.

'The whole thing is set in a nunnery,' she said. 'We gave Claudia – Hamlette's aunt – most of Polonius' lines, because she learnt his part by mistake.'

Miss Ripe added several new parts to the play – Joyce, Hamlette's sister and friend; Dinah, a blackamoor, whose part was made up of lines taken from the Nurse in *Romeo and Juliet*, 'with the dirt removed', and Louise, a girl disguised as a male deaf-mute, who drowns herself out of pique.

North Circular, Vol. 7 No.1 (n.d)

The column survived for thirty years.

RICHARD Ingrams' eyes were bright blue. At moments of heady amusement his laugh turned into a giggle, which, suppressed by half-closed lips, might become: 'He said that? And then fell over? Amazing. Use it,' blinking the while, looking straight at you over the top of his spectacles.

Although we never saw that much of each other, from our first meeting I felt that Richard and I were sympathetic. That is to say, we guessed each other's intentions. This may have been to do with his sharing my father's – and hence my own – admiration for Chesterton and Belloc. Since leaving home, I had never met anyone who knew, or could quote from, those writers.

He dressed badly. Corduroys in need of the cleaners. He disliked gambling, adultery, lies – except when the liar was caught out in a whopper. Many found him intimidating. His habit of looking over your head into nothingness when bored, or of not replying when you spoke. Save on the telephone he seldom used either of your names. He would have made an actor: Johnson or Cromwell his natural parts. Seemingly conservative, there was recklessness in him. You could never be sure which way he would jump. In a tight corner, he would be brave. Unlikely to quit. He loved the radio. He spoke quite slowly. You heard each word.

'What I find disconcerting about Ingrams,' Auberon Waugh volunteered, 'is his sudden changes of opinion. You are talking. You assume, legitimately – as you have spoken about it before – you are in broad agreement. Suddenly he turns on you. The chap you are talking about – if it is a chap – is a shit, corrupt, a boozer, not to be trusted.'

'Can you make him laugh?' I said.

'Rarely. Are you afraid of him?'

'If Ingrams came to power he would, if necessary, have the likes of you and me shot.'

I saw the distant look that comes into Auberon's eyes when you have said something he finds ridiculous.

'I don't like Ingrams,' my wife, Rosemary, said. 'He is a snob. He indulges his homophobia. He picks on people. He likes you a lot. Most freelance writers are dropped at least twenty times in their lives, whereas you, with an easy pitch, worked for him, a born editor, a genius at editing – don't interrupt – for ever. He increased your fee without your asking, gave you the same annual bonus as the *Eye*'s staff – though you were never more than a contributor. And instead of getting rid of you after goodness knows how many years, he gave you 'Pseuds' Corner' – a column with a rock solid future if ever there was one – to edit, so more money.'

I must say, I loved editing the Corner. Big heads. Big mouths. Big names. You'd be suprised how many of them, instead of keeping their heads down, would ring the magazine's office to say: 'Don't you see I meant it ironically?'

'Another pseud,' Richard would say, replacing the handset. True, when they were restored to their context, a few of the items I entered were not actually pseudish, just things that were difficult to say. And once, by listing an item of John Peel's, it was I who got caught, for Peel's sentence was purposely pompous. My apologies.

The nearest I got to making Richard laugh – intentionally, that is – was when Mary, his wife, asked me to be a godfather to their first son. 'Fred' was the name they wanted.

At the font, with Fred in my arms, watched by a largish congregation, when the baptizing priest asked: 'What do you name this child?' I answered 'Fred'.

Reaching for my godson, the priest told me he could not allow 'Fred'. 'Fred' was not a real name. It had to be Fredricus.

'No,' I said, stepping back, 'Fred.'

'Fredricus,' said the priest.

'No – Fred.'

In the pause, I looked at the parents. Richard was smiling all over his face. He looked really pleased. Then Mary gave me a nod and the priest had his way.

F OR those associated with authority – 'the establishment' – the autumn of 1961 saw a change for the worse. *Private Eye*, already popular in London, soon after, nationwide, was followed by the theatre review *Beyond the Fringe*.

As a form of entertainment, the review, with its assortment of sketches and songs, had lost its charm. Then Messrs Alan Bennett, Peter Cook, Jonathan Miller and Dudley Moore appeared, bringing their political-topical-satirical show from the

Edinburgh Festival to London, and reintroducing edged, often surreal, ridicule to the West End. Then, Cook and Nicholas Luard, a gentleman adventurer, opened The Establishment, a nightclub with a cabaret featuring stand-up, satirical comedy, free of censorship because – unlike the theatre – clubs were immune from that sort of interference. I was invited to write lyrics for the cabaret's songs.

To house The Establishment, Cook and Luard refurbished a building in Greek Street, Soho. Here I met Cook.

Long-legged, thin, suited, pale-faced, pushing a lock of dark hair off his forehead, Cook jumped up as Luard showed me in, offered me his hand – the opened pages of a newspaper hanging down from, as well as a lighted cigarette between, the fingers of his other hand – and said, in his ordinary speaking voice: 'Hello. I hear we are going to do as much to save Britain from its politicians as the satirical nightclubs of Berlin did to prevent the election of Hitler.' I specify 'ordinary voice', because, despite our spending a fair amount of time alone together, Peter often spoke to me in the voices of the characters he had invented. When using the voice he was born with he could be bitterly misanthropical.

Night after night, The Establishment was full. Not since the 1670s when Mr Julian the Reciter had delivered anonymous lampoons – composed, in fact, by Buckingham, Dryden, Rochester & Co. – to the patrons of Will's Coffee House in Covent Garden, had London seen such a venue. There were three bars. Upstairs: soft lights, sofas, etc. On the ground floor: bar, restaurant and stage. In the basement: a jazz trio or a discotheque, plus dance floor.

At Aldermaston, and then on television at the Anti-Uglies demonstration, I had caught glimpses of Pauline Boty. Now, as she and her friend and fellow artist Derek Boshier were often at the club, I got to know her. She was astonishing. A big, bright girl with a confiding laugh. Snug headband holding a toque of silver-blondé hair. Hoop earrings, jangling when she turned her head, shoes she decorated on the run – searching her handbag, out with the gold spray, whssp-whssp-whssp, then on to the dance floor.

Pauline introduced me to David Hockney, a serious-looking lad in National Health spectacles, handing out CND leaflets. A day later, lo and behold, the same young man, his hair now a gold-yellow cloud over pink-framed owl-eye glasses, wearing skin-tight jeans, white and green platform boots with Dayglo laces – but still leafleting.

Now and again, after he had finished performing in *Beyond the Fringe*, Peter came over to The Establishment. Funny as he was in a theatre, cabaret strengthened his work. Striding on to the club's tiny stage, rolled newspaper like a swagger stick under his arm:

Now then: when the bomb goes off and the entire country is destroyed – *get right out of it*. You understand? Get-right-out-of-it. Out of it, is well out-of-it. In it, is really in it. Is that clear?

If by chance you are caught in it, for God's sake don't move. Stand absolutely still. Stock still. But not next to a house or under a tree. That would be extremely dangerous.

And pay no attention to those cowards who say the four-minute-warning of a nuclear attack is inadequate. Let me remind you that there are already four people in this great country of ours who can run a mile in four minutes.

Alone with him, ah, the embarrassment I felt when my turn had come to say something funny or apt to keep the conversation alive. I was not even a good feed. Ingrams and John Wells were.

Once, while Peter, Wendy – his first wife – and I were on holiday together, he invented my wife-to-be, a wholly soulful, completely humourless, sandal-and-long-skirt-wearing woman called Deirdre.

'Oh, there she is, Deirdre of the Seven Poems. She's seen you. She's coming over . . . ' And Wendy would look at me and say: 'He's right, you know. Deirdre is your fate.'

I began to believe in Deirdre. Each time I went to a party I looked around to see if anyone like Deirdre was present. I hoped that Peter would not mention Deirdre in case others began to believe in her. Then she would appear and I would be lost.

Peter's resort to alcohol came from his isolation. An ethical satirist, he wanted to be of use. He died of boredom that came from despair.

One empty New Year's Day in the late seventies Peter rang me and suggested we go to the early show of *Apocalypse Now*, a childish film deadened by pseudo-philosophic chat.

The cinema was quarter full. About an hour after the opening scene, Peter – at first in a whisper, then, as the laughter spread around him, in a slightly louder voice – began to mock the film. In next to no time, those who could hear him were treating the picture as a comedy. Then the manager came in and, rightly enough, asked him to be quiet. So we left.

'Let's have a drink,' Peter said.

Ingrams had told me that, influenced by his second wife, the model Judy Huxtable, Peter had stopped drinking. We walked north. It was dark. It was cold. Everything was closed. Eventually we came across a place near King's Cross called The Crown. Dreary, smelly, empty, with a sullen barman. I had whisky. Peter, lemonade. I longed to go home. At the same time I could not leave him.

A taxi driver popped in for cigarettes. 'Let's go to my place,' Peter suggested.

At Hampstead he turned on the television, disappeared upstairs for five minutes, came down, and we watched a wildlife programme in silence until Judy Huxtable came in. Peter introduced us and she went upstairs. A moment later she returned, upset, saying that Peter had broken his word to her. He had been drinking. He had drained the contents of a box of chocolate liqueurs she had been given.

Nothing is more annoying than to be told, 'Cook was the funniest man alive', and then given no evidence of his fantastic gift. Had he written, or drawn, his humour would have been in the tradition of the seventeenth-century nonsense poets John Taylor and Richard Corbet, and after them, Carroll, Lear, Morgenstern, Gorey and Andrew Lanyon.

Neither Cook nor Luard was business-minded. Members of The Establishment were allowed £50 credit. 'Not a few of them cashed £50 cheques at each of the bars on each night of the week,' Wendy said. 'The bar stock was seldom checked against receipts.' A year after opening, the club's lease was sold to a Lebanese gold smuggler. When he was caught by the Japanese customs and given two years' imprisonment, his wife reopened the premises as a strip club.

A LETTER from Mother – 1962. 'Your aunt Margaret is dead at eighty-six. She died in Ireland as was her wish. Never forget it was she who taught you to read and write.'

I see myself aged five, standing, repeating my multiplication tables, and Aunt Margaret in her chair, her ruler laid on the plum-coloured velveteen cloth covering the table between us, my mind wandering, as it still does, wanting to get to the next thing, and Aunt Margaret saying: 'Come, come, John Christopher, or you will hear me tell your mother you declined to concentrate.'

Thinking of Margaret, of my parents, a wave of detached love, of loyalty, together with a sense of absolute loss, rises in me.

A picture comes to mind: my father brushing his hat before setting it on his head, my mother smoothing her gloves over her fingers, settling her fox fur around her shoulders, its long clip hidden beneath the snout, then taking the brush from my father's hand to give a few strokes across his shoulders, his back, the two of them checking themselves in the hall mirror before stepping out of the front door, arm in arm. Whereas all I do is tap my pockets – 'money, keys, nicotine' – and go.

I N every newspaper, many paragraphs over many pages reporting the death of Marilyn Monroe in Hollywood from an overdose of barbiturates.

In a single newspaper, a short paragraph saying that Xanthe Wakefield had been found dead in unsuspicious circumstances at her Kensington flat. Donald was in America long since. Why they had not gone together puzzled me. They were suited. Then I was told that Xanthe's father was infuriated by the suggestion that his daughter should marry a man who owned no land. Whereupon, for very little, Carne-Ross had bought a thousand acres of tundra below the Melville Hills of northern Canada.

Xanthe's death sobered me. I was certain she had not killed herself in my kind of hysterical, 1954 mood. She was intrepid on horseback. At Oxford she had won a double first in classics without having to try very hard. She hated the idea of reaching thirty. She loved Homer, Sophocles, Virgil. Donald said: 'She was the most brilliant person I ever knew.'

In the autumn of 1962, the programme of concerts, musical theatre, poetry and jazz-and-poetry readings Arnold Wesker had planned as Centre 42 at Drake Hall was ready.

Part of Arnold's intention was the revival of those lunch-time recitals in factories established during the Second World War. He was teased for his wish to bring 'culture to the workers'. But Arnold, who – as I did about me – believed that art had allowed him to discover himself, was sincere and undeflectable in his purpose: to offer anyone who might benefit from it, a door to the world that art can provide.

The first lunch-time reading/folksong concert was at Copeland & Jenkins Ltd, Wellingborough, Northamptonshire. I had never been in a factory. Our tour manager, Michael Kustow – later to become head of arts programmes at Channel 4 TV – was plump, polite, jolly, smooth, smartly turned out, and utterly confident as he stood outside C & J's canteen using a loud-hailer to announce the event to an empty yard.

On the canteen door a poster read: CHRISTOPHER LOGUE WILL READ HIS POEMS AT 1.15. Then an anxious middle-aged lady in white hurried up to us, drying her hands. 'Oh, here you are,' she said, and led us in.

The canteen, big enough for five hundred, was completely empty. On one wall was a second, larger poster, declaring IT'S A MAN'S LIFE! and carrying a photograph of a handsome soldier toting a machine gun. Across it someone had written: 'Piss off.'

'Are you the poetry reader?' said the lady in white. 'Well, in that case, I'm sorry to have to tell you there's been a mistake regarding time. They've all gone back to work. They get their lunches between quarter past twelve and a quarter to one.'

Next came the Raleigh bicycle factory at Nottingham. Alan Sillitoe, now my neighbour at the Gate, once worked there. When I asked him how to go about things at Raleigh, he relit his pipe, looked out of the window and said: 'Got any jokes?'

I had no jokes. I rang Miriam Karlin whom I knew from the Royal Court. 'Get the name of the factory's best-known foreman,' she said. 'Wait for things to quiet down. Then look around and declare: "I know you're all going to enjoy this – especially Mr So-and-so because he's such a great poetry lover."'

Then – quickly, sounding excited – "Ladies and gentlemen, before I start, I'd like you to give a big hand to this concert's guest star – Marilyn Monroe!" Pause. Then peering down into the crowd you say: "I'm sorry, it's two bald men".'

I followed her instructions to the letter. So far, so good. There were a thousand having lunch. Our stage was the top of a canteen table. I introduced Judy, the folk singer. She was shaking. She began in a small, polite voice:

> 'Two brothers going on their way,
> Two brothers going on their way,
> One wore blue and one wore grey,
> All on a beautiful morning.'

When the young men at her feet began to jeer, I lost my head. Climbing on to the table top I shouted: 'Shut up, you morons. She's fifteen. She's come a long way to sing you a song. I'm going to clap. When I do, you'll clap with me.'

I clapped. Nobody else did. Judy fled. In my head I could hear my heart saying: 'It's their factory. Their lunch hour. They did not invite us. Her age is irrelevant.' Seconds passed. 'Right,' I said to myself. 'No quarter given or taken.' And began with: 'The Second Chorus from *Antigone* – Logue version':

> There are many wonders on earth
> and the greatest of these is man . . .

Nobody stopped talking. To my immediate right, three men were playing cards. Beside them, two girls were sharing the *Daily Mirror*. After fifteen minutes I stopped. A small, sixty-year-old man in overalls helped me down. I, too, was shaking. Once down, I realized there was a pool of silence around us. The man said:

'Are you coming down to our end to do it?'

'No.'

'What's up with you, sonny?'

'Haven't you had enough?'

'Don't be so touchy. Our end couldn't hear a thing.'

'I'M not surprised you find it hard to write about yourself,' Isobel said. 'You never liked talking about what you call "personal things".

'We met soon after you became friends with Richard Ingrams and were in Arnold Wesker's "art for the workers" movement. Around 1962. You fell in love with me. You took me to meet your mother. I must say travelling with you was a nightmare. Everything you took had to be laid out on the floor five days beforehand. And we were only going to Bournemouth. You were small, aggressive, excitable, reckless, "an older man" – though you jibbed at the term when I mentioned it, saying you were "only thirty-six". You took yourself very seriously. You never thought to ask me if I was in love with you. You assumed I was.

'As soon as I began to fall apart, you turned away from me. I'm not blaming you. I was a nuisance. Continually drunk. Dangerous, even. Then not a word out of you for years.

'You've done the same to others. People mention it. You were so rude. So snobbish. Your pleasure was to exclude a person if they were titled, calling them ill-bred monkeys. But you told me that when Ken Tynan sat you next to Princess Margaret at one of his supper parties – he didn't like me, he thought I was stupid – you said you were amazed to find she had fingernails "the same as everybody else".

'Another habit of yours, if someone invited you to dinner – Rascomb and me, Christina and Bamber Gascoigne, Michael and Sarah White – halfway through, often at the time when your hostess was about to produce her pudding, you would leave the table and go to sleep on a sofa in the sitting room, if there was one, and if not, a few feet away from the table. Sometimes you snored.'

'I didn't . . . '

'You did. You said you wanted me to tell you things. Now you're cross. Please don't get cross with me. Please. Then you'd wake up, ask for a helping of pudding, eat it, and go home.'

'I'll never get cross with you again, Isobel. And I still love you. Are you sure about the snoring?'

'Quite sure.

'I have seen you walk away in the middle of something someone was saying to you, because you were bored. But if someone forgot your name, or after being told your name asked what you did, you sulked.

'I'll give you this: your sulks didn't last long because you couldn't be bothered to keep them going. You forgot what you didn't want to know. Christina told me that when you were staying in their house you scandalized the neighbourhood by eating the contents of a wrongly delivered Christmas parcel.

'It was not just my looks you liked. I was alert. Interested. When we met, I was twenty-two, poorly educated like millions of other young women. But companionable. Quick to see a point – and maybe cap it.

'Besides you, I was seeing Rascomb. What you didn't, or didn't want to see about me – though I gave you a few hints – was my interest in marriage and money. Having money meant a lot to me. Then Rascomb proposed. Then – this was typical of you – as if you guessed that something of the sort was coming, you proposed to me at the top of the stairs of Notting Hill Gate underground, and I said no, I am going to marry Rascomb. I prefer his way of life to yours.

'As a matter of fact, though I have heard you say the opposite, you were always proposing marriage. You proposed to Letia – who really liked you. When she didn't jump at the offer – though she would have said yes if you'd persisted a little – you never spoke to her of marriage again.

'You know what happened to Rascomb and me. You and I wouldn't have lasted a week, let alone ten years. You had things just so. Very neat. Pencils everywhere. Coins in piles according to size. Regular habits. Very kind to your mother. At the same time I found the look of relief on your face when I turned you down disconcerting. You did not want to throw your lot in with somebody else. You said you did, but you didn't.

'You were one of our witnesses. There was a scene in the registry office. You wanted to sit in a chair that had arms. Chairs with arms were reserved for the happy couple. I said you could have mine. You moved the bride's chair to the witness's place. The registrar insisted on it being moved back. My mother was scandalized. She said you behaved like a Labourite – her worst sort of person.

'When Rascomb and I began to separate you were my only male friend. I would call at the Mews – you lived at the top of a ladder, very romantic – for coffee and you would insist on my sleeping with you. I would go away having done no such thing. If you had been serious, well, that might have been another matter. We had slept together before I married Rascomb. Nothing much happened. You minded. I didn't. Then we would meet a day or so later and it was as if your demand for sex on my last visit had never happened.

'Now I come to think of it, the first time we were alone together the first thing you showed me was a new pencil sharpener you had just bought. Then you read me a poem I thought was too long. I looked at your clothes cupboard just to prove we had something basic – clothes – in common.

'With people who didn't know you you had the reputation of being a demanding sensualist. I was never sure why. Most of the time the only regular demand you made on me was for lunch. Perhaps it was those *Red Bird* poems on your record. Very fleshy. There may have been a bit of boasting about those poems. Christina said you left a big card with your poem 'Although I like to wallow on her belly / The dog-position's best when viewing telly' written on it in their sitting room.

'Letia – like other young women who fancied you – told me – oh, it's all so long ago who cares who slept with who? – that first of all you made a great fuss: "You have to stay the night or there's no point in our meeting again", etc. And the moment she arrives with her overnight bag and her favourite LPs, practically at the lights-out, clothes-off stage, you suddenly remember something you have to write down. Then I told her about your finding a subject to talk about as soon as I had my knickers off, and we had a good laugh about it. We both loved you. Only I was hopeless. Talk about women with their headaches and not-feeling-too-wells – and Letia had pregnancy to worry about. We all did pre-pill.

'Lots of people knew about your wriggling. You thought nobody knew because you never, ever, gossiped. Which is another reason you find yourself so hard to write about. You were not interested in people, including yourself. In people for their own sake, I mean. Not just because they were friends. But everyone else gossiped, so everyone else knew. It was a subject. Christopher has fallen in love with so-and-so. How long will it last? Answer: Until she says yes.

'You always looked away at the right moment.'

DIARY SCRAP:
To an exhibition of pictures by Joanna Carrington. Most English. Charming landscapes, some with sheep. I get fonder of sheep all the time. The pictures too expensive for me I'm afraid. Walking away from the gallery Michael Hastings – he was at the show, he knows a lot about painting – rushes out after me and puts a framed drawing of Carrington's into my hands, saying: 'This is for you. Keep working.' I have done nothing for months.

ALEX was in London. We saw each other occasionally. For all that he had been through, there was little change in his appearance. Still handsome. Burly. His laugh, his confiding voice, as charming as ever, at the centre of a group who thought that drugs would rid the world of its pain. When he was invited to appear on television to justify his views, he began by announcing his self-appointment as Drug Addict to Her Majesty the Queen. Then defended his right to take any drug he chose to take. The murderous behaviour of most modern states – Auschwitz, Katyn, Hiroshima, Dresden – having led him to find contemporary societies so vicious, any drug that weakened the loyalties they aroused was holy, a blessing. And that his drug took him on voyages through inner space which were every bit as interesting as those of Columbus, Magellan, Cook and Livingstone. The only difference being that his voyages would not bring death to the less well-armed peoples of the earth.

On one of his visits to me, Alex asked if he might inject himself. He produced his syringe, armband, teaspoon and heroin, drew blood from his arm, made a pink mixture, warmed it, drew it into the syringe, then sent it into his upper arm and lay down on my bed. I was glad we were alone.

Discussing my own use of drugs with Michael White, I surprised him by mentioning that, as far as my memoir was concerned, I was in two minds about mentioning the matter at all. 'You must,' he said. 'You really must. If only to avoid the charge that you funked it.'

Very well. From the late fifties to the mid-seventies I smoked marijuana in the evenings. Marijuana is a temporarily exhilarating, essentially bland vapour, overwhelmed nowadays by gales of common nonsense. Moreover, it was cheap, cheerful, and exotic. The only time I smoked marijuana during the day was at Christmas, when, before Lionel and Gladys moved to Felixstowe, Mother and I went to them for Christmas Day lunch in Finchley.

'I must say,' Gladys said (several years running), 'John Christopher's temper has improved with middle age. No thanks to the money you and Jack wasted on his fine education, though.'

'No, Gladys,' I said to myself (at least once), smiling, as I chewed her tasteless turkey in her bookless house. 'You are wrong. It is only what I smoked in your dreary garden that prevents your hearing me say that unless you stop criticizing my Dad I'll sneeze into your trifle.'

There being so much silliness in the air concerning drugs, it may be worth mentioning that I did not 'give up' marijuana. I just drifted away from smoking it. As never happens with nicotine. I have heard likewise from others.

During the mid-sixties, Christmas evenings took a turn for the better. The Tynans would throw a party. Twenty to thirty people of the kind usually with more than enough to do, completely stuck for anywhere to go. In my case, having spent the preceding year relishing my solitary ways while everyone else was busy with the affairs of the world, I would, suddenly stranded in the quiet, be forced to recognize the oddity of my position.

Thank God for the Tynans. From 9 p.m. to long after midnight Ken ruled as champion of family exile. Outrageously dressed – fluffed-out orange shirt, blue velvet, bell-bottomed toreador trousers, the jacket from his suit of lights – DJ-ing the complete Top Twenty, pouring out drinks on drinks for everyone. Then tap-tap on a glass – games time had come. For Ken liked nothing so much as to set his Christmas-night guests to word games. There were always well-sharpened pencils and pads to hand. And Ken always won.

On holiday in France, my irritability peaked. Energyless, discontent, I lay in bed. The outward signs – I could not, for instance, taste the difference between red and white wine – told me nothing. For thirty-seven years my physical sufferings had come from colds, breakages, burns. Whatever I had now came from within.

Back home, I wrote out a list of my symptoms and telephoned Patrick Woodcock, a doctor friend. After I read them over he said: 'What colour is your excrement?' I had not looked. 'I'll come over.'

'Have you been?' this, as he climbed the stairs.

'Yes. It's like porridge, my piss is reddish.'

He arranged my blood test by telephone.

'If I am right, it's hepatitis. If it's the infectious type, you'll be in hospital for three months.'

Kenny drove me to Harley Street. It was non-infectious.

'Go to bed,' Patrick ordered. 'Eat only fish, lean meat, Complan, Ribena. Drink water. No alcohol of any kind. Only get up to visit the lavatory. Now let me speak to Mr Carter.'

That afternoon I turned yellow.

'I am not kidding, Mr Logue,' Alice said, 'one moment you looked like rice pudding and the next like custard. I could hardly believe it.'

Ken and Alice looked after me. Patrick called in once a day for a week. I was not so much the one who was living, as the one being lived. When I got better, my description of myself to myself while ill depended on this contrast: from time to time when abroad, my companions having gone to visit a museum or a church, I have found myself alone in the hilltop graveyards of provincial towns, when, from nowhere, the certainty that, peaceful though the place was, I did not belong here, came over me, and I have tried to think of where I did belong. In England? Well, yes . . . but that was too broad a notion to suit. In London, then? Of course, but that, too, was, if not vague, so very diffuse. Finally, it came down to my house, my room, my table, and these, too, produced a negative answer. Under my skin, between my ears, then? Or nowhere? And I supposed it to be nowhere, and felt worried, depressed, until at last I said: 'Don't be vain. You are the same as everyone else.'

Now, lying on my bed in Denbigh Close, I felt the opposite. That I belonged everywhere. Day followed night followed day in their continual alteration, me sensing them, for the first time, as one thing. Regular in my habits, now, untroubled by habit I lay awake in the small hours with no urge to occupy myself with thoughts. I had submitted, something I had never done, and, save once, and that by accident, I have been unable to do so since.

I studied the darkness. Impatience left me. Each day Alice brought me her newspaper. I read the stories as a stranger might – it was easy to understand them, difficult to give them significance. Attempting to do so reminded me of my attempts to believe in God when I was a child.

In a detached way, I became newly fond of various of my possessions: particularly my Wordsworth silver teaspoon, its handle topped by a shield on which, immediately above the word 'GRASMERE', a lion was emblazoned in silver on a blue ground.

I had begged the spoon from Diane Aubrey, then married to Troy Kennedy-Martin, at the same time as he – then earning good money as a Hollywood script writer – gave me £300 to get on with my Homer poem, the second time that anyone professionally unconnected with my work had shown practical support for it.

After four weeks in bed I could walk about the house without my knees trembling.

One day when she brought me the paper, Alice said: 'I'll tell you something about Minky Warren, Mr Logue.

'When Ken and I started going out, I was living over at Pimlico, just seventeen. I'd said hello to Minky once or twice. Then he decided on a Friday tea for me to meet everyone. His family, that is.

'I'm off the bus twenty minutes early, so I think I'll walk around the block – Denbigh Terrace, Denbigh Road, the Portobello, blah-blah. On my second time around, there he is at the top of the Mews. Hat tipped, fag on, standing by his old brown and green Ford van.

'"Oi, you," he shouts. "Get in the fucking van."

'As you know, I don't like language, Mr Logue. But I got in for Ken's sake. And would you believe it, there is Ken, and his brother Alan – now living in Australia – sitting in the back of the van as quiet as mice, and when I look at Ken, he puts his finger to his lips.

'Off we go. Well, I say off, but Minky's hardly got the van going when we stop because his and Glad's place is only fifty yards down the Portobello.

'"Right," he says. "Upstairs. You" – me – "first."

'Now, in time I got to know Glad, and she's all right. You can trust her. But there was one thing she could not do, she absolutely could not do it, and that was, cook. Glad could not cook to save her life. Never.

'We had steak for tea. Terrible. Black. Curled up. You could not have worn it. I kept my eyes on my plate, but I couldn't get my knife into it. Everybody was the same. Even Minky – who, by the way, had taken off his shirt and was sitting at the table in one of his string vests. Suddenly he jumps up. "Right," he says. "I'm taking this fucking lot back."

'And he goes around the table taking our steaks off our plates and putting them into a paper bag. "Ken?" he says, and off they go in the van.

'When they got to Davis's – according to Ken the best butcher's in the neighbourhood – he's straight through the door, still in his string vest, shouting: "Oi, you" – that's the manager – "this meat is like fucking boards. Fucking floor boards," pushing his way through to the front, with Ken, fit to die, behind him. Then he tipped the steaks on to the counter. So he's given six fresh steaks. Back they come. Glad takes the steaks into the kitchen. Ten minutes later, she's back with them as black and hard as the others. By which time Minky has gone down to the pub. Then Ken takes me home. All this time hardly anybody has said a word.

' "He'll be home about nine," Ken said. ' "He'll belt Alan, then Glad, then he'll go to bed."

'I thought: Ken, the sooner you and I are married, the better. That Minky'll not raise a hand to me, I can tell you.'

MICHAEL White brought me a leg of cold lamb and a large jar of redcurrant jelly.

'Where are you going after this?' I asked.

'To see –' naming a famous West End theatre manager. 'I need a small theatre. I'll have to lick his arse for an hour. Then I'll get it.'

'What's the play?'

'Gogol's *The Government Inspector* – don't laugh.'

Isobel said:

'You're much nicer like this than normally. Now you know what being ill is like.'

VANITY returned with health. In Alice's newspaper a manufacturer of fluids for cleaning kitchens offered £25,000 to whoever got the most words out of a longer word. It's in the bag, I thought, opening my dictionaries. With their list of words, contestants were required to enclose three kinds of the competition setter's container tops – cost to acquire, £2.1s.2d.

A week later, with an entry of three hundred words behind me, I began to make plans for the £25,000. I would invite twenty people to supper at the Ivy, buy a broad-tyred Mini-Cooper, live in New York for a year. However, to preserve the dignity of my profession, and to conceal the unfair advantage of brains plus literary insight – not to mention guarding against the jocular publicity when my name as the winner was announced – I asked Alice to enter my list under her name.

Three weeks later, Alice came up the stairs with a serious look on her face and a letter from the manufacturer's head office in her hand. The front of the envelope said: YOU HAVE WON – OPEN AT ONCE!

'You open it Alice,' I said, casually.

'Dear competitor,' (Alice read)

'We are delighted to inform you that you are among the 16,321 who found over three hundred words in our set word. As so many of you succeeded, the judges, whose decision is final, have chosen to divide the prize-money between you. I have therefore the pleasure of enclosing a Postal Order for £1.10s.6d.

Yours sincerely'

Diary note:
Invited to drinks by George Martin at his new, independent recording studio. We talked about *Red Bird*, which had been deleted from EMI's catalogue.

'The management thought I was daft to do it. There was a monthly meeting where the heads of each label proffered their wares to the distribution and sales people. On their scale of one to ten, *Red Bird* came out at two. We pressed several thousand and they sold well. Then I met one of the directors in the lobby.

'"I'm on the Board, Martin. I see the figures," he said. "Last year EMI released 632 disks of which only 27 reached the top ten."

"Oh."

"And they made 95 per cent of our profits."

"That's good."

"Then why did Parlophone make so many of the other 605?" he said, and walked off.

'*Red Bird* was one of those.'

'George, if it was selling well, why did you delete it?'

'Because we ran out of sleeves and it was not selling enough to justify producing a new batch.'

A call from Tynan, or rather from Clive Goodwin, his assistant on *Tempo*, a television arts programme Ken was editing. He wanted some poetry on the show. He expected me and Adrian Mitchell – well known for his lyrics, his readings, his political poems – to provide it. We did. As, in 1980, we read at the burial of Ken's ashes in an unkempt Oxford graveyard.

Tempo's offices were a suite of rooms at the Piccadilly Hotel. Clive met me in the foyer. 'Ken is talking to Orson Welles about a programme on bullfighting,' he said. 'let's have a drink.' Settled, Clive asked for my ideas. I said poetry and television seemed mismatched. The visual ingredient was redundant. What usually happened when a poem was broadcast was that – if it included rural scenes – viewers were given stock shots of burbling streams, peaceful hills, and so on; if it had an urban setting, we got rooftops and cranes. It was no better to show a poet or an actor reciting the poem. What did the reader's face have to do with the words?

'So?' said Clive.

'I think we should put nothing but the text of the poem on the screen and scroll the lines upwards like the end titles of a film while a voice reads them,' I said.

'Nobody's going to like that,' Clive said.

'Well, that's my idea.'

His response was to order me another drink, put his feet up on the ottoman in front of him, lean back in his sofa and close his eyes. So we stayed until Celia, Ken's second assistant – soon to marry Adrian – came down to tell us that Orson Welles had agreed to the bullfighting story and Ken was in a bouncy mood.

I was shivery. I had never worked with Ken. Jobs with friends are difficult. You can end up losing both.

Clive said: 'Christopher has had a good idea for the show. That poem of his you liked in the *Statesman*, 'Professor Tuholsky's Facts', remember?'

'Um . . . '

'Why don't we ask Richard Williams to make a film to go with it – the words as the script?'

'Great,' Ken said, putting his arm around my shoulders. 'We'll do it. Let's have a drink.'

'No time for drinks,' Celia said. 'You are meeting Jonathan Miller *re* his item on the meaning of satire.'

Richard Williams was a friend of Lindsay's. He played the trumpet in a jazz band.

'Hope you didn't mind my taking your name in vain,' Clive said. I mentioned the drink.

'Sorry,' he said. 'I'm off to Birmingham. I've a trio of black girl singers, The Poppies. They're playing at the Crystal Room tonight. See you later.'

Williams made the film. We called it *Essay on Man*. My first script. It won a prize. £300. Though it was not the film that brought Clive and me closer.

EVERYONE wanted to date Pauline. Then she met Clive at a party. The next thing we knew, they were married.

'It was a shock,' Roger Smith – now down from Oxford, a script editor at the BBC television – said: 'No one knew where Clive came from. He had been an officer in the RAF. Then an actor. Then he worked for Tynan.'

Pauline found a kind, clever man who loved her. Above that – and rarer – one gratified to have a wife more famous than himself, pleased to advance her career as a painter.

And Clive had found his inspiration. 'On our first evening out,' he told me, 'Pauline said: "You are wasted in television – you should be an agent. For playwrights. Playwriting is all you have mentioned for two whole hours." ' Which is what he did.

It was typical Clive that, of the women who worked for him as secretaries, three became successful independent film producers.

'I was an ordinary, ignorant, upper-class English girl with a silly, expensive education,' Margaret Matheson, one of them, told me. 'I got a secretarial job at the BBC's drama department. Fairly boring. Then a playwright called Tom Clarke advised: "Work for Clive Goodwin. You'll never get anywhere here." I had never heard of Clive. His agency was not established. On the telephone he admitted: "Yes, I need someone. My last has just moved on to better things."

'I was anxious. If I got the job I hoped my room would not be too small. Clive opened the door. It was his flat. There were drawings and framed prints all over the walls: Patrick Proctor, Warhol, Hockney. I could not stop gawking. Clive was wearing frightful Marks & Spencer jeans, a pink shirt and sneakers. My mother would have died. We crossed the hall into a large airy room with two desks.

' "I'm not very experienced," he offered in an apologetic way. "The wages are below national average. A decent government would shut me down. The pictures come from good-cause auctions, CND, Anti-Apartheid. You can start now, if you like. Here's some money. We'll have a few people over for drinks tonight. Get some French bread, cheese, fruit. I'll do the drink. There's the address book. Start ringing round when you come back. Oh, yes, you'll need a key."

'He was my hero. "Margaret," he'd offer, "whenever you answer the telephone you always say: *Well?* How about: *Hello*, or *Goodwin Motion Pictures?*" Again: "Margaret, you have a fine, broad, forehead. I appreciate it. Is wearing the hair back such a good idea?" "Stuff this," he'd say, meaning work, "let's go to the Tate." Or "Let's buy some decent bread and cheese and eat it in the park." He made people happy. He saw their gifts. That's why he did so well.'

IT is hard to pin down changes in mood, the sensibility of a time, but towards the end of 1962 I felt that the spirit of the fifties had vanished.

One evening I was invited to a party by the *Private Eye* lot in a house belonging to James Callaghan, the future Prime Minister. The party typified what in next to no time became the norm: it was mixed, crossing boundaries of both class and age. Quite different from the one where, six years earlier, I had met Nell. In those days you knew what the crowd would be; now you could not be sure. Sexiness was flaunted and prized. There was a hint of freebooting, of danger. The music was extraordinary – and extraordinarily loud. Its effect reminded me of the thrill I had felt when seeing *Rock Around the Clock* and the audience had danced in the aisles of the cinema.

Ever since – at the same time as I studied under Miss Crowe – Molly had sent me for dancing lessons dressed in patent-leather shoes, a well-pressed blouse, and I had to 'lead' Lorna – wearing a bottle-green velvet dress with a white bow-at-the-back sash – through the foxtrot, quickstep, polka, I had kept well away from dancing. Tonight, the room was doing a sort of free-style cross between jitterbug and African tribal. You didn't have to touch anyone unless you wanted to.

At this – and, I guess, several thousand similar parties – an act of will was evident: this party is going to last. Then we went home. Someone gave me a lift from Blackheath to Notting Hill. It was getting light.

People ask what the sixties were like. For a start, there was plenty of work. Hence there was money about. Not that much, but enough to merit quoting Arthur Clough:

> They may talk as they please about what they call pelf,
> And how one ought never to think of one's self,
> And how pleasures of thought surpass eating and drinking –
> My pleasure of thought is the pleasure of thinking
>> How pleasant it is to have money, heigh ho!
>> How pleasant it is to have money.

For the first time in London's history a fair share of that money was in young hands. Colin MacInnes had noted in 1958 that 2 million 15- to 23-year-olds each had £3 spending money per week, £312 million a year. The new mood was friendly, self-centred, improvisatory, carefree, frivolous. It was obvious that those who were creating it did not want what the likes of Lindsay and me wanted them to like – a frugal, lyrical, unmaterialistic humanism.

Milk and honey were demanded: stylish clothes for both sexes, labour-saving machines in the kitchen, holidays abroad. New forms of self-knowledge. New, sometimes revolutionary and painful attitudes to personal relationships. Denunciations of old wrongs – racism, tyranny, cruel punishments.

Every month there was a different show of painting by the likes of Rosenquist, Warhol, Poons and Oldenburg from New York, or Hockney, Blake, Boshier, Colin Self from home ground. Better Books, Bumpus, Indica, and Bernard Stone were bookstores where you could find the literature regular publishers ignored. Independent cinemas showed French, German, Brazilian, Spanish and studio-free American films.

And music was everywhere, live and recorded. Music – about which I do not know how to write – was the heart of the time.

Needless to say, these happy days produced a deal of silliness. The conviction of its enthusiasts that they were about to create a perfect society. The incense trays, the religiosity, Hobbits, giggling gurus, the lyrics of the bands that aped Indian music.

Alex became one of the period's theorists. His schemes for social redemption were outlined in a collection of essays, *The Invisible Insurrection of a Million Minds*. The world was to be enlightened through the influence of a set of wizards of which he was one.

There were disappointments and material worries. Richard told me that the circulation of the *Private Eye* was falling: 'We have had to cut down to one telephone line. You had better think of something else to do.' On the way to the bus I bought a survival guide. On the bus, I discovered that a sack of soya beans would last me for a year. From America, Luard had brought me eight denim shirts, three pairs of denim trousers and two denim jackets. Ten years' worth at least. I had my stapler.

By the time Cook returned from performing in New York, the magazine had lost 40,000 sales. Fortunately for the *Eye* a businessman called John Bloom – one of the first to sell vacations – had just gone broke, leaving many people stranded. Peter put a reproduction of Géricault's *Raft of the Medusa* on the cover with one of the doomed saying 'This is the last time I go on a John Bloom holiday' and the circulation recovered.

In years gone by – unless well-to-do – you ate out as a treat. Now, inexpensive restaurants proliferated. Style stores opened. Notably, Biba, just around the corner from me, with its navy-blue walls.

'You must come and see it, you simply *must*,' Pauline said, and Michael, Clive, Roger and I went with her. And, yes, the place was full of lively young women listening – music in *shops*? – to the hits their money had made, buying democratized fashion, while as often as not the staff wore CND badges – *badges* on the staff? – pinned to designer clothes now accessible to the low-paid. Style, as an expression of *joie de vivre*, just as I had noticed it in Paris fourteen years ago, now in London. And, as said, music everywhere.

WHEN it was all over and the Blue Witch and her imps had come to power I was puzzled by the number of people – other than those who enjoy goading the timid – who made surly comments on what, almost immediately, the world christened 'the sixties'.

To set the record straight by pretending to be an historian for a paragraph or two: 1959 saw book censorship restricted by the Obscene Publications Act; 1967's Sexual Offences Bill removed the threat of prosecution from homosexuals making love in private; in 1968, the laws governing abortion were liberalized and censorship of the theatre ended; capital punishment was abolished in 1969; by the end of that year, chemical contraception had become the norm for sensible women; and by 1973 changes similar to the foregoing improved our laws with regard to immigration, divorce, gambling and drink sales.

Did the people who complained about those years actually want the freedom to publish abrogated? Homosexuals prosecuted for living together? Coat-hanger abortion reintroduced? A committee of army officers – however charming – to say what plays could be put on in GB? The Home Office to advertise for potential hangmen? Surely not.

For me, one of the most influential figures of that pleasant time was Roy Jenkins, now Lord Jenkins of Hillhead, Home Secretary for two years from 1965. In 1959, in his pamphlet *The Labour Case*, Jenkins wrote:

> First, there is the need for the State to do less to restrict personal freedom. Secondly, there is the need for the State to do more to encourage the arts, to create towns which are worth living in, and to preserve a countryside which is worth looking at. Thirdly, there is the need, independently of the State, to create a climate of opinion which is favourable to gaiety, tolerance, and beauty, and unfavourable to puritanical restriction, to petty-minded disapproval, to hypocrisy, and to a dreary, ugly pattern of life. A determined drive in these three directions would do as much to promote human happiness as all the 'political' legislation which any government is likely to introduce.

In some measure, often thanks to him, these aims were achieved.

Without using words like resentment, envy and vindictiveness, I find it hard to describe those who, almost half a century later, still complain about the years from 1956 to the early seventies. Perhaps they hold their views for medical reasons. In one way or another, most of the half-dozen modest reforms listed at the beginning of this section had to do with sex.

ON Sunday afternoons, a number of us, Michael and Sarah White, Roger Smith, Derek Boshier and his girlfriend Jo Cruikshank – the kind of friendly girl who, when walking by, gave you the eye from the corner of her eye as she drank from a can – gathered at Clive and Pauline's flat. It was a tonic to see them together. Pauline in a pinky-blue, six-foot fake-feather boa and white, knee-high boots handing round fudge, pouring out tea. Clive, anxious that she did not take on too much.

Pauline's thoughts on the fate of her own sex were alarming in their friendliness. 'I think us women should demand a lot more of our men than fertilization, protection and leadership. I don't object to giving birth to a child or two, or using a dustpan and brush occasionally, provided I can produce paintings at the same time. I want to be desired, but not only for what women will always be desired for. Hard to explain. It seems very big-headed to say it, but some of the things I am trying to say have never, ever, been said. There are no worked-out words for the thoughts. See? Love women who stand up for themselves. Respect and protect those who cannot. Apart from that, there is little for you men to do.'

It was the day of 'happenings': provocative, one-off quasi-theatrical events, given in odd non-theatrical settings. Clive said that Mark Boyle and Joan Hills, two artists Pauline swore by, were to put on a happening at their Queen's Gate flat.

'It had better be an improvement on the one in that field at Hemel Hempstead, Clive,' I said. 'Dennis Potter said he would not have you as an agent if you continued to support right-wing anarchist nonsense.'

'Be there. Just be there,' Clive said.

By the time that he, Pauline, Roger, Derek, Jo, the Whites, Hercules Belville and I arrived at Queen's Gate, fifty people were present, gossiping, drinking, admiring the art. Then Mark Boyle announced that the happening would begin with a film called *Ends*. This was bc shown in their large basement room which, aside from a projector waiting to be fed by an outsize 16mm reel, was empty. Down we sat, on came the film, projected against the far wall.

Ends was exactly that: short lengths of developed film retrieved from the waste bins of cutting rooms, spliced together accompanied by a tape-recorded 'soundtrack' of distant traffic. It lasted for twenty minutes. Then someone turned on the lights and out we trooped, looking for another drink. However, while we had been watching, without making a sound, the Boyles had moved. Chairs, tables, sideboards, carpets, beds, kitchen equipment, pictures, books, crockery, clothes, television, drinks and glasses – all gone, the house empty, the front door open, the keys in the lock.

TALL, very thin, blond – if born female, ideal for the catwalk – Hercules Belville had an authoritative voice, a love of art, particularly that of cinema, and a passion for organization. A confirmed bachelor with a fine house in Chelsea, handsome, capable – as a film producer's/film director's adjutant – of earning good money, our Herky was the target for many a domestically minded young woman. Nothing doing. Beauties came, beauties went. One actually moved in. Hercules has remained free.

'I'm very particular,' he would say. 'I like to sit at the same table, laid in the same way, in the same – four, five at the most – restaurants most days of the year. I am religious. I do not talk about it. I do not drink, but I like those who do. I read a lot, but I enjoy the company of those who never read.'

Hercules once organized a party to hear the Beatles at Hammersmith Odeon. I bet the film director, Claire Peploe, that when I gave her the word she would not stand up on her seat and shout: 'Fuck me, Ringo!' at the top of her voice.

I reckoned to lose. Claire was one of the best-looking women of her time – Michelangelo Antonioni was helplessly in love with her, Bertolucci married her – and not short of nerve. The trouble was, after Herky shepherded us: 'This way, my party. No straggling. That's the spirit. Keep together... Chloe' – Claire's sister – '... I am not doing this for fun. If you do not keep up, you may well be left behind in the foyer' ... into our third-row seats, the screaming from every part of the audience was so continuously astounding I never had the chance to give Claire the word. The ten of us left the auditorium completely stunned.

'MY beginning to drink coincided with your becoming discontented with yourself and everybody and everything, in late '64,' Isobel said. 'People would tiptoe around you. "Don't upset Christopher."

'You became obsessed with things that had nothing to do with your work. You never mentioned your work. I once said: "Translucent is one of your favourite words, isn't it?" Giving you what I thought was an encouraging smile. Nothing back. Just "Yes."

'You had never been any good at judging the effect of your words, but now you were hopeless. I have seen people on the verge of hitting you because of something you said, some dreadfully rude thing. Or if it was a woman, they would leave the room and cry. But you would say: "Nonsense. It'll all be forgotten in a minute", or "Don't be silly. Everything is all right. Pay no attention." It cost you a lot. It was as if you wanted people to hate you. As if you thought that to be honest you had to be rude.

'Some people said you thought you were too good for anybody. Too stuck up. They weren't clever enough. That was wrong. You liked women who did things. You wanted them to act. It was why you admired Nell Dunn, Pauline Boty and Sophie Baker.

'I made myself a winter coat. It was good. In fashion but different. My tailoring was top class. You were delighted. Next, why didn't I do this, then that? You never noticed I was depressed. I made the coat to show myself I still could do something.

'When we met after my drinking started you sat with lowered eyes. I would say "Why don't you look at me?" You would reply: "I looked at you when you arrived." Or something like it. My looks were all I had left. Why didn't you see it? You were evasive. You just didn't want to know.

'I remember one of our last conversations. It began with you making me laugh to myself: "I have decided to give up sex," you said.

'"Oh?"

'"Yes. It's a great relief."

'"Really."

'"Yes. It's safer."

'"What on earth do you mean?"

'"Well," you said. "One might go to a party, meet someone you fancied, take them home, and they turn out to be a psychopath and murder you in the night."

'Instantly I thought: "He means me. He was my friend. The one I could turn to. He has guessed that I think about killing." Then you went on:

'"For God's sake use your brains, Isobel. Do something."

'"Thank you for your advice."

'"You know what I mean."

' "I have to go."

' "Why?"

' "See you later."

'Later was twenty years later, as I said. How could you?'

Isobel began to cry.

'Don't cry, Isobel. Please don't cry.'

'Let me cry if I want to cry. You haven't changed. You just want me happy and active. You don't like it when I am upset, because it upsets you. You are the same as Rascomb. At least he had money. You don't want to be seen with a weeping woman in case someone thinks you are to blame, one of your famous friends, Lindsay Anderson or Nell Dunn.'

'You would be better off with either of them than with me,' I said.

'You were my friend. As soon as I began to fall to bits you turned away from me. I was an alcoholic. A bore. I couldn't stand the sight of Rascomb. Or the children. You noticed nothing. There was always a half-bottle of vodka in my handbag. I had two handbags, remember? When I needed a drink I went to your bathroom taking one of the bags with me. Why did I turn my face away when you kissed me goodbye? So as you didn't smell my breath.

'You have no idea how nasty you could be. Sometimes out of nowhere you have attacked me – verbally – for something I have said, some inconsequential thing, probably from my trying to think of a topic that would interest you so as we wouldn't sit facing each other in silence in a restaurant. You would go on and on until you had reduced me to tears. Then you would be sorry. Wanting it to be "all right", as if I was your mother.

'You do nothing to make other people happy. You think that your effort for other people is taken care of by your "work". Your "work" – such as it is – is your justification. Other people must put up with you for the sake of your "work". You are like that Dickens character who spent her time worrying about African tribes.'

'Mrs Jellaby.'

'If you say so. When did you go along to the local state school and offer to read poetry aloud to the children? Or give blood? You know exactly what I am talking about.

'I'm going. You wanted to know the truth about yourself. I hope you got what you came for. Goodbye.'

'Please don't go, Isobel. Please don't go. I'll think of something to make it better. We'll go to Italy. Stay with the Kings. I'll get some money from somewhere. Write a film or something.'

'You are useless. I don't want a solution. I just want to be listened to. Don't you see? Can't you get it into your head? I want sympathy. Not trips abroad. I've been abroad.'

'Do you know that slot-in-the-wall poetry bookshop in Kensington run by a bloke who looks like a tortoise with glasses?' Kenny said. This was to be my third bookseller friend, Mr Bernard Stone.

The size of a large bed, Bernard's shop was so cluttered I was unable to open the door. Looking up from behind his counter, Mr Stone – who did, indeed, resemble a bespectacled tortoise – edged doorwards between shelves laden with books, booklets, postcards, cardboard tubes, piles of envelopes, photographs, drawings, folders and magazines – poetry, art, music – reached the door, and, me pushing, him pulling, admitted me to the ting-tong-ting of the shop's bell and the slither of a waist-high pile of poetry pamphlets on to the floor.

Then – as always, with an 'Excuse me' – Mr Stone restacked the pamphlets, and shifted one pile of books off another pile on to a third pile. By the time, two minutes later, I had reached the counter, I understood that his entire stock was on the move from moment to moment, so that if, for instance, you wished to make a purchase from the items he tidied as he passed, you had better grab it there and then in case it slid away before you left.

Among his long-haired, sheepskin-waistcoated, black-lipsticked, mini-skirted customers, Mr Stone's mien was one of full Midlands respectability. Always in a suit. A freshly laundered shirt forever at the ready in a transparent dry-cleaner's envelope behind his counter.

Short-sighted and shy – though, like most second-hand booksellers, wiry-strong from lifting and carrying – Bernard was immediately, on conscription in 1940, marked for Stores. And it was at the main Quartermaster's Stores for the army in East Africa at Lagos that he decided to become a bookseller specializing in poetry. 'It came over me from nowhere. As some things do,' Bernard said. 'Yes, I would be a poetry book-seller.'

After a stint as a book dealer's runner he used his army gratuity to acquire a comprehensive stock of poetry books and his shelf of a shop – two paces from the flat where Pound had written *Cathay* – in Kensington.

Moderately successful as a dealer in mail-order limited editions and modern literary manuscripts, the moment he moved (two doors down) to larger premises, Bernard hired an assistant. Bernard's relations with his assistants were all on the same pattern. Usually dour-faced, middle-aged women, once engaged, they seldom left. This may have been because they were not allowed to do anything but sit and read, Bernard getting flustered if they moved an item from its present place.

So there they sat, year in, year out, reading. If there was a paying customer – now and then there was – and the assistant stood up to do some assisting in pursuit of, say, a rare 1920s pamphlet, Bernard materialized as from nowhere to lead the, usually endless, search himself.

My first buy from him was *UNICORN* by Angela Carter. *A Tlaloc print-out: 150 copies.*

> I have sharp teeth inside my mouth,
> Inside my dark red lips,
> And Lacquer slickly hides the claws
> In my red fingertips.

'A treasure,' Bernard said. 'An absolute treasure.'

That was/is Bernard. Always enthusing, always doing you a favour, giving you a present, asking after your work. In this respect, like George Devine, more mindful of others than of himself. One of his many gifts to me: *The Rifle and and the Man, or the art of Musketry: a Didactic Poem* by Andrew Steinmitz, 1863, 'to help with your Homer Poem' – a rarity Charles did not have.

BY 1965, the stallholders of Denbigh Close had begun to arrive each Saturday morning at 5 a.m., for the Portobello Road street market was becoming the rage it remains. The bargain hunters of old were replaced by Italian dealers. Furniture conversion became antique restoration. Mad John was dead. Harry Dust had a council flat. Middle-class people had bought the cottages that they had lived in. Having introduced decorative mirrors, Kenny put a number of art-school students to work painting furniture, turning out pictures to resemble naïve art. HMS *Victory*'s and Battles of Portobello sold well. I borrowed money to raise the roof of No.18. It meant the addition of a large room with a terrace overlooking the Mews.

Living at the blind end of the Mews was Mr Eric Jones. Since 1934 he and his mother had occupied a cottage with a third floor the height of my planned extension. Eric was a cross-dresser with dyed, orange-blond hair. On summer Saturdays before the road boomed, he would tie an apron over his pink dress and sweep the Mews from end to end when the marketeers had left.

'I was down the far end when I heard this terrible row coming from Eric's place,' Kenny said. 'There was Eric and his mother – she must have been eighty – having a fight, both wearing dresses. Eric was just about getting the best of it.'

' "Eric," I said, "that's no way to treat an old lady, especially as she's your mother."'

' "Fuck off and mind your own business," Eric said.'

'So what did you do?' I said.

'I fucked off.'

My extension was built. My new room! Eric saw me surveying the Mews from its terrace.

'You all right up there, Chris?' he said. 'Pleased with your top floor?'

'Come up and have a look,' I said.

'Nah,' he said. 'You come and see ourn.'

Eric introduced me to his mother.

'Evening.'

'Chris wants to look at our upstairs.'

'Stair-door's key's in the drawer.'

'Why do you keep the top floor locked?' I said as he gave me the key.

'Well,' Eric said, 'we've never been up there, have we, Ma?'

'Nah. More cleaning.'

As Isobel said, I became discontented. Idle. Poetry readings took me around the country.

Adrian Mitchell and I were invited to read at Hintlesham Hall, a mansion in the depths of Suffolk. A bed for the night was offered. Celia drove us.

Beyond its porch with fluted columns the Hall's front door was opened by a liveried footman. Hearing we were the poetry readers, he told us to go to the servants' entrance. I said, let's leave. 'No,' Adrian said. 'We've come all this way. We'll earn our money.'

In the servants' hall a housekeeper said that high tea would be served at 6 p.m. Meantime, she would show us to our rooms. As it was customary at the Hall for entertainers to be treated as single, Adrian and Celia were given separate rooms. High tea was served by a housemaid. Two pieces of Spam, sliced bread, margarine, an apple, a piece of seed cake. Water and/or tea to drink.

Adrian and I decided to give our best. The audience knew its place. Long dresses and dinner jackets at the front, suits and twin-sets behind, estate workers at the back. A Lord Mayor sat in the front row wearing his chain of office and a three-cornered hat. We read. By best, we meant bluntest. I added a number of 'fucks' and 'cunts' to otherwise quite decorous poems. Then we left.

It was dark. We were among high-sided lanes. After an hour, we reached Nayland, twenty miles from the Hall, where we gave a lift to two Boy Scouts going south. A few miles further on, I lost my temper with them and said they were no different from Hitler Youth. 'It was exactly like the Sunday morning in Nottingham,' Adrian said, 'when you gave the man behind the bar in the hotel lobby a dressing-down because the kitchens were closed on the Sabbath so there was no breakfast. Then it turned out that he, too, was a guest looking for a telephone number.' Hintlesham paid by post.

It was at a poetry reading in London that I met Belle, the young woman who tamed my fear of sex. Half-Finnish, half-Welsh, the daughter of an oil-company executive, Belle had done various jobs: cookery, fashion modelling, animal welfare.

Belle had an income from her mother, and no concern for social status.

Recently – 1994 – I was shocked when a woman friend said (we were alone): 'When I was first married, the only way my husband could bring himself to fuck me was by putting an open *Playboy* centrefold over my face. We loved each other enough to talk about it. That – and *Playboy* – saved our marriage. We laugh about it now. At the time it was humiliating for us both.'

Partly because of her nomadic background Belle lived without regard for, or resentment against, the sexual conventions of the settled. Uneducated, barely able to spell any of the five languages she spoke, she accepted without question her physical nature.

After the reading we had supper. When we got home to her mother's flat she said: 'Would you like to see me naked?' Her tits were like torpedo heads. They stood straight out. 'I get my rubbery flesh from my mother,' she said as she wandered about eating a bowl of cornflakes. 'Would you like to suck my breasts?' And when, trembling with frightened excitement, I did, she said: 'Why don't you play with yourself?' Which was, of course, exactly what I wanted to do. 'I like a man to suck my tits. It brings me alive. Sometimes it makes me come.'

Later, as she pulled back the duvet prior to our going to sleep, I saw that the undersheet was stained with menstrual blood. I am squeamish. Now, though, for the first time in my waking life, I hallucinated. The stains turned into goldfish that leapt about for a moment, then flew away. On only two other occasions – eighteen years before that, in Acre Central Prison, when I heard the sound of music coming from the governor's office window, and years later when recovering from hepatitis – have I felt so at peace as I did when I fell asleep next to Belle.

Thereafter, my sexual embarrassments vanished. My disgust, to the point of nausea, at the taste of cunt. Cole Porter's performing seals. Gone. 'You're so funny about masturbation,' Belle confided. 'I have been masturbating since childhood. My Thai nanny taught me. We used to do it together. Sometimes for hours on end.'

All I remember of the worldly things we said is Belle's reply to my question: What do you do about ironing?

'If I see something that needs ironing, I don't buy it.'

Our lovemaking continued for three days. We left the flat to buy food. Now and again the telephone rang. Her mother, her brother, a photographer. I was in a light, sensual coma. There was nothing I dared not say or do. I ate strawberries and cream off her cunt.

'OK. Let's do it on the kitchen table.'

I discovered I could talk to Belle about anything. Any fantasy. Any shameful urge. She would say: 'Don't worry. You're not alone. When I was young' – she meant fifteen – 'I had an affair with my closest friend's father, an engineer of fifty at the top of his profession. In charge of establishing a new telephone system for Surinam. He confessed he had wanted to make love to his daughter – my friend – for years and years. He would think about her while masturbating. Then he told me that he suffered from the most wicked racist thoughts. He would walk alone in the fields shouting out foul insults about people he liked and worked with.'

One evening, Belle said: 'I am off on a modelling trip. I have to meet Henry, the photographer, outside his flat in an hour. Will you drive me? The locations are in Bermuda.' Henry, dressed in black leather, was waiting on the pavement beside a black Aston Martin, the shelf of its boot covered with glittering equipment.

Belle sent me a card from Miami showing an avenue lined with high-cost bungalows set back from the road, and captioned: *Beautiful Negro Homes*.

Once a week for six months I called her mother's London flat. Then her brother answered. He was emptying the flat, selling it. Having the telephone disconnected. He hadn't seen her. 'Dad's managing the company's Lagos refinery.'

'Have you got her number?'

'Only my mother has it.'

'Would you ask your mother to remember me to her – Christopher, in London.'

'Certainly.'

'Goodbye.'

E ACH Saturday lunch time, I visited my mother. One day I was
hardly through the door when she declared:

'I have received the most upsetting news.'

'Oh.'

'Well might you "Oh". Hilda called in. Up from Felixstowe for
a day's shopping, she has decided to take your cousin Nora' –
Jimmy Logue's sister – 'home to Felixstowe for a holiday.'

'Ah.'

'A holiday! – after all those two have said concerning each
other. She's doing it to upset Lionel. They are bound to meet at
the shops. Not that there are any decent shops in Felixstowe.'

The coolness between Nora and Lionel had begun in the late
forties when Nora responded to his praise of Sir Oswald Mosley
by saying: 'Then why don't you join him in exile?'

'And then Hilda mentioned *last year's* Christmas presents,'
Mother continued.

'Surely not.'

'Yes. She said for the other half of my last-year's Christmas
present' – the first, as I had heard, had been a plastic chalice filled
with bulbs – 'she was giving me writing paper. Basildon Bond. "I
am no longer able to write as a result of my arthritis, Hilda,"
I reminded her. "Then give it away," she said, and left.'

We sat for a while in silence. Then Mother said: 'It's time you
married. What became of that young woman Isobel who gave me
the colour television?'

'That you returned because you preferred black and white?'

'That's as may be.'

'She is married.'

'In my day, a single man who saw too much of a married
woman got himself into trouble. Thank God the Pope has granted a dispensation allowing Catholics to be cremated. Good news
for you too. I'll have no such thing as a final resting place for you
to neglect. If nothing else, you can thank me for your health. I see
you can't wait to get away. Pass me my glasses before you go. Oh
yes, Hilda left this for you.'

It was a chocolate-liqueur box filled with dated clippings of
every review that my books, plays, or radio programmes had
received since 1953. How differently they read now. At the time,
oh, the complaining: that fellow failed to praise me for this, this

fellow blamed me for that, another positioned his comments on my book underneath so-and-so's book, or so-and-so's book had been given fifty words more than my book, and why was there a photograph of so-and-so but not of me? Now, how fair-minded their words appeared, how sensible their suggestions for my improvement.

BERNARD and I began to work together soon after my first visit to his shop. He produced a roll of 'To My Fellow Artists' posters – forgotten since I had left the last of them on a table in the foyer of the Royal Court in 1958 with a 'Please Take One' note. When I had signed them, Bernard said: 'Why not do another? We can publish it from the shop.'

A general election was due. The left-wing weekly *Tribune* had asked several writers, me among them, to write 200 words on why they were going to vote for the Labour Party. I settled down to do as requested, giving the usual (correct) answers: redistribution of wealth, reform of the Commons and the Lords, fairer taxation, increased expenditure on public education, health and policing systems, as much freedom of information as was compatible with a reformed defence policy, plenty of money for arts and sports, etcetera.

Suddenly, I was sick of the irritating pleasure this list of wants gave me. To replace it I wrote a poem called 'I Shall Vote Labour' consisting of some silly, some sarcastic, reasons for doing so. Thus:

I shall vote Labour because
    God votes Labour.
I shall vote Labour in order to protect
    the sacred institution of The Family.
I shall vote Labour because
    I am a dog.
I shall vote Labour because
    upper-class hoorays annoy me in expensive restaurants.
I shall vote Labour because
    I am on a diet.
I shall vote Labour because if I don't
    somebody else will:

AND

I shall vote Labour because if one person does it
    everybody will be wanting to do it.
I shall vote Labour because if I do not vote Labour
    my balls will drop off.
I shall vote Labour because
    there are too few cars on the road.
I shall vote Labour because I am
    a hopeless drug addict.
I shall vote Labour because
    I failed to be a dollar millionaire aged three.
I shall vote Labour because Labour will build
    more maximum security prisons.
I shall vote Labour because I want to shop
    in an all-weather precinct stretching from Yeovil to Glasgow.
I shall vote Labour because
    the Queen's stamp collection is the best in the world.
I shall vote Labour because
    deep in my heart
I am a Conservative.

True to their word, *Tribune* printed it.

The republication of this poem on a poster was our first venture. Rumour said that it sold 10,000 copies.

Doing business with Bernard was instructive. Nothing was too much trouble. But everything took a long time. Bills were paid. But money was never made. Reprints were promised. But not produced. Records were kept. But no one knew where.

Bernard loves secrecy. Once, under pressure, he admitted that he came from Nottingham, from a lace-making family. This said, he began to hum, look up in the air, then head for the cellar in pursuit of a book. On another occasion, Nicholas Luard's wife, Elizabeth, demanded to know: 'Bernard, are you in fact Mr Bernard Stone, the person standing before me now, this very minute?' No answer. 'Everything is in his head,' Elizabeth complained, 'but at the same time he knows nothing about it.'

I FETCHED Austryn from Heathrow. I told him that Maurice had been in London, a guest of honour at a Foyle's Literary Luncheon. Supposed to talk about censorship and the Olympia Press, he was drunk and made a fool of himself. One of the ladies who paid to hear him said: 'I thought he was going to talk about the Olympic Games. Most disappointing.'

I asked him what he was working on.

'I love good writing,' Austryn said. 'It makes the world a better place and I always thought of myself as a writer until my daughter Cassie was born. Then my wish to write – not the love of literature – went. No regret, no relief, no resentment. It just went. I am told many women feel similarly if the longing to become mothers takes them. Most reasonable. Something like that happened to me.'

I mentioned money. 'Dick has been my mentor,' he said. 'Translators are treated like dirt. Bad contracts. Invisible royalties. Agents won't touch you. For the Sade translations, Dick wrote my contract with Grove. Seven and a half per cent on all sales world-wide. That's what you call a friend. And you?'

'Nothing much. A few poems.'

'Why is that, Christopher?'

'I'm not sure. I'll get your bed ready.'

I did not know what had come over me. My work was published. I broadcast. Was invited to read. I might have reviewed books, exhibitions of painting. My fortnightly piece for *Private Eye* left me plenty of time. I did not have to go into the office. Richard's secretary sent me the clippings submitted for 'True Stories'. I rewrote those suitable. Posted the copy to Bert Kitchen, the column's illustrator. I said it took a day. It took a morning.

I WENT round to see Alan Sillitoe and said: 'Set me a task. Write out ten to twelve one-line chapter headings for a novel, between ten and thirty pages per chapter. I'll write it.' He obliged. I kept his list for years without writing a word for it.

As well as looking from time to time at this or that translation of the *Iliad*, I sat on my terrace, read, listened to the rain at night. I wished Belle would turn up. I knew she would not.

KENNY had put the posters carrying my poems in his shop window. On summer evenings from the terrace I watched people read them. There was a version of Villon's 'Ballade des dames du temps jadis' that had given me a lot of trouble. Particularly the last stanza, where I could not get the rhymes right. Impatient, I decided to rhyme 'reverie' with 'territory'. It works on the ear – just. Not on the eye. I watched a couple reading the poem.

'It's all in old English,' the man said.

'All the same,' the woman said, 'you must admit territory and reverie don't rhyme.'

MARQUAND passed through London on his way to Greece. *Commentary,* an American journal specializing in political analysis, had suggested that he should write an essay covering the question: 'What effect have the various US/UK anti-war movements had on public opinion?' So far, his reading for the piece has produced the answer: none whatsoever. 'Very reassuring for our right-wing friends. Inevitably,' he went on, 'the public supports any war involving itself. Demands for retribution surface along with the first casualty lists. War resisters are called "traitors", "cowards", and so forth. All the Allied leaders agreed that the atomic bomb should be dropped on Japan. And according to various surveys, both our publics agreed with them.'

John spent a day in the British Library looking into the fate of British conscientious objectors – 'whose ranks, around 1914, included your fellow poet Basil Bunting' – in both world wars. Apparently, during the first of these, over seventy men who had refused active service died in, or as a result of their being in, our prisons.

'Shouldn't their names be on your war memorials, Christopher?'

WHAT else can people do when they are attacked?' Kenny asked.

'Then war must be made illegal.'

'Don't be daft, Mr Logue.'

When Rosemary and I married he was my best man.

ISOBEL had left Rascomb. Wretched, she was staying the night at No.18. We were asleep when it started to rain. Then the rain became torrential, the sky chucking it down. Moments later I woke to the sound of water pouring into the house. Leaves had blocked the roof's pedimented back gutter, and, mounting under the bottom row of slates, the rainwater had begun to gush into the house through the kitchen ceiling.

Naked, I climbed from the terrace on to the flat of the roof, slid down the slates and cleared the leaves from the mouth of the drainpipe. The rain was as heavy as ever. Cold and stinging. Then – partly because the rain was streaming down it – I found I could not clamber back up the roof-slope.

There was a light on in Brigit Vaughan's house – she of the matchsticks. Standing in the gutter, glistening with rain, I yelled out for Reg, Brigit's husband. Nothing. Then the light went out.

I started to bang my fist on the slates above the bed. After a long two minutes Isobel put her head through the kitchen window, began to laugh, then came back to say she had telephoned Alice and that Kenny was on his way with a rope. Up which I climbed.

The odd thing was, after all that I felt very sexy.

OCCASIONALLY, interesting events materialize from a general mood. One person says to another: 'Let's do so-and-so,' and things begin to move.

The Albert Hall poetry reading of 11 June 1965 was like this. Alex called at No.18. Realizing there were a number of American and European poets in London, he and Michael Horovitz had formed a Poets' Co-operative to plan a large public reading.

'We met in Trocchi's flat,' Michael said. 'The Americans – Corso, Ferlinghetti, Ginsberg – were reading here and there in London, all seats sold. Then we heard that Andrei Voznesensky, the Austrian sound-poet Ernst Jandl, Simon Vinkenoog and Anselm Hollo were in town, with Pablo Neruda expected. "What is the biggest hall in London?" Vinkenoog said. The Albert Hall. Free in ten days' time. A £600 bond for the day.'

Jill Richter, the wife of Daniel – he choreographed and led the hominidae sequences at the beginning of 2001 – put up the money, and during those ten days the Co-operative covered the town with publicity. Better Books sold out of tickets. 'Still,' Alex said 'we were nervous. We had sold 500 tickets at five shillings and ten shillings each. 500 people are lost in the Albert Hall.'

To promote sales Alex suggested holding a press conference on the steps of the Albert Memorial. Everyone turned up: Ginsberg, with Harry Fainlight dancing around him, Simon wearing glasses with sunflowers painted on the lenses, Michael Horovitz, Julie Felix, Ferlinghetti, Barry and Sue Miles surrounded by a fantastically dressed, handsome collection of obviously happy young men and women. All this to the delight of a BBC-TV outside broadcast unit that delivered enough good material for the nine o'clock news to include a minute-long item on the conference, with full details of the First Great International Poetry Reading about to be held at the Royal Albert Hall, announced in the sunshine by Alex in his caftan.

I had put the date of the reading in my diary, and forgotten about it. I missed the press conference, but saw it broadcast, wishing I had been there. I was sure that it would add at least two thousand to the number of tickets already sold.

Came the day – a Friday – I rang Clive in the afternoon. Pauline had bought six tickets. 'We'll see you there,' he said. 'Either at the interval or when you come off. Do well.'

The weather had held. About 6.30 p.m. I walked up to the Gate, then, in the warm evening light, across the park to Kensington Gore with some of my poems in a folder. There were a few people buying tickets at the outside box-office. A doorman directed me to the artists' entrance – my first time behind the scenes in this famous building. Another doorman had my name on his list of readers. Good old Alex. In I went.

Simon's was the first known face I saw. 'This way,' he said, in a serious tone.

We went through a tunnel. Seconds later, we stepped into the light of this vast domed space where thousands of faces looked down on us, breathtaking banks of them, filling the Hall – a place intended for the performance of works of enduring beauty – itself suffused with a light that was like candlelight in its effect, though stronger, while here and there, a spot travelled over the audience – a sight that drew a silent gasp from me, as had my first visit to the British Library's round reading room.

Between seven and eight thousand people had come. Photographs show the Hall full. Helpers bought what remained of the stock from the Covent Garden flower market. As the audience arrived, they were given daffodils, tulips, roses and greenery. People sat where they chose. 'You sensed expectancy,' Alex said. 'We were astonished. Delighted. The evening centred on the poets. We half-emptied the arena' – the Hall's central floor-space – 'of seats and arranged a horseshoe of tables set with water and wine for the readers. At the middle of the space was a low, microphoned podium, beside it a high stool with lectern and a second microphone.' From which Alex, as master of ceremonies, announced each reader.

At Alex's flat, he, Ginsberg, Horovitz and Vinkenoog composed an Invocation beginning with a quotation from Blake's 'Jerusalem':

> *'England awake! awake! awake!*
> *Jerusalem thy Sister calls!'*

And now the time returns again:
Our souls exult, & London's towers
Receive the Lamb of God to dwell
In England's green & pleasant bowers.

So the evening began.

My awe was warmed by the happy buzz rising and falling as Alex called poet after poet to the stand, detaching the microphone from the neck of the one departing, attaching it with a 'Don't be too long now', to the next.

For me – perhaps only for me – to see my now distant friend Alex as his early fifties self again was a boon. Relaxed, confident, humorous, very much in charge. As the press said: 'A model chairman, introducing the speakers without fuss and exercising a kindly but implacable "guillotine" when the minutes allowed for each poet were up.'

Time makes short work of bad verse. Literary standards were not high that day. It did not matter. It was the moment that spoke. A big, discrete, concentrated, four-hour moment, wishing poetry well in the city that had sheltered a number of its fairest voices.

For me, the high point of the Albert Hall event – it can be seen in the video of *Wholly Communion*, Peter Whitehead's film of the reading – was the performance of Kurt Schwitters' sound poem, 'The Furore of Sneezing', by Pete Brown, Jandl and Horovitz. The text (or score?) of the poem goes:

> Tesch, Haisch, Tschiiaa
> Haisch, Tschiiaa
> Haisch, Happaisch
> Happapeppaisch
> Happapeppaisch
> Happapeppaisch
> Happapeppaisch
> Happa peppe
>   TSCHAA!

which the trio, led by Jandl – a superb verbal technician – gave in about a minute. Starting

> *'Tesch . . . Haisch . . . Tschiiaa . . .'*

the suspense rising through

> *'Haisch . . . Happaisch . . .'*

to the almost unbearable

> *'Happa . . . Peppe . . .'*

all 8,000 of us dying for the release of

> *'TSCHAA!'*

Ginsberg was the star. As much a priest, a rabbi, as a poet. By any standard, an impressive man at the height of his reputation, surrounded by those he inspired, he shuffled away under a cloud of thrown rose leaves as the show came to a close, while Alex, at whose invitation I came to this unique event, unhooked his microphone, and lit up.

THE Albert Hall audience was the largest I had ever read to until the Isle of Wight Festival in 1969 when I stood up in front of a crowd of over 100,000 people.

Then followed years of depression. A decade and more.

Hard to put my finger on what was wrong. I had my routine. Most days I saw Kenny and Alice. There were amusements. I wrote one film, acted in two or three. I read. Made notes. Day followed day. I had no obvious complaints. Still, I was depressed.

Isobel was in London.

'I hate to see you like this.'

'Like what?'

'Like me. You were the one who got up in the morning and did something that made people like me get up. Now you haven't done a thing for months except your *Private Eye* piece. Never mind who said so. More than one. People who like you.'

'I'm thinking.'

'Rubbish. When you've thought of something you come out with it like a child. Go and see Donleavy in Ireland. He likes you. Or go to America and see George Plimpton. He likes you. I can't help. I would if I could.'

Then things improved. I met Rosemary Hill. We arranged to meet outside the British Museum. She was carrying a frightful bag, one of those now long-vanished nets made of plastic strips with bamboo handles, hers making a cubist bunch of books, files, pencilcase. She had a most beautiful smile. Open, friendly, sceptical. We went to the Russell Hotel and had champagne with smoked salmon sandwiches.

1998

So far, my life has been pretty easy. I have not been driven away from my own country, or emotionally betrayed. Nor have I had to face a debilitating illness, or poverty, or professional neglect. I have not seen one close to me suffer terrible damage, or go mad, or kill themselves.

Indeed, sex aside, I have done more or less what I fancied doing, and the greater part of my time has been passed in the company of those who have done likewise.

Not for me a consciousness of having no special talent, of taking the best job my capabilities allowed, knowing that it was no more than an honest way to earn decent money in the company of those whose fate in life was similar to mine. Today, finding myself among those who have lived in this way, the sound of my own voice makes me uneasy. I find my opinions about almost anything other than this or that piece of verse, my number one subject, not worth so much.

Involvement with Homer, however distant, teaches you never to count your chickens. As Milton says, just when things seem to be moving in a favourable direction:

> Comes the blind Fury with th'abhorred shears,
> And slits the thin spun life.

'Yes,' said Bamber – he, his wife Christina and I were discussing Milton's 'Lycidas' – 'but earlier in the poem he gives the most perfect quietus in English.'

> So may some gentle muse
> With lucky words favour my destined urn,
> And as he passes turn
> And bid fair peace to be my sable shroud.

1967

PAULINE was pregnant. In hospital for tests. Clive and I were going to the Tynans. Nothing special. Drinks. He had visited Pauline at lunch time.

'Do you mind if we call at the hospital?' he said. 'I'll just say hello.'

'I'll come in too.'

'No, don't. I'll only be a minute.'

After half an hour I thought: 'What does he mean – just saying hello?' Then it was an hour. Then well over an hour. Then he came out, crying. 'She has lymphatic cancer. She's going to die,' he said.

Pauline was sent home. She grew thin. 'It's nice being thin. I've never been thin before,' she told Roger.

Clive moved their bed into the sitting room. Ken Russell brought his projector round and showed her films. She weighed less and less. Sarah White told me: 'I visited her on a sunny day. "Shall I move you into the sun?" I suggested. "No," she said. "I don't want to be in the sun any more."'

After she returned to hospital Roger and I visited her only once. She lay back, two pillows under her head, shivering, her face covered in sweat. Her legs were like sticks. A day later she died.

AND now (1998) Mr Carter, my Kenny, twelve years younger than me, the elder brother I never had, is dead of a similar affliction.

He loved walking, often alone, over Dartmoor, across the Fells, through the Lake District. The year before last, when he returned from the Lakes, he told Alice he had buried his walking boots at his favourite spot.

23 *de la Salle Brothers* An order of Christian Brothers founded by St
Jean Baptiste de la Salle (1651–1719) at Reims. Its members took
monastic vows; they did not become priests.

32 *The Irish Christian Brothers* Founded by Edmund Rice
(1762–1844), a merchant from Waterford, the Brothers – an
illegal organization until Irish independence in 1920 – educated
poor male children. Seven of the leaders of the Easter Rising
(1916) executed by the British were Christian Brother boys, as
have been all but two of Ireland's Prime Ministers. The Brothers
are in decline. Their use of corporal punishment (unlike their
founder) damaged many of their pupils, and other forms of
abuse have brought them into disgrace.

46 *Popski's Private Army* No.1 Special Demolition Squadron raised
in October 1942 and commanded by Lt-Col. V. Peniakoff. A
raiding party operating with considerable success behind enemy
lines in Tunisia, Italy and Austria.

55 *My diary says* – and, subsequently, *Diary Scrap(s)* – I have a
selection of abandoned diaries.

60 *Lehi* The Lohamei Herut Israel, or Fighters for the Freedom of
Israel, a breakaway faction of the Irgun Avai Leumi (the Irgun),
formed by Palestinian Jews for their self-protection. The Lehi were
led by Abraham Stern, and so were known to some as the Stern
Gang.

74 *Tuinal* A combination of equal parts of quinalbarbitone sodium
and amylobarbitone sodium, a schedule D drug requiring high
security.

116 *'Means of Love' exhibition* Actually, 'An Liebesmittel Eine
Darstellung der geschlechtlichen Reizmittel-Aphrodisiaca',
curated by Magnus Hirschfeld and Richard Linsert, Berlin, 1920.

145 *'I, the undersigned . . .'* *Merlin* 3, Winter 1952/53, pp. 159–71.
This extract, translated from Hungarian into French by M. Tibère
Kremer and published in *Les Temps Modernes* in 1951, was
translated from French into English by Seaver and Wainhouse.
A second extract from Dr Nyiszli's text, also translated by
Seaver and Wainhouse, was published in *Merlin* 4 Spring/Summer
1953.

164 *'When Gwendolyn left the house . . .'* From Alfred Chester's
     'Rapunzel, Rapunzel', in *Here Be Dragons*, stories by Alfred
     Chester, Editions Finisterre, Paris, 1955. See, too, Cynthia Ozick,
     Alfred Chester's Wig. This fine biographical essay on A.C. was
     published in *The New Yorker*, 30.3.1992.

202 *Mr Warren* For more on A. J. C. 'Minky' Warren, the Carters,
     and the Portobello Road street market, see Alan Carter, *Carter
     Bros. and Dad*, The Australian Antique Trader, 599 Pacific
     Highway, St Leonards, Sidney, 'Minky' being the 'Dad' of the
     title.

214 *The* Times Literary Supplement *published . . .* 'Classic
     Inhumanism' 2.8.1957, p. 214. *Four issues later . . .* Eliot's letters
     appeared on 9.8.1957, 23.8.1957 and 13.9.1957, mine on
     6.9.1957.

229 *attracted support enough . . .* Supporters of the Campaign in its
     early days included: Sir Richard Acland, John Arden, Lindsay
     Anderson, John Arlott, Pat Arrowsmith, Dame Peggy Ashcroft,
     John Berger, Robert Bolt, Pauline Boty, John Braine, John Bratby,
     Vera Brittain, Benjamin Britten, Reg Butler, Ritchie Calder, James
     Cameron, April Carter, Canon John Collins, Dr Alex Comfort,
     Frank Cousins, Constance Cummings, Shelagh Delaney, George
     Devine, Peggy Duff, Dame Edith Evans, E. M. Forster, A. S. Frere,
     Victor Gollancz, Stuart Hall, Jacquetta Hawkes, Barbara
     Hepworth, Patrick Heron, David Hockney, Laurence Housman,
     Revd Trevor Huddleston CR, Edward Hyams, James Kirkup,
     Bernard Kops, Marghanita Laski, Doris Lessing, Ben Levy, Joan
     Littlewood, Professor Kathleen Lonsdale, Dame Rose Macaulay,
     Hugh MacDiarmid, Sir Compton Mackenzie, Wolf Mankowitz,
     Ethel Mannin, Denis Matthews, George Melly, David Mercer,
     Sir Francis Meynell, Ralph Milliband, Spike Milligan, Adrian
     Mitchell, Naomi Mitchison, Henry Moore, John Neville,
     Ben Nicholson, John Osborne, Michael Randle, Sir Herbert
     Read, Vanessa Redgrave, Karel Reisz, Dame Flora Robson,
     Professor J. Rotblat, Revd Michael Scott, Alan Sillitoe,
     Dr Donald Soper, Professor E. P. Thompson, Michael Tippett,
     Ken Tynan.

231 *'The marchers were mainly . . .'* Alan Brien, the *Daily Mail*
     8.4.1958. Cited by Christopher Driver in his book *The Disarmers*.
     This and *Middle Class Radicalism* by Frank Parkin are the best
     British accounts of the history, the arguments and the motivations
     of CND and the Committee of 100 I have read, and I have drawn
     on them in my own reminiscences of those days. Those interested

by CND may care to read *Resisting the Bomb*, volume two of *A History of the World Nuclear Disarmament Movement* by Lawrence S. Wittner, 1997.

234 *... except for that in the* Daily Mail *...* Daily Mail 10.3.1958 and 1.4.1958.

235 *Artie Shaw* Artie Shaw was married to Lana Turner from 1940 to 1941 and to Ava Gardner from 1945 to 1947.

248 *The Lily White Boys* a play by Harry Cookson with songs by Christopher Logue and music by Tony Kinsey and Bill le Sage. First London performance 27 January 1960. *The Boys*: Albert Finney, Monty Landis, Philip Locke. *The Girls*: Georgia Brown, Shirley Anne Field, Anne Lynn. *The Upright Citizens*: Willoughby Goddard, James Grout, Geoffrey Hibbert, Barbara Hicks, Ronnie Stevens. Directed by Lindsay Anderson. Assistant Director, Anthony Page. Dance Director, Eleanor Fazan. Music Director, Anthony Bowles. Produced by the English Stage Company and Oscar Lewenstein Ltd.

267 *Macmillan, not a panicky ...* The government files covering the actions of the Committee of 100 show that behind their apparent calm the Cabinet feared that the armed American sentries guarding the aircraft loaded with nuclear weapons would open fire on any demonstrators who tried to immobilize the aircraft by sitting around them, which was what, according to the spies who joined the Committee, the Committee planned to do. Between 1960 and 1962 the government worked hard to frustrate CND and the Committee of 100. The September jailings are to be seen in this context.

Ernest Rodker, a member of the Committee's planning group, said: 'I was discussing government spies with an ex-National Front organizer who had police contacts. He said that one of our planners, an elderly man who claimed to be deaf – I knew him quite well – was working for MI5. "At your sessions he'd say: 'Speak up! Speak up! My hearing aid is on the blink'." In fact his hearing aid was a recorder and cassettes of your sessions went straight to MI5.'

For the analysis of the government files vis-à-vis the influence of CND on Cabinet thinking, see Stephen Ward's article in the *Independent on Sunday*, 9.1.1994.

284 *... seventeenth-century nonsense poets ...* See *The Origins of English Nonsense* by Noel Malcolm, 1997.

332 *Wholly Communion* Directed by Peter Whitehead, Hathor Video Publications. www.demon.co.uk peterwhitehead.

332 *'The Furore of Sneezing'* See *Pin and the Story of Pin* by Raoul Hausmann and Kurt Schwitters, edited by Jasia Reichardt, 1962.

INDEX

Abbey Road Studios, London, 242
Acre Central Prison, 64–8, 312
The Adventures of Robin Hood (film),
    xi, 35, 81
Agence France-Presse, 165
Ahamad the Butcher, 65, 66
Akademika Duncan, 113
Alazard, M. and Mme, 139
Albert Memorial, Kensington Gardens,
    320
Aldermaston March, 230–33
Allen, Ralph, 32, 34
American library, Rome, 131
Amsterdam, 117
Anderson, Lindsay, 83, 84, 195–6,
    207–8, 224, 225, 227, 230, 245,
    247, 262, 298, 301, 307
    and *Look Back in Anger*, 199, 200,
    211
    meets CL, 198–200
    The Lily White Boys, 248, 257–60
Andorra Star prison ship, 119, 160
Andraeus, Hans, 184
Anti-Uglies campaign, 233, 257, 282
Antonioni, Michelangelo, 305
Apollinaire, Guillaume: *The
    Debauched Hospodar*, 161
Arator of Liguria, 243
Archer, David, 183, 185–7, 188, 189,
    225
Arlen, Harold, 129
Army Education Corps, 53
Army Education Scheme, 71
Ashmoleon Museum, Oxford, 244
Astaire, Fred, 9, 35
Atomic Weapons Research
    Establishment, Aldermaston, 230,
    283
Attlee, Clement, 211
Aubrey, Diane, 294
Auschwitz, 146, 190, 191, 291
Austen, Jane: *Emma*, 93
Auteuil, Paris, 118, 120, 121

Bacon, Francis, 187, 212
Baker, Sophie, 306
Bal des Quatz' Arts, 175–6
Baldwin, James, 167
Balzac, Honoré de, 174
Barber (Samuel Johnson's servant),
    174

Barker, George, 185
Barnett, Dame Henrietta, 6
Barthès de Ruyter, Georges, 95–6, 103,
    104, 105
Barthès de Ruyter, M., 103, 104, 125,
    237
Barthès de Ruyter, Mme, 100, 103, 109,
    110, 237
Barton, Bernard: *The Convict's Appeal*,
    188
Basie, Count, 195
Bath, 32
BBC, 182, 183, 187, 212, 240, 242,
    247, 248
    Third Programme, 76, 162, 189, 190,
    203, 213, 225, 239
    World Service, 203
BBC television, 299, 320
Beales, Mary, 230
Beatles, 305
Beckett, Samuel, 123, 135, 141, 173–5,
    176–7, 204, 210, 213, 215, 235
    Echo's Bones, 177
    En Attendant Godot, 135, 221
    Endgame, 215
    Malone, 135, 144–5
    Molloy, 135, 144–5, 176
    Watt, 142–3, 144
    Whoroscope, 176
Beddoes, Thomas Lovell: *Poems*, 90
Beech's Bookshop, Salisbury, 200
Beirut, 58
Belloc, Hilaire, 280
Belville, Hercules, 304–5
Bennett, Alan, 281
Berger, John, 262
Berlitz School of Languages, 107,
    110–11, 115, 117, 120, 121,
    124
Bertolucci, Bernardo, 305
Bertram Mills' Circus, 214
Betjeman, John, 5, 257
Better Books, 186, 188, 301, 320
Beyond the Fringe, 212, 281–2, 283
Biba, 302
Bicycle Thieves (film), 156
Bikini Atoll, 200–201
Binyamina, 57, 76
Black Watch, 46–54, 62
    4th Battalion, 56–7, 58, 62, 66, 67
Blake, Peter, 301

331

Logue, John Christopher, *selected references*:
education, 16, 17–18, 22, 23–5, 31–4, 36–8, 42–3, 45, 48, 202
juvenile court, 16, 45
enlists (1944), 46
eye injury, 53, 54, 66–71, 87
court-martialled, 60–63
in prison, 64–73, 81, 155, 189, 312
suicidal, 86–7, 154, 155–60
makes three close friends, 88–92
disability pension, 87, 93, 109, 136, 219, 256
death of his father, 98–9
starts to live in Paris (1951), 103
lives in Rome, 130–4
Wand and Quadrant, 134, 137, 143, 146, 151, 183, 188, 189
meets Beckett, 173–5
returns to London, 177
Devil, Maggot and Son, 183, 184, 188, 193
meets Lindsay Anderson, 198–200
meets Donleavy, 203–4
moves to Denbigh Close, 205–7
Xanthe Wakefield's influence, 209–10
War Music, 126, 209, 226, 228
'Achilles and the River', 221–4
Patrocleia, 225, 226, 248–9, 272
'To My Fellow Artists', 224, 225, 315
the Aldermaston March, 230–33
Twenty Poems based on Pablo Neruda's Los Cantos d'Amores, 239–41
Red Bird recording, 241–2, 257, 290, 297–8
Songs, 247
Songs from The Lily White Boys, 248, 249, 250, 257–60
Committee of, 100 court case and imprisonment, 265–72
Private Eye, 279–82
marries Rosemary Hill, 318
hepatitis, 293–4, 312
the Royal Albert Hall poetry reading, 319–23
Isle of Wight Festival (1969), 322
depression, 131–2, 323
Logue, John Dominic ('Jack') (CL's father), 3, 4, 5, 11–12, 24, 37, 57, 60, 75, 79, 82, 87, 96, 99, 200, 202, 213, 279, 280, 285
Catholicism, 6, 34
career, 6, 9, 14, 16, 45
and politics, 6–7
holiday in Germany, 15, 19, 22

retires to Southsea, 15
in the Second World War, 20, 41, 42, 54
at the juvenile court, 45
death, 98–9
Logue, Margaret (CL's aunt), 7–12, 40, 49, 98, 285
Logue, Molly (Florence Mabel; née Chapman; CL's mother), 3, 4, 5, 7, 13–14, 22, 31, 60–61, 75, 82, 98, 99, 108, 188, 202, 203, 218, 219, 274, 285, 288, 300
in the Second World War, 20, 41, 42
takes in student lodgers, 87, 95, 100
death, 99
and CL's leaving for Paris, 100
CL visits, 201–2, 314
Logue, Nora (CL's cousin), 314
Logue, Rose (née McCloskey; CL's grandmother), 10, 11
Loiguire (alleged ancestor), 9
London, 80, 87, 104, 124, 164, 172, 182, 272
compared with Paris, 182–3, 301–2
London County Council, 256
London Library, 219
London Postal Service, 9, 14
Lottman, Herbert: *The Left Bank*, 124
Lougee, Arthur Fogg, 121, 126–7, 135, 137
Lougee, Jane, 118, 119, 120–21, 126, 127, 128, 130, 135, 138, 141, 159, 160, 173–4, 176
Luard, Elizabeth, 316
Luard, Nicholas, 282, 284, 301, 316
Lubbock, Basil, 38
Lucretius, 93
Lutyens, Sir Edwin, 6, 86
Lynn, Anne, 258, 260

McCarthy, Joseph, 127, 157, 166, 171
McCloskey, James Michael, 10
McCloskey, Rose, 10, 11
McCormack, John, 8
McGrath, John, 243
MacInnes, Colin, 301
Macmillan, Harold (later 1st Earl of Stockton), 225, 255, 266, 267, 269
Mad John, 216, 252, 310
Magdalene College, Cambridge, 83
Maiden Castle, near Dorchester, 88
Manwaring, G. E., 82
Mao Tse-Tung, 156
March to Aldermaston (film), 230
Marciano, Rocky, 163
Margaret, Princess, 289